A Bowl Of Cherries

A Memoir

Tekla Dennison Miller

PublishAmerica

Baltimore

First printing

ISBN: 1-59129-690-0
PUBLISHED BY PUBLISHAMERICA BOOK PUBLISHERS
www.publishamerica.com
Baltimore

Printed in the United States of America

Dedicated to
my mother Marion Kolk Dennison,
my sister Alyce Bonura
and
my brother Chuck Dennison

I'd like to thank my family, friends and writing colleagues who both supported and encouraged me to complete this project. Especially important to me were my sister Alyce, my husband Chet, and friends Elizabeth, Joyce, Joan, Judith, Maudy, Karl, Susan, Leslie and Jill who not only had the patience to critique the work, but never gave up on me.

CHAPTER ONE

The 4:10

When I heard the first explosion, vibrations shot through my body. A chair bounced into my chin and the kitchen table pitched. A bowl of potatoes my mother had been peeling plummeted to the floor.

As a second explosion thundered through the house, my mother dropped her paring knife: "Oh God," she said. "It's the 4:10."

Dad worked on that train. We were getting supper ready for his return.

Mom grabbed my hand and pulled me through the front door. Outside, our neighbors, mostly women and children, streamed from the doors of their houses. They converged onto Kinne Street like a swarm of bees. Mothers toted babies on their hips, dish cloths still in their hands. Others clutched the small fingers of confused children. Mom and I joined them.

No one spoke. We moved in one large wordless mass. Looking from one face to another, each tight with worry, I searched for an answer to our silent movement. Maybe talking would confirm something awful had happened. Although Mom held my hand, I felt adrift in a black nightmare. To my seven-year-old eyes, every person was a mute, faceless blur.

Except for her white, terry cloth turban covering her head and her tight grip on my hand, I wouldn't have known even my mother from the others. Like them, like every mother in the 1940's, she dressed in a plaid house dress, white bib apron, black-wedge shoes and white ankle socks. Like the others, her face was ghostly and pale.

The closer we got to the depot, the larger the procession. We walked faster. The faster we moved, the more frightened I became. I tugged at Mom's hand to get her attention. She just kept her eyes focused straight ahead toward the depot, two blocks away, in the center of town.

I looked for some comfort in each stone face. My eyes stopped on Father Kelly's. The Catholic priest in our neighborhood hurried to the front of the group. Sourness slid into my throat and my stomach did a flip-flop. Father Kelly never missed dinner unless someone died.

Thick, greasy smoke billowed into the air as we approached the depot. Soot showered down coating me in grime, covering everything with a black film, even the newly budded trees along the street. My eyes stung from the particles in the smoke-laden air.

For several minutes the nerve-splitting noise of metal scraping against metal reverberated. The clamor intensified and climaxed in a final thunderous explosion. At last we arrived to see the pieces of mangled metal coming to rest in a heap. Two trains had collided head-on.

I wiped my eyes with my soot-covered hand. My tears painted a web of smudged streaks across my palm. I wanted Mom to wake me up and tell me I was having a bad dream. Instead, blaring ambulance sirens interrupted the stillness and jolted us from our stunned inspection of the smoldering pile. Frenzied questions erupted from the disbelieving onlookers:

"What happened?"

"Is anyone dead?"

"Where's Joe, where's my husband?"

"How could this happen here?"

My eyes darted from one moving mouth to another. I heard jumbled, nonstop hysterical words from mouths stuck on automatic: nothing like this had ever happened in our small, rural upstate village. The only things we could boast about were miles of tracks and being home of the New York Central Railroad's round house.

When one woman murmured, "There's never been an accident before in our peaceful valley," I nodded in shocked agreement.

As the ambulances came closer, the large crowd parted to make room. Then we rushed the wreckage as though the sirens had ordered an assault.

Rescue workers brought out the bodies from the smoking metal debris and laid them in a row on the scorched grass. Mom squeezed my hand and dragged me from one unidentifiable body to another. She maneuvered through the throngs of hysterical women, their bewildered children hurrying behind. We eyed each other as though relief would come from our everyday sameness.

Every few moments I heard a woman's mournful wail. Mom's head tilted in the direction of each sound, but she didn't stop to offer comfort. I struggled to see toward the commotion, while Mom tightened her grip.

When we reached the caboose, Mom dropped my hand and staggered toward the emergency team extracting my father from the wreckage. They lowered him to the ground and held Mom back from gathering Dad into her arms. She cried, "Denny, can you hear me?"

I didn't understand any of what was happening. I backed away from the area that looked more like a scene from a war movie than anything that should be happening to me.

Choking on tears and smoke, I was still backing away as the emergency team lifted Dad's unnaturally bent body to a waiting stretcher. His listless arm brushed against the ground as though it wasn't attached. Mom picked up his hand and held it tightly to her chest as she ran alongside, releasing it only when they lifted the stretcher to slide my father's body through the double ambulance doors. She climbed in, sat on the side bench and held Dad's hand again.

One of the attendants closed the panel doors, shutting me out. The ambulance sped by me. Mom peered out the window. The look on her startled face told me that only then she'd realized I was still there. I pressed my lips together and tried to fight back the fear of being left behind. As the ambulance siren announced its departure, I knew our lives would never be the same.

Too terrified to move, I remained in the same spot, paralyzed by the chaotic scene that continued to unfold in front of me. If I did move, I thought Mom wouldn't be able to find me when she came back. Or maybe she'd send my sister Alyce for me. Mom had always taken care of me before.

When a woman placed her hand on my shoulder, I jumped. Disappointed that the person touching me wasn't Mom or Alyce, I didn't recognize her. Soot had filled the creases in her face and coated her hair. She looked like a cartoon character who had come up against a fire cracker. Thinking I was dreaming, I searched her face for something familiar. Finding it in her eyes, I cried, "Oh Mrs. Thorpe, Mom and Dad left me."

She bent down and took both my hands in hers. "Your mother needs to be with your father," she said. "You understand, don't you?"

I nodded, but I didn't understand anything. She tugged at my hand and led me away toward her home. I kept turning around to look at the wreckage as though Mom would come running out from the smoke. "Will Mom know where I am?" I asked.

Mrs. Thorpe must not have heard me because she didn't answer.

After dinner Alyce appeared at the Thorpe's front door. "I've come for Tekkie," she said, sounding exhausted.

I ran to the door yelling, "Where were you?"

"At school and the hospital." Her hand brushed my cheek. "But I'm here now and we can go home."

"Why don't you stay the night?" Mrs. Thorpe asked as she reached out to Alyce and tried to coax her into the house.

Alyce stepped away. "We'd better go home," she said in a grown-up, controlled voice as she gazed off toward the depot.

As we walked the mile to our house, I asked my older sister a thousand questions about Dad and why Mom left me alone. Though smoke filled the air and coated my tongue, I wasn't sure what part of that day was a bad dream and what was real.

"We need to sleep," Alyce answered. Her eyes fixed on something in the distance. "We'll talk in the morning." Her hand tensed like a vise squeezing the life out of mine.

Dad had broken his back in three places when he was thrown across the caboose. Two weeks later as Mom opened the door to Dad's hospital ward, she cautioned me along with Alyce and my older brother, Chuck. "Keep your voices down," she said. "And no monkey business. Do you understand?"

The three of us nodded in unison. Mom marched forward, clutching her purse under one arm. With her head held high, she gave her full attention to the wall at the end of the ward. The three of us children stopped just inside the door. I searched for Dad in the vast dormitory, a room lined with white metal beds. Each time a patient moved, the stiff white sheets sounded like a cat scratching at a door. Each bed rested under a window letting in enough light to create a glare on the well-shined linoleum floor.

When Mom discovered we weren't following her, she stopped and motioned to us impatiently. We inched forward, Alyce clenching my hand. Mom came to an abrupt halt and turned toward a figure in a body cast. Dad forced a smile and winked at us. His bruised arms and shoulders exposed above the top of the cast contrasted with the stark whiteness of the plaster holding him together. The cast had transformed my father's Irish good looks and robust six-foot physique into a mutant. I leaned against my sister, taking comfort in the familiar scent of her freshly laundered dress.

Eyeing my father's scary image, I wondered whether he would ever be the same again. He used to awaken us in the early morning to share hot jelly donuts. The bakery was a regular stop for him on his way home from work or after a night of drinking. Would he ever do that again?

I raised my hand to my chin as if to wipe away some warm strawberry jelly oozing down it. When I found none there, I wanted to run from the ward to vomit up the memory along with the hospital smell of rubbing alcohol. Instead with my mouth hinged open, I gawked at the strange figure that had become Dad.

Alyce and Chuck tried not to show any emotions. But when Dad stretched his shaking arms out, the three of us crumbled into teary-eyed greetings. Dad chuckled first when we tried to circle our arms around his chest. It wasn't easy to embrace a man in a body cast and our attempts at hugging Dad made us giggle.

Dad took Alyce's hand and rested it against the cool sheet. "I'll be home soon," he said. "But you'll have to live with this monster." He jabbed at the cast. "And it looks like I'll miss your graduation next month, Alyce."

Alyce's body stiffened and she dropped Dad's hand. It thumped against the bed. She pursed her lips as she faced the wall. When she met Mom's reproachful eyes, Alyce turned back to Dad. She leaned over and kissed him, "That's ok," she whispered.

Dad caressed her face and said, "You can practice your salutatorian's speech on me."

Alyce, Chuck and I laughed self-consciously when Dad added, "I'll be a captive audience."

Mom didn't join in the laughter. For the first time I noticed the fear on her face.

When visits were over, we walked the mile to our home, crossing the tracks over a bridge that sliced our town in half. From the bridge we could see some uncleared remains of the wreckage. But there was little other evidence of the devastation. In that short time slivers of grass were already poking through the scorched ground.

Since the accident, the town had strained to get back to normal. We all wanted to erase the tragedy and pretend it didn't happen. All day and night I could hear the trains moving in and out of the roundhouse and depot as usual. The air smelled of burning coal.

Once we got to our house, I noticed that the curtains were drawn tight as if to prevent any further evil from sneaking in rather than tied to the side or dancing in the breeze through an open window. A week before the accident, Dad had hosted his baseball team for the annual spring celebration and barbeque, opening another season. Since then, the yard had become a muddy, abandoned patch of unkept earth. I strained to hear Dad laugh, see him drink beer and smoke Camel cigarettes with his friends on the back porch after work. But the yard was silent.

Mom squatted down to face me. Although thinner than usual, she was still a stunning woman who reminded us of Greta Garbo. She seemed to always read my mind. "It's going to be ok, Tekkie," she said. "You'll see. Everything will be the same. I promise."

"Will Dad still wake me up to give me a quarter after a week on the road or after winning a baseball game?"

Mom cupped my face in her hands. "Of course he will."

"But," I said, trying to fight back my tears, "will he still talk about places he's been like Poughkeepsie and Tarrytown and tell me we'll go there some day?"

I didn't tell Mom that I wouldn't miss Dad waking me up in the middle of the night. I didn't tell her that I hated the smell of stale beer and cigarettes when he hugged me and sang, "Who's my little darling?"

I always had to play along and answered, "I am."

"Who's my turtle dove?" he'd ask and wink.

"I am."

"And who does she love?"

My final answer was our little joke. "Somebody."

If he had donuts, Dad would hoist me off his lap and lay the pastry on napkins, one for each of his children.

Mom wiped the single tear that slipped from my eye. She patted my head and went inside the house. In the kitchen, she put on her apron as she always did. But that day she prepared us canned tomato soup and grilled cheese sandwiches rather than her usual fare of stews, roasts and lots of gravy and mashed potatoes. We gathered around our kitchen table and ate in silence.

CHAPTER TWO

Denny

My father, Merton Charles Dennison, Denny for short, loved drinking with his friends at one of the fifteen bars on Manlius Street, our town's two-block-long main road. He loved drinking almost as much as he loved pitching for the town team. Before I was seven years old, I spent a lot of time in Thorpe's Bowling Alley Bar watching Dad buy rounds for the guys, knowing all the while Mom was struggling to pinch pennies for decent meals, clothes and shoes for us. When she'd complain, about his "spending money on those bums," Dad responded, "Ah, Marion, they're good boys. Join us for a couple of rounds."

Bill and Margaret Thorpe, the owners of the bar, were my godparents and Mom and Dad's best friends. Unlike Mom, many afternoons I sat on a stool in the dim light at the end of Thorpe's dank bar sipping Coke, eating potato chips, watching the bowlers and listening to Dad and his friends exchange baseball statistics and local gossip. Most of the men worked with Dad on the railroad or played baseball with him on the town team. Often they'd come straight from work in grimy denim overalls or a game in striped baseball uniforms. Dad showed up in clean slacks and a shirt only a few times. All the men were hard drinkers and heavy smokers.

I studied each man as he challenged another to the tallest tale or most outrageous baseball memory, words slurring as the afternoon wore on. Eventually I'd turn to the smoke-filmed mirror that lined the wall behind the bar. It was easier to watch everyone.

Usually Dad did most of the talking: "You shoulda seen me, boys, when they called me Cannonball and I pitched that no-hitter for the Triple A's back in the thirties." Dad turned to me. "Met your mother then."

I smiled and crunched a potato chip.

"Denny, didn't you play for the Yankees too?" My eyes followed the voice to the end of the bar.

Dad raised his glass to a man in denims, one of the regulars. "Sure did, off and on. But you know, boys, their rules were tight."

The group of ten or so men sitting around the bar nodded, lifted their beer glasses and drank.

"Yeah, too tight to keep you around, right Denny?" One man shouted out. The others laughed.

Dad took a long sip of beer, put the glass down and wiped the foam from his lips with the back of his hand. "Well, boys," he said, "if I stayed with the pros or semi-pros, I wouldn't be here drinking with my buddies, would I, now?"

"The fact is, Denny, you could never take orders," my godfather said. "You've always marched to your own drummer."

"Maybe so, maybe so," Dad answered as cigarette smoke billowed around his head like a fog. "Pour me another beer, Bill."

Bill Thorpe would listen to the patrons as he pumped drafts and wiped the bar with a damp, threadbare towel. He'd slap the rag against the counter every time a point was made and wink in my direction as though I understood or cared. Every so often he'd yell out, "How ya doing, Tekkie?"

"Fine," I'd answer in a meek voice, trying to stay as unnoticed as possible. Other than the few times Chuck was there, I was the only child in the bar.

Dad always defended his beloved Yankees, while the working men sitting around the bar defended the Dodgers, known as the Blue Collar Team. A few women, but never Mom, sat at one end of the bar and drank and smoked right along with the men. Their heavily painted lips left deep red mouth prints around the rims of their beer mugs. When those women laughed at the jokes, their ruby mouths opened wide, making them look like Bozo the clown. Though they made sure to acknowledge each man's banter, the red-lipped women never once offered a bit of information. They smelled like day-old Midnight in Paris perfume and stale beer and had names like Honey, Sweetheart, or Toots. None looked like Mom, and I wondered if that had husbands at home worrying about the money they were spending like Mom did

If I had to go to the bathroom, one of the women would take me. When we returned from the lady's room, the woman sat on a stool alongside the boys and usually commented, "Blondie there," she'd light a Camel and nod in my direction, "is a cute little girl, Denny."

He'd nod, but never interrupted the tale he was telling.

I hated being called Blondie. It was bad enough when Chuck called me Chicklets like the chewing gum. But I could retaliate with loud, witchy screams when he also sang the commercial jingle, "Chiklets candy-coated chewing gum." I couldn't mouth off like that though when red-lips called me Blondie.

Listening to Dad brag about his semipro and pro-ball years reminded me of the story I had heard Mom tell more times than I could count. She told me that after Dad pitched for the Newark Bears, the Yankees AAA Farm Team, the Yankee management brought him up as a relief pitcher several times to test him. The management gave him a choice: stop partying and pitch for the Yankees, or continue partying and not pitch. Dad chose to quit pro-baseball, go to work for the railroad, and join the town team. Mom should have know then there was no sense complaining about being penniless.

Once I asked Dad if he ever bowled at Mr. Thorpe's alley. "No, Tekkie," he chuckled. "Don't want to waste my good pitching arm, now do I?"

"Guess not," I answered. "But maybe I could try it once."

Dad ruffled my hair and lifted his beer. As I watched that motion repeat itself so many times I wondered if that was part of his exercise routine to maintain his toned muscles for baseball.

Feeling tired, I'd often lay my head on the bar. Sometimes I'd fall asleep on my curled-up arms listening to the rollicking ball bounce into pins that wobbled to the wood floor.

"Denny," my godfather would ask as he handed him another draft, "don't you think it's time to take Tekkie home?"

"Naw. She'll be better off resting her head on the bar than listening to Marion's high-brow music."

The boys would snicker. I was glad he said that in the bar and not to Mom's face. For sure she would have had a few heated words in response.

When my godmother was working the bar, she'd take me home, leaving Dad there until closing. The days Mrs. Thorpe didn't take me home, Mom would stomp into the bar around supper time. Her presence was made known by the abrupt halt in conversation among Dad and his friends as their heads lowered, eyes focused on their beer. The red-lipped women slipped from their bar stools and scrambled for the ladies' room like a herd of cattle.

In those moments Mom's graceful footsteps were replaced with harsh, forceful treads. Not a word, not even in angry Polish, came from her mouth as she strode, shoulders pressed back, to me. She'd nudge Dad aside, placing her back to him, between him and me. For a few moments she'd scowl at me, mouth turned down so that the corners almost reached her chin. Her expression accused me as though I had a choice in all this, as though I was old enough to pick one parent over the other.

I in turn appraised her through wide, pleading eyes appealing to Mom's more understanding side. Instead she'd circle her hand around my upper arm and whisk from my perch. The quick motion flung the potato chips from their bag, spreading them down the bar. The skittering noise they made in the silent room sounded like a thousand fingernails scratching against the wood top.

Homeward bound, Mom's furious pace and ever-tightening grip did little to brighten my spirits even though I had been freed from the bleak, smoke-filled surroundings. She had to know I would have rather been outside playing. She had to know there was no way I could tell Dad I didn't want to be with him.

Once inside our house, Mom tossed me into a chair where a lukewarm meal awaited on the dining table. Pushing the food around the plate, I dreaded the idea of eating it when I had a stomach filled with potato chips and Coke. While forming little sections of untouched morsels into mounds, I again tried to make sense out of why Mom seemed to blame me for my absence. I also prepared myself for the inevitable—Mom's harsh accusations when Dad finally showed up at home.

On those evenings I was sent to bed early. Again I thought I was being wrongly punished. Yet I am positive Mom wanted to protect me from the events that were sure to follow.

The moment Dad came through the front door, they hurled bitter words at each other. Mom's were clear and thought out, while Dad's were slurred and defensive. Neither were kind.

"Do you think only of yourself, you selfish bastard?" Mom would shout before Dad closed the front door. I cringed at her unusual cursing.

Dad often didn't respond. I could hear his unsteady plodding into the kitchen and Mom pattering behind.

"How can you continually subject your daughter to that hell hole, Denny?" Mom's voice screeched. Embarrassed, I wondered if the neighbors sharing our duplex could hear my parents.

"There's nothing wrong with her being with me, Marion. She needs to see and hear more than those damn operas of yours." A chair scraped against the floor and I listened to Dad's body, heavy with drink, plop into it.

"You think nothing of spending every dime on those bums," Mom screamed as she pounded her hand against the table to keep his alcohol-cluttered attention. "What about decent shoes for your daughter? What about enough money to pay for milk and food? Are those so-called virtuous drunks you say are your friends going to pay for them?"

"Now Marion." Dad's words sounded as though he couldn't get them out, as though he was pushing them through a wad of cotton.

"Don't you 'now' me. You're nothing but a no-good, selfish drunk who'd rather play baseball and drink with other no-good drunks than support your family."

I could hear something crash and then Dad yelling, "And you, Miss Prima donna," his voice sounding more clear, "you and your high and mighty ways, you think you're better than everyone."

"What about the money, Denny? What about the bills? We can hardly pay the rent? It all goes to your drink and those, those..."

"Friends, my buddies, the ones who think I'm somebody, Marion."

"Those lousy good for nothings who use your ego to support their bad habits, while all along knowing your kids are starving," Mom fired back without taking a breath.

When I'd hear a slap and more thrashing I'd poke my fingers into my ears and hum away the horror, while tears streamed down my face.

In the morning Dad would be gone. I assumed to work, back on the road. As always Mom, wearing her apron, would be at the stove preparing breakfast. Though I craved an explanation of the events of the day before, I dared not disturb the normalcy of the moment that I desired even more. Watching Mom maneuver cooking utensils in her matter-a-fact way gave me hope that last night's meanness would be the last of those episodes.

Having spent the better part of my childhood in a bar, I thought smelling like stale beer and cigarettes was normal. Even at seven, I was convinced that cigarette smoking was the way to be sophisticated. One day when my parents weren't home I pilfered a pack of Camels from the carton Dad had stored in the drawer of his bed stand. After I tucked the pack under my waistband, I met Kay, my next door neighbor and best friend, behind the garage. We sat on the ground with our backs against the rough wood. I pulled the pack out and handed it to Kay.

"You take the first drag," Kay said as she crammed the pack in my hand.

"Where'd you get that word, 'drag'? From some movie?" I accepted her challenge. I unraveled the narrow red tie that kept the cigarettes sealed. I took a cigarette from the pack and tapped it against the cellophane wrapper like I saw Humphrey Bogart do. After striking a third match I lit the cigarette and took a puff. I immediately choked and spit out pieces of tobacco.

Kay snatched the cigarette from me in disgust. "Here, let me show you how it's done," she said, puckering her lips.

We both coughed up our lunches and decided that smoking might look glamorous when Lauren Bacall did it, but it wasn't fun and the cigarettes didn't taste good. The day following my secret meeting with Kay, Dad called me into his bedroom and said, "I'm missing some cigarettes, Tekkie. You don't know where they could be, do you?"

Biting my lower lip, I shook my head. I was stunned he knew I was the thief.

Shortly after that incident, I decided it would be wise for me to live somewhere else. Once again Dad discovered me. This time I was caught in my room filling a suitcase. "Why are you packing?" he asked.

"I'm running away."

"Where're you going?"

"Hollywood with Kay. We're going to be actresses."

Dad walked toward me and carried a few pieces of clothing from my dresser drawer. "Here," he said, "let me help you."

A lump the size of a potato formed in my throat as he piled clothes into the suitcase. "I've changed my mind," I said, unpacking. I went next door to Kay's to tell her there was no use running away when no one would miss us.

Dad was the third oldest of nine children, three boys and six girls, born to Frank John Dennison and Myrtle Abbott. His older brother, Dell, and younger sister, Julia, were the only two of his siblings I knew. Uncle Dell was a dairy farmer outside Binghamton, New York and Julia was a housewife in Pennsylvania. The rest of his siblings settled in Pennsylvania along the New York border.

The original Dennisons arrived on American shores from County Cork, Southern Ireland, just after the American Revolution. Grandpa Dennison owned a sawmill and a construction business in Hancock, New York, Dad's birthplace. When World War I broke out, Grandpa was conscripted to build ships. While Grandpa worked for the government, the sawmill burned. Shortly after he died in a work accident. Having no insurance or any other means of support, Grandma Dennison and the children moved to Hawley, Pennsylvania to live and work in the family-owned Dennison Hotel in the Pocono

Mountains. They went from riches to rags.

Aunt Julia told us, "We had to go barefoot to save our only pair of shoes for school." She also told us that Grandma Dennison was forced from a life of relative leisure to taking in laundry.

Looking at my covered feet and sure the laundry Mom did was ours alone, I thought we were lucky to have more money than Aunt Julia.

Grandpa Dennison's brother and his heirs fared better. He started the Dennison Crepe Paper Company, which became the Dennison Paper Company and finally the Dennison-Avery Paper Company. Our family had no contact with them. Aunt Julia believed it was because of my father. She said, "Your father was a rascal. He did things his own way." She added with some reluctance, "He never even knew his mother died until a year later."

Dad eloped with my mother, Marion Kolk, in 1932 after knowing her only three weeks. He was pitching for the Newark Bears when they met. She was smitten by that handsome, sweet-talking, twenty-eight-year-old Irishman with a thick head of black curly hair and smiling lapis blue eyes. Though more serious and intelligent than Dad, Mom had been prepared for marriage all her life, and Dad had a steady job and a happy outlook. She was only eighteen and loved to dance. He literally swept Mom off her feet the night they met at the Orpheum Dance Palace in New York City where Mom worked as a taxi dancer. For ten cents a dance, Dad waltzed, charlestoned and lindy-hopped into Mom's heart.

CHAPTER THREE

Marion Kolk Dennison

As much as Dad loved baseball and beer, Mom loved dancing and the opera. Mom danced and exercised to Benny Goodman and Verdi. Though bright and an avid reader, she didn't go beyond the eighth grade in school. Like many in immigrant families, she had to go to work as a maid and seamstress to help with the family's support.

There were nineteen children in Mom's family, including nine boys born to her father's first marriage and nine girls born to her mother's. After Grandpa and Grandma had been widowed, they married each other before leaving Poland for the United States and settling in Newark, New Jersey after World War I. Neither ever spoke English, and Mom, the nineteenth child, was the only one born in the U.S. When the family was processed at Ellis Island, Grandpa's name was Americanized to John Kolk.

Grandpa was fifty years old when Mom was born in 1915. She was christened Manya, later Americanized to Marion. The next youngest sibling, Steffany, was fifteen years older than Mom. All the girls were considered beauties, and Mom was thought to be the most beautiful.

When Dad met Marion Kolk, she was a tall, elegant strawberry blonde. Mom wore her hair in a '30s style which revealed her high, intelligent forehead. She parted her hair on the left and let it hang in soft, natural waves around her face.

Mom's seamstress skills allowed her to always be in fashion. She could copy any dress she studied. For instance, Mom once showed me her wedding picture. She wore a floor-length black sheath dress trimmed in sequins and fringe.

"We were on our way to a party," she said. "I had copied the dress from one I saw in the window of Saks Fifth Avenue that cost $1500." A pleased smile spread across her face.

She cut a stunning figure in that dress. It draped in several folds from shoulder to shoulder and covered her bodice. As was the style, it was a clinging affair cut on the bias and revealed Mom's perfect figure.

I never knew Mom's mother, Tekla, after whom I was named. Grandpa, once a soldier in the Polish Army, died in his sleep at the age of 94 when I was fifteen. He managed to survive to that age on little more than black bread and strong black coffee laced with bourbon. When he was in his late 80's he moved in with our family on Kinne Street. After Grandma died, Grandpa had been passed from one of his children to another. Mom's older and wealthier siblings, the men graduated from college in Poland, decided it was her turn to care for the old man. That was the first time I saw him.

When I met Grandpa, I asked, "You're an old man, aren't you?" Mom translated my question in Polish. He laughed at me, exposing teeth browned by too many years of smoking, and patted my head. We became great friends after that.

Each day after breakfast Grandpa went to his bedroom, closed the door and held his own Mass. With the help of Mom I impatiently waited for him at the kitchen table. She'd place her forefinger to her lips and whisper, "Sshhh," making sure I didn't bother Grandpa until he came out. I was just four years old, and the ticking minutes seemed like an eternity as I lingered nearby listening to his muffled voice coming from behind the door.

One day when his bedroom door didn't close all the way, I peeked in through a slight opening. I saw Grandpa, lips moving, kneeling at his bed and holding a rosary.

Finally the door would open. Grandpa would put on his hat and grab my hand. Through the whole neighborhood I'd walk with him, his frame stooped, hands clasped behind his back and gait slow. No matter what the weather, Grandpa wore the same brown tweed overcoat he had since I could remember. It smelled like moth balls.

Being a scavenger myself, I never was embarrassed by Grandpa's rummaging through trash, whether in cans or laying in our path. Grandpa made stick people from cast-off wood, filled bottles with dried flowers, polished stones or refurbished unwanted toys for me. All of them were treasures and made me feel I had to be someone special to him.

Grandpa spoke Polish the whole time we walked. Though I didn't know Polish, I understood every word. He talked nonstop, often spitting through spaces between his full set of teeth. I marveled at his high cheek bones, which emphasized his sunken cheeks that puffed as he spoke. He pointed to buildings, trees and plants, and appeared to be explaining their importance. Grandpa's fingers were long and narrow and stretched out from transparent hands lined with prominent blue veins. When not pointing, his fingers combed his full head of white hair away from his narrow, filmy eyes. He was most animated when he showed me where he'd found my gifts; his arms flailed and circled as he tried to portray the discovery.

I envied Alyce and Chuck for having known Grandpa when they lived in Newark. When they visited him, Grandpa served them coffee laced with bourbon and canned milk just the way he drank it. I doubt Mom knew he was giving bourbon to Chuck and Alyce, and apparently they were smart enough not to squeal on him.

Other than Aunt Julia and Uncle Dell, Dad's sister and brother, the only relatives I had ever heard about or knew were Mom's sister Frances and her cousins, Jean, Johnny, Andy and Eddie, and their families. Of the three boys, I had only known Johnny. Jean and her brothers were raised by Grandma and Grandpa when their mother, Steffany, died of TB. My middle name is Steffany.

All told Grandpa and Grandma raised twenty-three children. Since Mom was closer in age to her cousins and was raised with them, they thought of each other as siblings. Grandpa's sons were all successful professionals—doctors, lawyers, businessmen—while all grandma's daughters were like most women: they married young and had children. I had thought the age differences kept Mom's siblings estranged from her.

When I met Aunt Frances, Mom's sister, she lived in a two-story row house in Newark. She was the only one of my Mom's real siblings I knew. She spoke with a Polish accent and had lost her second husband. Her first husband left Frances a wealthy widow, while her second husband squandered the money on alcohol and gambling.

All her life, Aunt Frances banked on her beauty for survival. She aged poorly and became obese. Yet she continued to see herself as a twenty-year-old beauty, whom jealous people were trying to poison. She ate only food she prepared and often badgered exasperated grocery clerks about where the store's food came from.

There were no full-length mirrors in her house. So Aunt Frances could only see her face, which she painted like Bette Davis' in the movie *What Ever Happened to Baby Jane?* I was never sure what Aunt Frances beheld in her mirror. I, however, saw a woman whose dyed hair was the color and texture of straw, except for the dark brown roots, and styled as it had been in a 1930's photo I saw of her on her living room mantle. To her credit she did wear clothes appropriate to her size and age, usually a floral printed house dress covered by a bib apron.

Aunt Frances had four children: one alcoholic son, one normal son, a promiscuous daughter who dyed her "big hair" platinum, and a son, Marty, who suffered with Down's Syndrome. On one of Mom's and my visits, Marty almost killed me by beating my head against a pillar while we played on Aunt Frances' front porch. I just knew I was going to die as I counted to nineteen thumps before I was rescued by his older sister, Barbara. Though my head ached, I laughed when I saw her racing to the front porch on spindle legs sticking out from leopard-print short-shorts.

Jean's brother, Johnny, whom we called Uncle, was far removed from Aunt Frances' insane world. He was a fine, hard-working, optimistic man who loved life and saw good in everyone. Uncle Johnny always wore dark slacks held up with suspenders over a white shirt and Greek-style sailor's hat. Though he was born in the United States, he was the exact likeness of the Polish immigrant being herded through Ellis Island that I had seen portrayed in my history texts. His usual Polish- accented ending to any statement was, "Enjoy. Enjoy." He often said this as he lifted a jelly glass filled with red wine. His devout Catholic heritage was passed onto his daughter and my favorite cousin, Genevieve. She became a nun.

Many Thanksgivings we gathered in the unfinished basement of Johnny's Long Island house. Thirty-plus relatives and friends showed up for a potluck served on long tables laden with food before pushing the chairs against the walls to make room in the center of the floor for dancing the polka into the night. Even at my age I was allowed a glass of wine with that dinner after which we polkaed to "Roll Out the Barrel."

Though Mom joined in the festivities, she always appeared reserved, quiet and perhaps more sophisticated than her relatives. Yet she and I danced every *schottische* and polka played.

I have no recollection of Dad joining us at Johnny's. Dad took us to the Syracuse Chiefs games or fishing on DeRuyter Lake, usually close to a bar so he could drink beer, but never to Mom's relatives'.

To save us from being too much like Dad, Mom took each of us children to the opera. Mom didn't go to the ball games and Dad didn't go to the opera. Except for the railroad picnics, firemen's fairs and Mom's annual surprise birthday party, they did very little as a couple. She counted every penny while Dad was in search of a good time, no matter the cost.

My turn to go to the opera came when I was just seven. Dad mocked Mom's bent toward the more intellectual forms of entertainment. "Why'd you want to see some high-brow boring opera, Marion? Besides, Tekkie's too young to understand it." He nodded at me. "Hell, I don't understand that junk."

Despite his scorn, Mom managed to squeeze money from Dad's paychecks before he squandered it at Thorpe's Bar. Verdi's *Rigoletto* was my first opera. We went to see it on Mother's Day. Mom dressed me in my Easter outfit which she had made: pink cotton dress with puffed sleeves and full skirt, a navy blue coat with a pink cotton collar trimmed with lace, pink socks and gloves, black patent leather purse and Mary Jane shoes, and a straw hat with navy blue and pink streamers hanging down my back. Most of the ensemble had once belonged to Alyce and been updated for me. The opera was one of the rare occasions Mom let me wear fancy shoes, rather than sensible, ugly oxfords. She knew when fashion counted.

I had also worn that outfit the day I shopped for a Mother's Day gift at Flah's Department Store in downtown Syracuse. A photographer took my picture as I picked a handkerchief for Mom's gift. The photograph appeared in the *Syracuse Herald* on Mother's Day. When we went to the opera I felt like a celebrity and believed everyone knew who I was when we entered the theater just a few blocks from Flah's.

Although we sat in the cheapest seats at the very rear of the theater's balcony, nothing could stop the enchantment of my first time at the opera. Mom had told me the whole story the night before so I would have some idea what was happening. I was captivated the moment the curtain opened on the ball held at the palace of the womanizer, the Duke of Mantua. From that first scene, the flamboyant costumes, and the exhilarating sounds of the performers' extraordinary voices intoxicated me. Every note felt as though it traveled in my veins. The entire event went beyond anything I could have imagined, and to share that excitement with Mom was a treat, especially since she could only afford to take one of the three of us children at a time to the opera.

When the last scene ended, Mom wasn't embarrassed when I cried as loud as I could, "Pleeeease let me stay to watch it again. Pleeeease."

While the audience seated near us clucked with disapproval at my whining, Mom seemed delighted that I enjoyed the opera. Her eyes lit up as she laughed when I told her I thought it was like going to the movies where we could stay and see the feature over.

The image of Rigoletto in the last act tearing open the bag to find his dying daughter remained with me. As I stood in front of a mirror, I often hummed the quartet in the last act—or thought I was—pretending I was an opera star.

My sister Alyce Marion was born on July 7, 1933, nine months after my father and mother married. Alyce—pronounced Aleese—was French for Alice. My brother Charles Merton (Dad's name in reverse because Mom refused to name him Merton) was born on September 17, 1936 in Newark. The four of them lived over the Market Street Bar until they moved to East Syracuse in 1940 when Dad became a railroad brakeman. By the time Alyce was three years old, Dad had taught her to pitch. By the time they left Newark she knew how to keep score and was well on her way to being a baseball whiz kid. Chuck learned to catch by the time he was three. Both became Dodger rather than Yankee fans because the Dodgers played in Brooklyn where Aunt Jean lived. Also during their warm-ups they entertained the kids sitting in the bleachers, tripping over their bats and falling over when catching balls. Dodger players often tossed the kids balls, saying, "Sshh. Don't tell anyone."

CHAPTER FOUR

The Neighborhood

Three years after Mom and Dad moved to East Syracuse, I was born. I came into the world on Sunday August 8, 1943 in one of two duplexes that were nestled among several single family homes stretching around the corner of Kinne and Yates Streets. I was born at home because Dad was on the road and Mom had no way to get to a hospital.

Our home was across the street from the gray stone St. Matthew's Catholic Church and two blocks from the newly built Catholic school. Shoddy and crowded East Syracuse High was another block beyond the Catholic school on Kinne Street. The public high school had an open campus. For the students, eating greasy french fries for lunch at Tony's, the fish-and-chips place next door, almost made up for the high school's old and drab structure.

Nearly half of the county's population lived on farms, while the poorest families lived in the only green-painted building in town, a two-story apartment. It was a few buildings down Yates Street around the corner from us. So when the Morrelli family built the first three-bedroom brick ranch house with a picture window, I thought they were the richest family I'd ever know. They owned the market under the bridge near the train tracks. Based on their newly built extravagant house, business was probably good.

One time when I was five years old, ignoring Mom's lectures, "Don't go near that apartment building," I sneaked inside the forbidden building. Fearing nothing, I walked through the front entrance. Shoes lined the dimly lit corridors outside each door. Most were heels and work boots and appeared only to need cleaning. So I collected about ten pairs and carted them away in a paper sack I found near one door. I presented them to my mother saying, "I found them in the hall. I guess no one wants them." I held the bag out to her. "I thought you could use them."

Mom's face formed a web of angry lines. "How many times have I told you not to go near that apartment?" She shook me with such force I dropped the bag, spilling the shoes down the porch steps.

I gave one of my best wide-eyed innocent looks and said, "Dunno."

"The last time was when you toted all those dishes home to me in your wagon," she said as I picked up the shoes that had fallen out of the bag. "Remember?"

I nodded. Those dishes were stacked outside the green apartment house in cardboard boxes from Morrelli's Supermarket. I believed someone had thrown the perfectly good multi-color collection of plates and cups away. I didn't want them wasted. Like the shoes, I took them home to Mom.

"Those poor people had just moved in and searched all day for the only dishes they owned," Mom reminded me. "What am I going to do with you?" she tisked as she nudged me off our porch.

"You're going to take each pair of those shoes back," she said as she led me toward the apartment. "And you'll apologize for being a thief."

"A thief?" I asked her. "Will I go to jail?"

Mom just pushed me forward.

I knocked on every door as Mom stood behind me making sure I didn't shirk my sentence. When each door was answered, Mom nodded to the renter and shoved me forward as I sobbed out my apology, "I'm sorry I'm a thief." I handed a pair of shoes to a faceless person. After that day I was so afraid of the green apartment building I wouldn't even walk on the same side of the street.

All the other structures in town, including our house, were painted brown to hide the soot from the coal-fed, smoke-spewing trains. Other than the roundhouse, the Medieval-looking St. Matthew's church across the street was the largest building in the area. Its stone steeples loomed over the neighborhood, which was made up of Irish, Polish and Italian Catholics.

The street gutters in front of our house always contained an odd mixture of wedding confetti and rice and black soot. Kay and I sorted through the mixture weekly. We collected the rice and confetti and stored them in empty peanut butter jars. We threw the carefully prepared blend at the brides and grooms getting married each Saturday at St. Matthew's.

One Saturday I got my hand stuck in the jar and charged through the middle of the wedding party screaming, "Mom, Mom. My hand's stuck." The alarmed group divided like the parting of the Red Sea, as they watched in amazement the little girl dressed in dirty shorts and t-shirt streaking through the congregation waving a jar above her head.

Mom greeted me at the door with that look she always gave me when I was in trouble, her eyebrows narrowed into a V over her nose and her mouth turned down at the corners. As she dried her hands on her apron, I thrust my glass-enclosed fist at her face, pleading, "Mom."

She shook her head and made a clicking sound. "I should never have let you off that harness."

About a week after the shoe incident, Mom had put me in a harness and tethered me to a tree in our backyard. One day before the tethering, she spent an entire afternoon searching for me, starting at the green apartment building. After several hours of frantic searching, she discovered I had walked to my Godparents' home—Bill and Margaret Thorpe. I told Mrs. Thorpe, "Mom sent me here to eat."

We had no phone so Mrs. Thorpe couldn't call Mom to tell her I was at their house. After she fed me, Mrs. Thorpe walked me home. When Mom met me at the door, she pointed toward the dining room table, where a congealed plate of food was waiting.

"Sit," she said, "and eat your dinner."

I swallowed hard trying to cram the dinner I had already eaten as far into my stomach as I could and sat down. Mom showed no mercy and made me eat the cold mashed potatoes, peas and meatloaf. If I started to fall asleep, she'd poke my shoulder. "Finish up. Then you can go to sleep." I had a long night, but managed to choke down the cold food.

Mom tethered me to the tree the next day. Though she never mentioned my adventure, I didn't visit the Thorpes on my own after that, fearing I would have to face another unappealing meal. Besides, they moved several miles away to DeRuyter Lake, making that decision easier.

After the peanut butter jar incident, Father Kelly tried to bar me from future weddings, but since I stood on the public sidewalk, his crusade to get rid of me failed. Kay and I were at our usual post the following week.

Those weddings were the closest I had been to the Catholic Church since Mom threw Father Kelly out of our house for telling her she should have more children and donate more money to the church. His timing was definitely off, because Mom had just gained back her strength after battling with what was thought to be hyperthyroidism. It had sapped her energy and left her bald, forcing her to either wear a wig cut in a page-boy style or a white terry-cloth turban. She also had a difficult delivery with me and had lost twins at birth three years before I was born.

"Who do you think you are to tell me how I should run my life?" she asked Father Kelly.

Before he could answer, Mom tossed him out the door. I watched as he tumbled down our front steps. I pressed my hand over my mouth to hide my smile at the image of the black ball rolling into the dust, shouting out his usual fire and brimstone diatribe.

As Father Kelly raised himself off the ground and brushed off his black priest's garb, he bellowed threats of excommunication at Mom. His reward was to watch her stalk off to join the Episcopal Church a block away.

I was baptized for the second time and later confirmed at the Episcopal church by a soft-speaking man, Father Absent. After that, I felt absolved from any threats of Father Kelly's, including his favorite, "You're all going to hell."

I responded, "I'll see you there." And under my breath, "Wherever hell is."

While Mom, Alyce, Chuck and I never missed attending Sunday services at the Episcopal Church, Dad never stepped a foot inside. "My religion is baseball," he'd often say when Mom tried to get him to come along with us.

Father Kelly's threats seemed to furnish me with the nerve to add to Mom's defiance. I'd sneak into the vestibule of the Catholic Church and make notes about the movies posted on the forbidden-to-see lists. Once collected I would persuade my friends, especially the Catholic ones, to come with me to see those movies when they appeared at the "Pit," our town movie theater on Manlius Street. We'd often follow that daring escapade by sitting on the curb across from the pool hall and watching the fights, which was another of Father Kelly's "forbidden." Most brawls ended in a body being tossed through the large storefront window. The knowledge that the owner of the pool hall had to replace a lot of windows was better than any cliffhanger shown at the Pit.

The Pit, short for the Rat's Pit, was a ramshackle brown wood building crammed between the VFW Hall and my godfather's bowling alley bar on Manlius. The marquee often displayed only a part of the movie's title because the owner didn't have enough of those black letters. But if I could see through the scratched glass cases holding the movie bills, I would know what was playing and what features were coming next.

The Pit bordered the tracks, and every time a train went by, the building shook while the noise drowned out the sound from the movie. The building held about 100 moviegoers and smelled of burnt popcorn and urine. There was a two-foot jagged tear in the screen that often caused famous actors such as Bogart or Dietrich to look like deformed monsters. When we sat down, we sank into the holes of the brown vinyl seats where the stuffing had been removed during prior popcorn fights. When there was no more popcorn to throw, we used the stuffing for ammunition. These fights worsened if the film burned through, leaving a break in the movie. What else could we do while the projectionist repaired the film strip? Despite these disadvantages, my friends and I gave up twenty-five cents every Saturday to see the matinee and stayed through two showings.

We always called Mom's cousin Jean Ferrara "Aunt." When I was four years old, she, her son Guy, and her husband Al spent one summer vacation with us near Ottawa in Quebec, Canada. It was one of the two lakeside vacations that our whole family, including Dad, went on. Our rented white clapboard cottage was owned by a French couple and sat on a hill overlooking Otti Lake. Bill and Margaret Thorpe loaned Dad their new Ford for the trip.

Guy was the same age as Chuck. He, Alyce and Chuck were able to walk the quarter mile on the sand bar to an island that the cottage faced. I either had to go by rowboat or be left behind. More often than not I was told, "You're too little," and was left to entertain myself. We spent many evenings playing poker, a game Dad taught us. I often beat that cohesive threesome, which made being left behind less painful. I spent my winnings in town where I learned American currency was worth more, which made the experience all the more thrilling.

Most of our lazy summer days at the cottage were interrupted at some point by Aunt Jean chasing the unruly Guy around the cabin and out into the lake, trying to hit him for some dastardly deed or prank like hiding worms in the coffee tin. I usually thought he deserved such treatment, especially after he killed our landlord's prize rooster with an errant arrow. One time Aunt Jean even broke a bottle over Guy's head. I could hear the "whack" echo across the lake.

Mom, Alyce, Chuck and I often visited the Ferrara family at their Brooklyn home. We took the train from the Syracuse Depot. Though Dad never came along, I looked for him in every man wearing railroad denims. At several stops along the way, including Poughkeepsie and Tarrytown, vendors boarded the passenger cars with trays laden with snacks, soda and coffee. Though I marveled at the mouth-watering temptations, Mom never purchased anything. She packed our food to save money.

Once in the city, going to Coney Island was a special treat. Mom would lay a blanket out on the sand and watch us romp in the ocean. She wore a two-piece, blue terry-cloth bathing suit and her white turban. After soaking up enough beach and sun, we headed over to ride the Cyclone Roller Coaster and the Steeple Chase. We'd finish the perfect day by riding the carousel. Mom always cheered me on, "Grab the brass ring, Tekkie, and make a wish."

I only won the ring once. Holding it close to my heart I wished that our days on the beach would go on forever.

Most summers, Guy visited us alone, giving Aunt Jean a needed break. Mom always said, "It's the least I can do for poor Jean. She has to put up with Guy's antics all year." It was during one of those summer visits Guy killed the rooster.

The year Alyce graduated from high school was one of the few times Jean and Guy traveled together. I envisioned her chasing him around the cake Mom would no doubt bake with Aunt Jean's frustration ending in something being tossed at Guy. I prayed it wouldn't be the cake.

CHAPTER FIVE

Leaving

The day before Alyce's graduation, an ambulance brought Dad home from the hospital. The two muscular male attendants struggled to lift his plaster-wrapped body onto the gurney and roll it into our house like some mass from outer space. All the neighbor ladies gathered to watch. Many said prayers on their rosaries, thanking God Dad wasn't one of their husbands.

The attendants cranked the gurney down so that it was even with the mattress and rolled Dad onto his bed, rotating him so he lay on his back. They covered him with a sheet and placed a white metal bedpan shaped like a kidney on the night stand. From where I stood looking into the bedroom through the doorway, I could only see my father's feet sticking out from under the sheet.

As soon as the attendants had Dad settled into his bed, he shouted to Alyce, "Let me hear your speech." Dad smiled and nodded as she stood beside his bed and delivered it flawlessly, just as she would during the graduation ceremonies the next day.

The following morning, Mom baked a cake for Alyce's open house. Dad, once a Navy cook, shouted orders from his bed about how she should decorate it. Chuck and his friends had rolled Dad's bed into the living room after breakfast so he could supervise the party preparations and enjoy the festivities that would follow the graduation ceremony. Fortunately, Mom and Dad's metal bed had wheels. If it hadn't been for the cast imprisoning Dad, I'd have thought our home was back to normal.

Friends started arriving in the late afternoon, bringing gifts to Alyce and gathering in a circle around Dad as though he was some tribal king. "You look ready to pitch a no-hitter," one male partier said.

Another pumped Dad's hand and chided, "Couldn't keep you outta the bars any other way, eh, Denny?"

Mom chuckled and pointed her finger at Dad as if saying, "He's got your number."

For her graduation, Alyce wore an emerald-colored dress that Mom had made from material Aunt Jean, a full-time seamstress in New York's clothing district, had given her. The dress accentuated Alyce's generous, naturally curly copper-red hair, green eyes and voluptuous body. She was the only redhead in our family, and I had jealously coveted her hair and body. But even more, I wanted the emerald dress, especially after years of made-over hand-me-downs. I frowned at my tomboy figure in the mirror and tried to perk up my straight, fine blond hair Mom had cut in a Dutch-boy style. I stuck my tongue out at the girl staring back.

Mom wore a powder blue shirtdress that brought out the blue in her eyes. Though usually timid, she managed the gathered group like the Queen of England on a walk-about. Mom flowed in and out of conversations like a pro. She leaned close to each person to whom she spoke and gave them her undivided attention. She never took her eyes off them and appeared to be completely engrossed in what they said as though he or she was the only person in the room.

Grandpa sat near the cake and watched the festivities. Once I caught him wiping his finger across the frosting and sneaking a taste. After cleaning his finger of any evidence, he placed it to his lips and said "Sshhh" and winked at me. It was our secret. Every now and then Grandpa would nod and smile to the newly arriving guests. Though he only spoke to Mom, Aunt Jean and me, I never doubted he was enjoying the gathering and the food.

As the party got underway, Dad told Alyce, "We know you will be a success." Mom nodded her head in agreement. "And you can live at home so you can save your money for college."

When we heard the motorcycle, Mom's head jerked up and tilted in the direction of the sound. Her face quickly changed from radiant to a frustrated flush as her eyes darkened and searched for a reaction from Alyce.

Dad raised his eyebrows and turned his head. He disregarded Mom's obvious concern. Instead he continued praising Alyce.

Alyce also ignored Mom's chastising eyes and looked toward the front door as Angelo, her boyfriend, walked in carrying a huge box wrapped in silver paper and red ribbon. As I watched Angelo's massive body fill the doorway, I could hear Mom's warning, "His Mediterranean good looks could charm the unwary."

I inspected him and agreed. Angelo could have been a movie star. He was over six feet tall and his well-toned and muscular body appeared intimidating rather than inviting to me. Yet I did envy his black curly hair and perfect white teeth. Both emphasized his dark complexion and deep rose-colored cheeks. Standing near him, I felt like an orphan in one of those workhouses from a Dickens novel who never had enough to eat to make them grow or reap the benefits from sunlight.

Mom leaned toward Alyce and said loud enough for everyone to hear, "I wonder what his excuse is this time for being late." She nodded in Angelo's direction.

Alyce walked away as Mom added, "And for not being at your graduation." Mom glared at Angelo.

Alyce rolled her eyes at me, while Angelo gave Mom a broad, self-assured, contemptuous smile. Mom's eyes darkened and narrowed with equal contempt.

Angelo handed Alyce the box and kissed her on the cheek. She blushed and glowed at the same time. "Congratulations, baby." He focused his attention on Alyce and said nothing to anyone else.

Alyce tore the red ribbon off the box and ripped the paper away. Angelo's boastful smile boldly exposed those flawless teeth when Alyce lifted the top off the box and took a full-length muskrat coat from it. "It's wonderful," she said, looking at Angelo through adoring eyes.

"A little warm to wear at this time of year." Mom's snide remark chilled the room.

Wrapping the coat tightly around her, Alyce ignored Mom and stroked the fur. The guests admired her as she twirled around and around. "I feel like a queen," she said and hugged Angelo.

After a few minutes of compliments, Alyce took the coat off and announced she was going with Angelo and his best friend, Tommy, for a ride. "We won't be gone long, so eat up, everyone." She rushed from the room to change.

A breeze filled the area when Alyce dashed by. In a flash Alyce changed from the emerald dress into blue jeans and a white shirt and pulled her hair into a ponytail. Her spirited retreat evidenced by both her energy and emotionally charged red cheeks left little doubt to whom she pledged her heart.

As my eyes followed Alyce out the door, I knew then I didn't like Angelo. He was taking Alyce away from her party. I also didn't like him for not paying any attention to the rest of us as though we weren't good enough for him. When I heard him pump the motorcycle to start, I sensed his actions that day were only the beginning of more unexpected and sad moments. I was losing my sister.

Standing alone in the middle of the room, Mom's intense face told me my intuition was all too accurate. When we heard the motorcycle leave, Mom brought her hand to her mouth as though to stop a scream. Lowering her hand, she turned toward Dad. Her brooding eyes signaled her displeasure. "That man is trouble," she said. "Besides, he's too old for Alyce."

"I'm ten years older than you, Marion, remember?"

Mom gave him a sharp look. "Things are different now."

The roomful of guests quieted as their eyes followed the sound of the fading motorcycle's engine.

"You should have more faith in her," Dad said with a wink. "She'll be all right."

Mom raised her eyebrows and shook her head in exasperation.

Feeling the heaviness created by Angelo's interruption, the guests began to leave. When the door closed behind the final parting person, Mom left the room and went to the kitchen. Sharing the hurt I saw in her eyes, I followed. Mom took the dish cloth from the hook over the sink and wiped the already-cleaned counter top. She sat down at the table and rubbed the cloth over and over the same spot.

A few weeks later, I heard a muffled conversation between Dad and Mom. When the door to their bedroom closed, I knew that talk was serious. So I tried to listen with even greater interest than usual and pressed my ear against the door. I heard Mom say, "We have no savings, and you know the railroad won't pay anything until the lawsuit is over." Mom cried out, "We have no money, Denny, except what social security gives us."

Alyce had begun work as a secretary right after graduation, but hadn't been paid yet. Chuck was only fifteen, so couldn't do anything but deliver newspapers. I wasn't even old enough to babysit. We children weren't much help.

I heard shuffling from behind the door and tried to sneak away. When Mom didn't come out, I returned to eavesdropping. I considered getting a glass and placing it between my ear and the door as I had seen the Three Stooges do, but I didn't want to miss anything if I left to get it. What I heard frightened me.

"Denny, you know Mr. Cossey is evicting us."

TEKLA DENNISON MILLER

I never liked Cossey because he was mean to Alyce, Chuck and me. So though I didn't know what evicting meant, I believed it was something to worry about. I heard Mom's footsteps stop abruptly when Dad said, "Ah, Marion, we've been through worse times."

"You're impossible, Denny." The door flew open too fast for me to get away. When Mom caught me there, she tightened her mouth into a thin line, followed by a huge open-mouth deep breath. She pressed pass me without a word and left the house. Mom went into the backyard and tore the drying laundry from the line.

One afternoon a week later, Mom gathered all three of us children around our kitchen table. "We're going to move next week," she said. "I don't want you to be alarmed by this. But until Dad is better...well, we need to watch how we spend our money."

Chuck spoke first. "I can get a job in September at Temple's Dairy or Tony's Fish Shack when I'm sixteen."

Mom patted his hand and smiled. "It's more important for you to work hard in school so you can get a scholarship for college. You know how important it is to get an education. It's your only ticket out of this poverty." Mom was calm and appeared resigned to cope with Cossey and his eviction.

"This is just a one of those vicissitudes of life and we must accept it," Mom explained as she always had. "Your dad and I will straighten things out," she said in a quiet, confident voice. "This is only temporary. No matter what happens, all my children will go to college."

As I listened to Mom's answer, I questioned whether Alyce could keep her scholarship and go to college if she was pregnant. Though I didn't understand everything about being pregnant, I knew it was important and confusing. Shortly before the train accident, I had overheard Alyce talking to her best friend Josie. They were sitting on the back porch thumbing through a bride magazine, planning Alyce's wedding. That was the first I had heard about any wedding.

Alyce whispered to Josie, "I'm pregnant so I need to get married."

"What will you tell your mother?" Josie asked.

"I don't know. But I have to get married or forever be labeled trash."

Alyce seemed excited, not at all upset. I was embarrassed and afraid for her, because from what I had heard you had to be married before you got pregnant. If it's the other way around, it's bad, and I didn't know what Mom would or could do.

Even I knew how difficult it was for girls to go to college, pregnant or not, because marriage was thought to be preferred. All young girls were encouraged to marry rather than get an education. Girls were raised to be good wives and mothers, not college graduates seeking careers. Knowing those facts, Mom's dream of all three of us having degrees and careers often seemed out of reach for Alyce and me, especially when Alyce had to get married.

I studied Mom's face. The serenity I saw clashed with the lines that had deepened in her forehead and between her eyebrows. Did we have to leave our home because I had spoiled that wedding at St. Matthew's? Or because I was a thief? Or because Cossey warned Mom about Chuck and me parachuting off the back porch to his garage on the clothesline pulley? And where were we going to live? Please not the green apartment building with the other people who had no money.

Alyce remained silent. I traced the lines on the table top where years of resting elbows had worn designs into the Formica. I wondered if we would take this table with us.

We heard Angelo's motorcycle arriving. Alyce's eyes followed the hum of the engine. "I guess this is as good a time as any to tell you." She took a deep breath.

Mom turned toward Alyce. Mom's eyebrows were arched, deepening the lines that formed above. She appeared to know what was coming next and started to say something when Alyce, without taking her eyes away from the direction of the motorcycle, began talking again. "Angelo and I are going to get married."

Mom lowered her head and shook it as though that action would shake loose and erase what Alyce said. When she lifted her head, the color had drained from her face. I could see the disappointment in it. "You don't have to do this," Mom whispered. "You're too young and have so much ahead of you. We'll get through this."

The sound from the motorcycle engine stopped. Alyce concentrated her attention on Mom. "It's too late," she said in almost as quiet a voice as Mom's. "I've made up my mind. It's the only way out of this mess for me...and he has money."

"He's not even working, Alyce," Mom said, giving her a cold stare. "And there are rumors that he's been in trouble."

"He has the truck farm." Alyce stood up from the table. "Besides, you don't understand." The freckles in Alyce's face darkened the louder her voice became. "People are jealous because I've caught a handsome, caring man who'll take care of me. Look at me, Mom." She held her arms straight out from her body. "I'm taller than most men and too smart for their liking. Angelo likes... loves me the way I am."

"What about your scholarship to Columbia University?" Mom asked. "It's all planned. You want to be an attorney."

"I can't." Alyce's answer sounded resigned. Her eyes filled with tears as she hopelessly asked, "Who wants an attorney for a wife?"

"Give yourself a chance," Mom pleaded as she leaned toward Alyce and tried to take her into her arms.

Alyce raised both hands in front of her to block Mom's nurturing. "I'm destined for the same life as you, Mom. What woman isn't?" She wiped a tear from her cheek.

Chuck's face reddened and mine heated up as we listened to their exchange. Even I knew that Alyce's self esteem wasn't the best. She was searching for acceptance of her 5'9" height, unruly hair, and brains. She didn't realize that she no longer had pimples or was no longer taller than the guys she went to school with or that her long, red, curly hair was the envy of all the girls and sought after by the boys. When she looked in the mirror, she once told me, "All I see is a gawky, freckle-faced teenager others make fun of and call 'carrot top.'"

I wanted to ask about Alyce's baby, but thought it probably wasn't the right time. I also didn't want her to permanently leave us either and believed telling the truth would keep her from going away.

Bewildered, but faced with having to do something, I blurted out, "What about your baby, Alyce?"

She was stunned and looked at me with more hatred than I had seen in anyone. She didn't take her eyes off me when she said, "I'm getting married with or without your approval, Mom." Such defiance was a new side I hadn't noticed in Alyce before. "I would marry him even if I wasn't pregnant."

Mom touched Alyce's shoulder. "Don't do what I did."

Alyce yanked away. As Alyce opened the door to leave, Mom stood up and yelled at her, "If you leave now, don't come back." Mom tilted her chin into the air. Her bullheadedness was overshadowed by the tears that formed in her eyes as Alyce slammed the door and was gone. Mom, Chuck and I were immobilized by the silence that filled the room. The stillness hinted at the regret we shared over what Mom and I had said.

CHAPTER SIX

Home is Where the Heart Is

Bill Thorpe parked a yellow moving van in front of our duplex one week after Alyce left. Mom had talked with the sheriff to stop the marriage. Sheriff McBride told her, "Alyce is eighteen. Nothing we can do. It's a family problem."

Kay and I sat on the front porch and watched as Dad's friends loaded the truck with all our possessions. I scrunched my face when I asked Kay, "Do you think there's a Catholic Church near my new home?"

She swept her dark curly hair away from her face and shrugged.

"I'll miss the weddings," I added as we both raised our eyes upward and focused on the gothic towers which menaced our neighborhood.

I was relieved when Dad's friends carried the Formica kitchen table to the truck, which was just before they loaded the last thing—Dad. His friends rolled him in his bed down a plywood ramp covering the front porch steps and up another ramp into the rear of the truck. Kay and I giggled when Dad waved at us like a king acknowledging his subjects from a gilded horse-drawn carriage. The men strapped the bed down so it wouldn't roll when the truck was in motion.

Mom followed behind and sat on the truck's tailgate, swinging her long, graceful legs. Even with her head covered in the turban, Mom looked like a young girl. She yelled to me, "Tell Kay good-bye and let's go. We've got a lot to do yet today."

Kay and I didn't budge. It was the first time I noticed how large Kay's brown eyes were. And the hundreds of freckles on her face reminded me of Alyce. That thought panicked me because I was afraid Alyce wouldn't know where we moved.

Words didn't come freely for Kay and me as they usually did. We had always lived next door to each other, gone to the same school and played together every day. We had no idea what this move meant, except she would go to Heman Street Elementary and I would go to Park Hill. Neither Kay nor I wanted to let our familiar lives go, which was like being in two different states.

Mom yelled, "Get a move on, Tekkie."

I finally said simply, "Good-bye."

Kay shrugged again and said, "Good-bye." She remained on the curb, and I watched her image shrink to a small, dark smudge and out of view as the truck took us to our new home.

We moved about four miles away to the other side of town, which seemed as far away as another city. The day before, Mom put Grandpa in the Onondaga Hills County Poor House, a home for the poor and elderly located on several hillside acres outside Syracuse. It was hard saying good-bye to him even though Mom vowed we would visit him often.

My whole world was coming apart.

Our new home was a gray cinder block garage that had been renovated into a one-room house. Two widowed Polish sisters, Tanya Zewkowski and Genka Tomascek, were our landlords. They lived in the house next to the garage with their four unruly children, three boys and one girl, ranging in age from four to nine. The widows scolded the children in an English-Polish combination language. That scolding was familiar to me. Mom often lapsed into that same combination when she was especially upset with something I did. When she began with, "Tekla Steffany Dennison," I knew I was in big trouble and she would forget some English words. Like the day she yelled, "This is the last time I'm telling you, Tekla Steffany Dennison, to *podnosic* your *odziez*." When I didn't do as she asked, Mom pointed to my clothes laying in a pile on the floor near the bed, stomped her foot and scolded, "You know what I mean."

If I ever dared to not hear what she was saying and ask for the hundredth time, "What?" Mom would tell me, "Cheese crackers got all muddy." It made absolutely no sense to me and I guess that suited Mom just fine at that moment.

The toilet was the only partitioned area in our new home, and that partition didn't go all the way to the ceiling. The door to the toilet was covered by a pink and green floral printed curtain. As I stood surveying our surroundings, I was startled by two eyes peering down from the exposed rafters that crossed at the center of the ceiling. Mom shouted for me to move out of the middle of the room and help unload the truck. When I didn't shift from the spot, Mom's eyes followed the direction of my upturned head and discovered a tabby cat. Since he seemed at home and not about to be moved, we decided to keep him. He no doubt had been used to roaming the fields that surrounded the garage and came through the open window whenever he wanted to get warm or sleep. I christened him Tiger.

Though aloof and apparently incensed that we were taking over his territory, Tiger remained in his lofty home until Mom bribed him down with a bowl of milk and liver left over from a chicken. Once the initial encounter was over, he decided sharing his quarters may not be all that bad and took up sleeping against Dad, an unmoving form, when not lounging on a rafter. As time passed everyone in our family gave Tiger a different name, so he became known as Tiger Pepper Rhubarb Boots Tom Whiskers Fatty Dennison.

We quickly settled into our new home. Unlike our duplex, the garage was located in the middle of fields where wild raspberries and strawberries grew. There was little soot from the trains, though I could still hear their whistles, especially in the quiet evenings. Every night I lay in bed and named the intersections—Hartwell, Bridge, Highland, James—the train crossed at each whistle's sound. This ritual was often interrupted by Dad's painful moans as he tried to find comfort in the immobilizing cast. After a while the whistles and the moans became one to me.

Our garage-home was cramped and had little privacy. Yet we managed to carry out our daily functions. Chuck and I slept on rollaway beds which were stored in a corner during the day. He once complained about being awakened by a rat running over his chest. I believed we had mice; rats I felt were an exaggeration. In either case, sleep didn't come easily most nights for me.

We took our weekly baths in a laundry tub that also served as the kitchen sink. Mom did our laundry in that tub using a wooden scrub board. When I watched her scrubbing clothes against the metal grooves, every nerve in my body responded to the scraping sound. She had scoured me in the same manner when Kay and I played in the newly tarred Yates Street, tarring ourselves as well. Though Dad had begged her not to, Mom had to cut my waist-length hair into a Dutch-boy style in order to rid it of the hardened tar balls.

The tub sat next to the gas cooking stove, and when the weather was cold, Mom lit the oven and opened its door to keep us warm while we bathed, dressed and ate, mostly breads, milk and eggs supplied on credit by delivery men. We sat right in front of the oven's mouth, sometimes propping our feet on its door. I was comforted by the warmth flowing from the oven and Mom's nurturing, so it never occurred to me that people lived any other way.

The times we had extra money, we ate fried potatoes, pancakes or oatmeal and the occasional rabbit or chicken from the Thorpe's coops. When I whined about our boring food, Mom reminded me that I was lucky. "During the Depression before you were born," she said, shaking her forefinger at me, "we lived in Newark with Grandpa, Grandma, Aunt Frances and her two sons, Adam and Artie." Mom put her hand on her hips. "And if that wasn't bad enough, we lived in a condemned house. We were lucky to get potatoes."

I stopped badgering Mom about our meals, but not about being sure Alyce had our new address—"In case she wants to visit," I told Mom. I missed Alyce and blamed myself and my big mouth for her eloping with Angelo.

Sue Zewkowski, the oldest of the four neighbor children and my new friend, walked to town with me once a week to offset the summer's boredom. One day at the end of August, we walked several miles to the library on the other side of town. Summer's humidity hung in the air like a fine mist of rain even though the first day of school was only a week away. We bumped into Alyce coming out of the sheriff's office located across the street from the library. She was crying and quickly wiped her eyes when she saw us. Ignoring her tears I smiled and waved as I jumped up and down with the excitement of seeing her. Alyce responded with a quiet, "Hi!"

Though obviously pregnant, she also was gaunt and pale. I attributed that to her pregnancy until I saw the bruises. When I asked about the black, yellow and blue marks on her arms, she said, "I fell." When she wiped a wisp of hair from her face, I noticed a fading dark patch over her right eye.

Before I could ask her why she was at the sheriff's office, she said, "I've got to go. Maybe I'll see you soon, Tekkie, but don't tell Mom you saw me here."

I didn't have to tell Mom. When I got home later that day, she was sitting on a kitchen chair next to Dad's bed crying and reading an article from the newspaper out loud to Dad. Angelo had been arrested on suspicion of raping a sixteen-year-old girl from the next town. "I told you, Denny, he was no good. What will happen now?"

"We can hardly do anything unless Alyce wants us to help," Dad said. "Besides, he's been arrested on suspicion. They don't know if he's guilty or not."

Mom gave him one of those icy frowns, wiped her eyes with the hem of her apron and was about to say something, but stopped when she saw me. She folded the paper and placed it on the floor between her and the wall as if she hiding it from me.

"I saw her today," I said as I twisted the hem of my shirt.

Mom turned to me. "Who?" Her eyes were red and puffy.

"Alyce. She was coming out of the sheriff's office."

"Did she say anything?" Mom stood up. Her forehead crinkled into canyon-size worry lines.

"Nope. Just hello and not to tell you where I saw her. She didn't look good." I had hoped by telling the truth that time, they'd break their silence with her. I was wrong. The only thing that came from Angelo's arrest was Mom telling me I could no longer hitchhike with the other kids to Green Lake to swim. School was about to start, so I thought she'd forget the new rule by the next summer.

A few weeks later, I entered fourth grade at Park Hill Elementary, a half mile up a hill from our home. Chuck was not so lucky. He had to walk two miles to East Syracuse High School. He joked about the distance: "It will help with my training for sports."

I agreed that participating in football, basketball and baseball, he needed help, but not much. He was a blond Adonis earning straight A's, along with a letter in each sport. Though the cheerleaders voted him to have the best legs on the basketball team, Chuck's physical attributes and academic and athletic abilities did not endear him to everyone. In fact, Ernie McBride, the sheriff's son, had a difficult time hiding his envy. Ernie was a local. His family helped establish East Syracuse. Our family had only lived in town for twelve years. To the old-time town citizens, we were recent arrivals and forever considered outsiders.

One Friday night after a basketball victory, the town's teenagers gathered as usual at Temple's Dairy on Manlius Street. When Chuck entered wearing his letterman's jacket, the group gathered around him cheering. They praised him for winning the game that night against Solvay High School, a major rival. Ernie, also a basketball player, followed Chuck into Temple's, but was ignored by the crowd. He couldn't accept being left out of the celebration. But even more, he couldn't tolerate all the praise going to an "outsider," even though Chuck was the best player on the team. Ernie never admitted it, but he could hardly dribble without tripping and was only allowed to play because he was the sheriff's son.

Ernie bulldozed through the crowd and pressed Chuck against the wall, holding him there with his left arm braced across Chuck's chest. "Just who do you think you are, Mr. Big-Shot, coming into this town like you own it?"

Ernie's face was inches from Chuck's.

"A better player than you, that's all." Chuck's face turned a deep red.

Chuck blocked Ernie's fist as it came up and aimed toward his jaw. He snatched Ernie's arm and used it like a catapult to fling him to the floor. Leaving him on the floor, Chuck left Temple's to walk home and cool off. Ernie shouted after him, "This ain't over. You can't do this and get away with it."

No one else moved. Like so many in that town, they feared the sheriff's retaliation if anything was said or happened to Ernie. Ernie probably took the others' lack of interference and silence as a sign of support.

Other than that day at the sheriff's, we hadn't heard from or seen Alyce since she stormed from the Kinne Street duplex to elope. We did learn from Sheriff McBride that Angelo had been released from jail because the victim wouldn't press charges. "Besides, she's a little tart, if you know what I mean," the sheriff said.

"What's a tart?" I asked Mom.

"Nothing you need to know about."

I looked up tart in the dictionary at the library so I wouldn't be so stupid the next time. It didn't help. A tart was a bitter small pie or a prostitute. I understood the pie, but had no idea what a prostitute was, even after I looked that word up, and I wasn't going to ask Mom.

Despite Angelo's release, I couldn't help thinking about those bruises I had seen on Alyce's arms. I wanted to tell Mom about them, but I wasn't sure why they bothered me. So I kept my mouth shut that time. Besides, I figured Mom probably would tell me again it was nothing I needed to know about.

Before I knew it Thanksgiving had passed, and our first Christmas in our garage-home was fast approaching. I was the angel in the school play on the last day before Christmas vacation. When the bell rang signaling the end of the day, I sprinted from the building and ran home still wearing the costume Mom had altered from the year before. I was always chosen to be the angel because I looked cherubic with my blond hair—not because of my behavior.

I was so energized by the cold air, thoughts of Christmas and just being nine years old, I bolted into our home, took off my winter coat and hurled it onto the hook to the side of the door. Mom, wearing her ever-present white apron and white terry cloth turban, looked up from where she sat at the kitchen table peeling apples. Light squeezing through the narrow window above her head bounced off the knife and danced across the cinder block wall behind her.

"Take off those boots before you go another step, young lady," she yelled without missing a single portion of the apple skin.

Though I didn't dare say it out loud, I wondered how much damage I could do to a cement floor. I knew not to badger her, though, and I didn't want to annoy her just before Christmas. She certainly wasn't my usual Mom, meeting me at the door with a smile, a hug and the offer of milk and my favorite sugar cookies, the ones filled with strawberry jam made from wild berries we'd picked during the summer. I scanned the room for what might be troubling her, but nothing seemed different. Even Tiger slept in his preferred perch in the rafters above Dad's bed. As I took off my boots, I realized what was missing. "Where's the Christmas tree, Mom? You promised we could decorate it tonight."

Mom stopped peeling apples and held the knife in midair. Her face looked as though she had just heard someone had died. "I'm afraid there'll be no tree this year." She glanced at Dad as though asking for guidance. "With your father out of work and no money coming in, we just can't afford it."

Mom might have been funny at times, but never lied. She had sworn we would have a tree.

She went back to peeling apples, so I looked to Dad for help. He was making pie crusts, a skill he had learned as a Navy cook. He was still in the body cast and lying on his stomach, parallel to the brown metal headboard, arms dangling over the side so that his hands reached the cement floor. Mom, no doubt, had rolled him to that position earlier.

"Tekkie," Dad called out to me. "Now that you're home, you can help me. Get me the rolling pin and four pie plates."

As ordered, I carried each item to him and placed them on the floor within his reach. I waited by the bed. The only sounds in the room were the shwooshing of Mom's paring knife and the clicking of Dad's utensils. The radio on the night stand rested next to the bedpan in an uncommon silence.

Dad rolled out the pie crusts on a wooden carving board that laid on the floor. When he was about halfway through, we heard a knock at the door. "Answer it," he ordered and continued to roll the pie dough into perfect circles.

I opened the door and faced a huge wicker basket that seemed suspended in midair. I stood on tiptoes for a closer look and discovered the basket was carried by one of three railroad workers flaunting huge grins. I recognized them as men I had seen with Dad drinking at my Godfather's bar. They were still dressed in coal-blackened, navy denim overalls just like Dad had worn before the accident.

The basket they carried was filled with every holiday delight imaginable. It was heaped with a fresh turkey, breads, cranberries, yams, tangerines, nuts and ribbon candies. The three gift-bearing men had laughed at me, an angel dancing around the basket as my sequined wings fluttered and a tinfoil halo bounced on my head. When I saw the tears in Dad's eyes as he turned his face to the wall, I stopped dancing.

No one spoke as Mom walked toward the men. When she faced the man carrying the basket, he thrust it at her as though he was caught with something he shouldn't have. She wrapped both her arms around it and quietly thanked the men, "This will mean a lot to the children." She placed the basket on the kitchen table and unpacked it.

Without the basket, the three gift-givers appeared ill at ease, putting their hands in their pockets and taking them out. In response to the awkward silence, one man laughed nervously. Finally, the man who had carried the basket let out a hearty good-bye. "Well, we'll be going, Denny. Merry Christmas to all of you."

Dad didn't answer, so I waved good-bye and shouted, "Merry Christmas to you, too!"

Mom, holding a bag of cranberries in her hand, answered, "Oh, yes, thank you."

When the men closed the door behind them, Dad returned to making pies. He maneuvered the last crust into a pie plate and filled all of them with the apples, pumpkin and lemon fillings Mom had prepared. His adept movements reminded me of the day he had pitched a no-hitter for the town team in the final game of the season. Now his powerful pitching arm had been reduced to pushing a rolling pin. Yet seeing him hanging over the side of a bed making pies, I believed he still had a lot of fight left in him.

The door suddenly burst open and banged against the wall. The commotion shocked Tiger out of his sleep. He let out a screeching, "Meeeooooowwww," and jumped onto Dad's cast. Though he tried to hang on with his extended claws, which sounded like fingernails scraping a chalk board, Tiger slid onto the bed and crouched behind the cast. While the cat hid, we looked at the door and saw Chuck displaying a silly grin. He was holding a Christmas tree.

I shouted and clapped. Mom stood up, wiped her hands on her apron and walked toward Chuck. "Did you steal that tree?"

Dad's eyes sparkled for the first time in months, returning them to the intense blue they had been before he was injured. He half yelled as if to hide this momentary emotion, "Tekkie, stop that noise, and Chuck, close the door. I'll never get these pies done. It's been like Grand Central Station here."

"Answer me, Chuck," Mom persisted as her eyes narrowed and she stomped her foot. "Where'd you get the tree?"

"It fell off a truck at the corner of Kinne and James Streets. I chased after the truck, but the driver kept going."

"Well, looks like there'll be a tree after all," Dad said with a wink.

Mom took a deep breath of relief and pointed to an empty space along the wall near the toilet. "Put it there." Then she went back to her task of unpacking the food basket.

That night, we brought out decoration boxes from under Dad's bed and trimmed the tree with scratched green, red and silver glass ornaments collected during my parents' nineteen-year marriage. We made stars and chains from newspaper and glue and sang along with carols playing on the radio.

The following night, snow fell as we walked home from the Christmas Eve service. When we got to our garage, we were greeted by glowing multicolored tree lights and Dad hanging over the side of the bed wrapping the last of four gifts, one for each of us. The comforting smells of homemade pies permeating the air that evening almost hid the musty odor that emanated from the cinder block walls and cement floor.

Mom, Chuck and I, our heads moving in unison as though choreographed, saw Alyce standing near the tree holding her one-month-old son, Kyle. I hadn't seen her since that day at the sheriff's office, and none of us had ever seen Kyle. Mom hastened to her as if physical distance was the only thing that had kept them apart since June. She hugged Alyce and took Kyle from her in one fluid movement. Mom's eyes glistened like the fresh snow in the moonlight as she cooed at Kyle, "Look at you. You're so beautiful."

Mom turned to Alyce. "I'm glad you came."

Alyce tossed her curly hair back and smiled, "I'm glad, too."

Chuck and I tickled the fat, rosy-cheeked baby in Mom's arms and marveled at the idea he was our nephew. "Do all babies have this much hair?" I asked as I patted Kyle's head.

"No," Alyce said. "But this one sure does."

Mom took Kyle over to Dad. She knelt beside the bed and held him close enough for Dad to touch. I swore I saw a smile on Kyle's face as Dad played with his chubby hands and tickled Kyle under the chin. Dad looked like the young baseball star we once knew him to be.

I sensed no one asked about Angelo because no one cared. Perhaps it was also because of the yellowing bruise we saw on Alyce's forehead which was exposed when she tossed her head back.

Mom handed Kyle back to Alyce and went to the stove. "This calls for a celebration," she announced.

"Show Kyle my tree." Chuck gently elbowed Alyce as Mom retreated to the stove. Kyle's eyes reflected the lights as Alyce carried him around the tree that stood in the middle of the floor. As Kyle's eyes followed the illumination, Chuck pointed to the decorations he had made, explaining in great detail how he had crafted them.

Mom made her special cocoa—boiled Hershey's powder cocoa, sugar and milk—in a huge saucepan and scooped it into mugs for us to drink as we opened our presents. She gave me my gift first. I removed the tape one piece at a time, taking great care not to rip the paper I recognized from the year before. I pulled the top off the box and removed the tissue paper. In the box was a beautiful dress, which I knew Mom had sewn on her cherished Singer treadmill machine, her single possession from better days. Made from used blue-striped mattress ticking Dad brought home from the railroad, the dress was trimmed at the neck and around the sleeves in white lace taken from one of Mom's own dresses.

Alyce handed me a tiny box wrapped in red. In that box was a silver cross on a chain. If I looked in the center by holding the cross close to my eye and into the light, I could read the Lord's Prayer.

Mom had also made two outfits for Kyle and gave them to a surprised Alyce. Perhaps Mom had hoped Christmas would bring Alyce's forgiveness, so she was prepared. Alyce's smile, however, could not hide her joyless eyes.

I raced to the toilet and tried on my new dress. I came back into the main room lifting the skirt out to the sides and curtsied. After Alyce clasped the cross around my neck, I twirled around and around the room. I felt like a princess.

Alyce laughed, "You look like an angel."

Mom chuckled, "Tekkie wasn't such an angel during church services tonight when she shouted 'When is Father Absent going to stop all that beseeching?'"

My face reddened as everyone else laughed. Dad motioned me to him and gave me a big hug as he laughed especially hard. Since he never went to church and probably thought I asked the right question.

By the time we finished our cocoa and opening presents, it was two in the morning. Mom tried to persuade Alyce to stay the night, but she said, "Angelo will be home soon. I should be at the farm when he gets there."

Mom crinkled her forehead. "Where is he?" she asked.

Alyce waved her hand as though to dismiss the question. "With family?" she asked and stated at the same time.

Mom smiled with only half her mouth.

We all hugged and vowed to see each other more in the new year. I was too excited to think much about their conversation or the fading bruises on Alyce. After Alyce left, I went to bed believing I was the luckiest person in the world and dreamed about eating a turkey drumstick.

CHAPTER SEVEN

Bombshell

One August night after that Christmas, Mom, Chuck and I were huddled together on my parents' bed listening to *The Lone Ranger* on the radio. Tiger as usual slept in the rafters above us. He laid his body horizontally along one beam and hung his paws at his sides down toward the floor. Dad had left about a week before to visit his brothers and sisters. He had been freed from the body cast, but because his back remained weak, he couldn't work and was compelled to wear a bulky brace of inflexible plastic and steel.

Dad and his friends didn't drink beer in the backyard and talk about baseball. He didn't take us on any more impromptu family picnics at my Godparents' home near Chittenango Falls or fish in the Butternut River. We never went to Thorpe's bar, and Dad even forgot Mom's annual "surprise" birthday party—a party to which he invited all his friends and supplied a keg of beer and cake. And since the train accident Dad never stopped for jelly donuts either, hot or cold.

It also was the first time I could remember that we didn't go to the railroad picnic or the firemen's fair. "What's the use?" he said. "I can't play in the ball game."

That summer his powerful pitching arm didn't win any more stuffed animals to add to my collection. Dad's upbeat, devil-be-damned personality turned into one filled with resentment and violent arguments with Mom. Often during these outbursts, I crouched behind the floral curtain of the toilet.

One time, scared by my parents' progressively more turbulent relationship, I stayed completely hidden. Music from the opera *Carmen* played on the radio.

"All you do every day is drown your self-pity in beer. You've been a bum since the first day I met you," Mom yelled.

Mom threw the alarm clock at Dad, missing his head by mere inches. He chased her around the kitchen table, pointing at the radio. "I have to do something to block that opera crap."

Mom hid behind a pillar. "All you want to do is play ball and drink with the boys," she shouted.

"You used to like baseball," Dad screamed, face turning red as his arms jabbed around the pillar trying to grab Mom. "You always thought you were too good for me."

In his brace, Dad could hardly keep up with Mom. She easily dodged him and taunted, "I did like baseball when it meant a paycheck. I think you'd rather die than be a father and husband."

"It would be better than listening to you and that high brow music." Dad stormed out of the house in defeat. When I was sure he was gone, I slipped to Mom's side to comfort her as though I was her parent. The whole time I wished Alyce was there to console me.

Those times were a far cry from Dad's old happy-go-lucky, let's-party days. Mom said it wasn't just because of having no money. Though her voice was filled with bitterness, she once excused his behavior, saying, "It's because of the constant pain he's in and his inability to play baseball anymore."

Dad's friends worked, played ball and drank in the Manlius Street bars as they always did, while he shuffled his gaunt frame from one corner of the garage to the other smoking cigarette after cigarette and chugging beer. Once the novelty of the accident wore off, Dad's friends had stopped coming around. Dad was no longer pitching shut-outs and no-hitters for the town team, so he stopped going to the games altogether.

After that last fight, he and Mom stopped talking to each other. He'd often use me for a sounding board. One day he hoisted me onto his lap and went into a monologue. "I miss the boys, Tekkie. I'd give anything to take my turn at bat or be buying groceries and cooking meals in that old caboose again." He nuzzled his face into my hair to block his crying.

Mom was used to Dad seeking solace from his friends and beers poured by my Godfather. So his abrupt departure that week didn't alarm her.

A loud knock at the door surprised us and interrupted the end of *The Lone Ranger*. Mom got up from the bed. Just before she reached the door, she stopped and glanced back at us. It seemed she knew what was coming next.

Mom opened the door, and I could see Sheriff McBride holding his brown uniform hat over his bulging stomach. It was the first time he had shown any respect to a member of our family. Mom nodded as he spoke to her in low tones. When Sheriff McBride left Mom went to the toilet area.

Chuck and I sat on the bed, hands folded in our laps and backs into the pillows, propped against the headboard. We watched in silence for a sign from the partition surrounding the toilet. I listened for a clue but could only hear the radio's drone. After several minutes, Mom came back into the room and stood in the center, staring at the wall behind the bed. Her eyes were barely visible in the dim light. The slump of her usually proud shoulders said everything.

Chuck and I swung our feet around and sat on the edge of the bed, legs dangling. We waited like that for Mom's next move or at the very least an explanation.

Mom opened and closed her mouth as though she was trying to formulate the right words. She straightened, walked toward us and sat on the bed between Chuck and me. Her arms felt heavy as she drew us to her and she simply said, "Dad died at Aunt Julia's. He had a heart attack."

I could feel my body tense as a lump as big as one of Dad's baseballs formed in my throat. I heard screaming as I thought Mom was wrong when she told me Dad would be taking me to Poughkeepsie as he had promised.

Suddenly I realized that the agonizing shrill I heard was mine. Mom released Chuck and wrapped both her arms around me. I nestled my head against her breasts. I squeezed my eyes closed and inhaled the familiar scent of Ivory soap. Once again Mom told me, "It will be ok. You'll see." She stroked the back of my head and gently rocked me. And once again, I wasn't sure it would be all right.

Chuck lowered his head into his hands and cried. Through his sniffles, he said, "Dad won't be at my graduation either."

We huddled together for what seemed to be hours until we heard only static from the radio.

Dad's funeral could have rivaled that of any national hero. The procession to the cemetery was a mile long, made up mostly of railroad men and their families. I half expected a twenty-one-train whistle salute. Other than those men, Dad's grave-site was surrounded by his baseball and drinking friends. Many railroad workers themselves had been victims of the same accident. Of his relatives only his older brother Dell and younger sister Julia attended.

At the funeral, we had found out from Dad's doctor that Dad had known he was going to die, which made sense of his pilgrimage to his relatives. Dad's statement to me about a month before also made sense. When he and

I went by the funeral home on Kinne Street, he told me, "I'll be there soon."

The idea he'd be visiting a funeral home seemed outlandish to me. "What do you mean, Dad?"

He smiled and patted my knee. "You'll see."

I cranked my head to try and look inside the building where Dad said he was going. All I could see was Boris Karloff in a black cape and denim overalls sitting in a coffin.

"But don't worry," Dad added as he stroked my hair. "You'll be ok." He winked like he always did, yet his tired eyes didn't convince me. Besides, I was sick of everyone telling me I'd be ok.

Everything was not ok.

The grave site was not like the ones depicted in the movies I had seen at the Pit. In those movies, the heroine and mourners wore smart black suits and the women wore veils covering their faces. Black umbrellas protected the mourners from drizzle falling from heavy gray skies.

The day we buried Dad was oppressively hot. The sun beat down on our bared faces as we squinted at each other. Hand-held cardboard fans from the funeral home replaced umbrellas. They did little to stop the sweat from dripping off our noses and chins. Mom did not hide her face behind a veil or fan, and she wore a floral shirtdress rather than the traditional black. Tears didn't flow from Mom's eyes, which seemed transformed from ones darkened by worry to ones that had found peace. Her rigid stance and the high angle of her chin projected arrogance and independence.

Dad's doctor was surprised we didn't know how bad his health was. That news should not have surprised any of us. It seemed we ignored all the signs. His once muscular body had been reduced to bone, and his sunken face had begun to remind me of an old man's without teeth. Dad had just turned forty-eight years old, but looked like a seventy-year-old in bad health. He also seemed determined to help his death along. Right after he was able to get around on his own, he went back to being a two-pack-a-day Camel man and drinking heavily, lamenting over not being able to drink with the guys or pitch ball. "I can barely get dressed, and when I do, this thing," he'd thump his brace, "gets in the way. What I'd give for one day back on the road."

A man approached us as we listened to the doctor. Mom's face brightened when she spotted him and waved. "Hank, thank you for coming."

The man kissed Mom on the cheek and said, "You know I wouldn't miss Denny's funeral after all he did for me."

Mom turned to Alyce and Chuck and told them to shut their gaping mouths.

"This is your father's friend Hank Borowy."

A partial smile was all I could muster as a greeting, while Alyce and Chuck said, "We know Mr. Borowy."

He leaned toward our family group and said in a soft voice spoke directly to we three children, "If it weren't for your father, I would never have been the pitcher I was. He taught me everything."

When Mr. Bowory left, I asked who he was and why everyone knew him but me. Alyce answered, "Hank Borowy played on the Newark Bears with Dad. He was a great pitcher who took the Chicago Cubs to the World Series in 1945. He shut out Detroit in 35 of the first 37 innings."

"You forgot to mention," Chuck stated with authority, "Mr. Borowy was also named MVP two years in a row." He scuffed his right foot in the dirt and looked at the grave. "Dad was a better pitcher," Chuck almost whispered.

After that explanation, I hoped Dad knew Mr. Bowory had come to his funeral. I also hoped Dad heard what he taught Alyce. She was a walking baseball encyclopedia and she was passing that talent onto Chuck. For me it wouldn't be until years later that I understood MVP meant the Most Valuable Player. I learned about MVP and that Hank Borowy was elected to the Baseball Hall of Fame when my school class made a trip to Cooperstown. Walking through the museum honoring men like my father, Cannonball Dennison, I was positive Dad's picture would have hung among those sports phenomena if he had stuck with baseball. Inside those walls I could hear him telling the story one more time about pitching a no-hitter.

As I listened to Dad's smoky voice tell his tales and studied the faces of Ty Cobb, Babe Ruth and the like, I fantasized about how different our lives would have been if he was a Yankee. Fingering the bats and balls collected from those heroes of summer, I dreamed about living in Newark or maybe in Brooklyn near Aunt Jean. In either case we'd have our own house and not renting a garage. Mom wouldn't worry about Dad squandering his pay at Thorpe's Bar. Alyce would be going to Columbia University. Chuck would probably follow in Dad's baseball footsteps after he graduated from college. And me, I'd have fewer hand-me-downs and wouldn't have to block out the arguments between Mom and Dad.

Wandering among the Baseball Hall of Famers on that day would be the only time I'd visit Cooperstown.

Alyce attended the funeral with Kyle. Angelo didn't come, giving the excuse he had planned a motorcycle trip with Tommy. When the four of us were alone, Alyce announced, "I'm pregnant."

Mom looked as disappointed by that news as she did the night Sheriff McBride delivered the message about Dad's death. "Don't you think it's too soon to have another baby?" she asked.

Alyce raised her hand as though to stop Mom's interrogation. "Kyle will be almost two years old when this baby's born," she said.

"Closer to a year and a half, but..." Mom didn't finish her statement. Instead she was distracted by a woman hovering with a young man in the shadow of a mature maple tree behind the group of mourners. She was dressed unfashionably in a gray forties style suit and hat. The young man, who seemed to be in his early twenties, wore a shirt scrubbed clean into fading plaid and pants that shined at the knees and seat and didn't quite reach the top of his scuffed shoes. He looked like the pictures I saw of Dad when he was about the same age, especially his intense blue eyes.

It turned out she was the third surprise of the day. The woman approached Mom as the last mourners gave their condolences and left the cemetery. The young man lingered beside the tree.

The woman introduced herself, "I'm Edna Dennison, Denny's former wife." She pointed in the direction of the tree and said, "That's Frank, Denny's son."

Mom's mouth dropped open and her eyes widened as she looked at the young man. I could hear only pieces of their heated conversation, yet I understood the gist of it. The woman wanted part of the railroad's settlement, whatever that would be.

"This is not the time or place to discuss such matters," Mom told the woman as she pointed toward Dad's grave. Mom turned away from her and scowled at the young man when she passed him on her way to the waiting mortuary car. Her manner translated into a silent accusation: "How dare you say you're my husband's son?"

Mom was so bewildered by this encounter she had forgotten Alyce, Chuck and I were there. We had difficulty keeping up with her long, determined stride. She was startled when we caught the car door before she could slam it on us. Mom's empty gaze told us she had no idea what she had done. Her face was the same one I had seen through the window of the ambulance the day of the train accident. I hugged Alyce and kissed the top of Kyle's head before Chuck and I sat in the car beside Mom. I peered out the rear window at Alyce as we drove away.

About a week later, Frank and the first Mrs. Dennison came to our home, again demanding some sort of compensation. "I have a right to it," Edna said.

Mom's answer was simple: "There's nothing." She waved her hand around the garage in evidence. "We have nothing, unless the railroad settles and gives us Denny's pension." Mom didn't tell them about the pending law suit filed by the families of the accident victims.

The first Mrs. Dennison and Frank surveyed our garage home. I was convinced they weren't persuaded by Mom's pleadings. Frank sucked in a great deal of air and said, "You better not be hiding anything from us if you know what's good for you."

Mom had enough of these two and shouted back as she shoved the woman out the door, "Don't ever threaten me, especially since I have no idea who you really are. And don't come back here if *you* know what's good for *you*." The scene reminded me of the day Mom threw Father Kelly out of our house.

Edna Dennison tidied her suit before she and Frank stomped off. I never saw them after that. We never saw any of Dad's relatives again. That didn't seem odd to me since we had hardly ever seen any of them anyway. None of us understood the reason for the distance between Dad and his family.

Aunt Julia tried to explain that estrangement when Chuck had questioned her about not seeing Dad's family, except for her and Uncle Dell, at the funeral. "Denny always did what he pleased," she said. "And after he found his first wife in bed with another man, he divorced her and disappeared. I guess our mother and siblings thought he was wrong for abandoning his children—and us."

"Children?" Chuck asked.

"Yes. There's a girl, Rita." Aunt Julia sighed. "She's a few years older than Alyce."

Standing with our mouths flopped open, none of us could give a response to that news.

For the six months following Dad's funeral, the Polish widows allowed Mom to pay half the rent until she could afford more. The bread and milk men delivered what little food we could afford and kept an on-going bill.

One day the widows stopped by to see Mom, standing at the door huddled together as though they were Siamese twins. Mrs. Zewkowski told Mom, "You're over three months behind in the rent and we can't afford to be nice any longer."

Her sister chimed in, "You're going to have to be out in a week."

Mom stared them down. "Who do you think you can rent this rat's nest to besides us?"

"Just be out in a week," Mrs. Zewkowski ordered. The two sisters, looking satisfied like predators who had just caught their prey, turned arm in arm and left. I let my imagination go wild over what had really happened to their husbands. Perhaps they poisoned them.

Within days of that confrontation, the lawsuit was settled and the railroad pension came through. It was as though someone had overheard the two sisters. When Mom found out about the settlement, she made plans to build the first house we ever owned. I called it the death house because it was constructed from the money the railroad agreed to pay in settlement for Dad's injuries. Mom also could collect Dad's meager railroad retirement benefits which had been withheld until that settlement. Suddenly we felt rich.

Having money didn't replace having a father. But I didn't find his absence as disturbing as I thought I would. I attributed that to his being gone for long periods of time on the road with New York Central when he was alive. Maybe it was also because by the time Dad died, the playful father I had known had been replaced by an unfamiliar angry man. Perhaps I was also grateful for not having to go to bed listening to my parents fight.

Many times I'd squeeze my eyes shut and try to conjure up the image of Dad in the casket. I couldn't. Usually all I could visualize was the day we passed by the funeral home when Dad told me he'd soon be there. Sometimes scenes from our many picnics at Chittenango Falls or the taste of hot jelly donuts would float through my mind in a haze. But even those memories were fading fast, especially since I don't remember Mom talking about Dad at all after he died.

Though I followed Mom around more closely than usual, afraid she too would leave me, at nine I had no way to express what was inside my head. In fact, for several months I had become more introverted. Mom was so preoccupied with coping on her own, I doubt she noticed any change in me. Shortly the guilt I harbored over my lack of remorse about Dad's death and Mom abandoning me were replaced by the excitement of our soon-to-be-built home.

At first in the months following Dad's funeral, Mom seemed more cheerful too. Though always frugal, she mentioned to me several times how thrilled she was finally able to provide well for Chuck and me. She was also looking forward to a house she owned rather living in rentals or a garage.

Though I questioned my lack of missing Dad as much as I thought I should, I was more uneasy about Mom's sunny disposition. Grief was short-lived for her, especially once the settlement money started coming in. After a while I decided Mom's upbeat disposition was due to her wanting to put her best foot forward to help her children get through those tough times and adjust quickly to our novel single-parent life.

CHAPTER EIGHT

Secrets

The same three railroad men who had brought us the Christmas basket built our new two-bedroom, 900-square-foot house. As I watched them labor in the summer's heat, I wondered where they had been when Dad needed them in his last days.

Instead of money, they labored for food and plenty of liquids. Mom carried frosty pitchers of lemonade and jugs of water to them, but no beer. It was one of the few times in my life that I saw Mom baking desserts and cookies when it wasn't a holiday. She carted huge trays filled with sandwiches and chocolate chip cookies, jam-filled sugar cookies, fruit pies and German chocolate cake to the building site.

I envied the workers as they gulped the treats down so fast it appeared they thought someone would steal them. I tasted every mouthful they took as though the treats were sliding into my very own stomach. I hardly had a chance to snatch a cookie before Mom scolded me, "You don't want bad teeth, do you?"

When I reached for one more sugar cookie, pleading with my eyes, she shook her finger at me. "That's the last one."

As soon as she retreated to the garage, I took another one. The workers scowled at me for taking their special morsel.

Dad's friends built our house after work and on their days off, so the construction took most of that bittersweet year. Early that summer Alyce stopped by late one afternoon on her way home from work. She told Mom, "I can't stay long. Angelo will wonder where I am," her eyes darting wildly as though looking for him. "I just wanted to see how things are going."

"We're fine, but you don't look well."

"It's just the pregnancy. It hasn't been as easy as Kyle's." Alyce balanced Kyle against her burgeoning stomach. She was wearing a straight black cotton skirt with a kick pleat at the lower back and red plaid cotton maternity blouse with large pleats that hung from her shoulders. Most days she held her long mass of curly hair clipped behind her neck in a tortoiseshell barrette. "It's easier this way," she told me when I questioned why she stopped styling it.

Mom bit her lower lip and took a few moments before she went on. "Alyce, are you sure everything's ok?" She took Kyle from Alyce and cooed, "You're sure a handsome guy, aren't you?" Kyle wiggled and grinned.

With each month Kyle looked more and more like Angelo. Kyle even held onto that mass of black curly hair he inherited from him.

Alyce half-smiled. "I got to go, Mom. I'll try to get by more often." She took Kyle from Mom and hesitated before she asked, "Do you think Tekkie could come over on the weekends and help me with Kyle and the cleaning?"

I shouted, "Yes!"

Mom gave me a scolding look, but agreed. I was sure Mom was remembering that when she had offered earlier to help, Alyce was quick to fluff-off the suggestion.

"I'll pick her up on Friday after work," Alyce said as she pressed her large stomach behind the steering wheel. "See you then."

Mom raised her right hand to her lips and held it there watching Alyce drive away in Angelo's blue Ford convertible. She turned to me and raised my chin with two fingers so I could see her stern eyes. "If there is any trouble at their farm," she said, "I want you to come home immediately."

"Nothing will happen," I whined. I didn't understand why she said that.

The following Friday Alyce picked me up. She, Kyle and I went grocery shopping at the new A&P in Eastwood, a small town on the way to the farm. Besides the supermarket, Eastwood also had a more modern and larger movie theater than the Pit. When I could save enough money, I'd hitchhike to the Eastwood Movie Theater. Once there I watched movies that Mom would have never allowed, like *Rock Around the Clock*, *On the Waterfront* and *Blackboard Jungle*. I had to sneak there pretending I was going to the Pit.

Alyce cashed her check from work to pay for the food. Along with the week's groceries, she bought snacks for what she called "girls' night."

By the time we got to the farm, it was dark. "Where's Angelo?" I asked as we carried the groceries from the car to the kitchen.

"Out. He goes out every Friday night." She dropped a full bag on the table and added in a dull voice, "With the guys."

Alyce and Angelo's place was actually a truck farm in an undeveloped area within the city limits. Angelo raised a few hogs and grew vegetables like lettuce, cucumbers and tomatoes. The two-story white clapboard house was set off the road down a steep gravel driveway. The next truck farm was a quarter a mile over and was owned by Angelo's oldest sister, Louisa, and her husband. They constructed a large fence to separate the two places after a feud. Louisa thought she should inherit the family farm instead of Angelo and their brother, Tony. It didn't matter that she already had a farm. After all, she was the oldest. The hostilities escalated into an armed confrontation which ended in the families not speaking to each other.

Alyce was the only person I knew who had a TV. Mom and all our neighbors only had radios. After we put the groceries away, we made dinner, which we ate from TV trays as we watched *Topper*, *The Loretta Young Show* and several other programs. I often practiced for hours swooping through a door like Loretta Young did at the opening of each show.

We followed dinner with large portions of bridge mix and ice cream. After Kyle had fallen asleep, we turned off TV and made fudge, taking turns hand-beating the gloss from the dark brown mixture. It was like a marathon of bad eating with me trying to make up for the years I went without such temptations. Unless I could sneak cookies from the men building our house, the only treats I got from Mom were rare—the occasional popcorn and ice cream. I must have had an iron stomach since I have no memory of ever getting sick from eating all the sweets.

Our "girls' night" was like a slumber party. We styled our hair, painted our nails and gossiped. That night Alyce became my best friend and confidante.

While I didn't miss Angelo that evening, Alyce kept going to the window facing the driveway every time she heard a car. Each time the car passed by the farm, she relaxed and returned to her seat in front of the TV or her turn at the fudge.

At the farm I slept in the bedroom off the living room. Alyce, Angelo and Kyle slept on the second floor. The narrow, steep, wooden stairs typical in old farmhouses were next to the only bathroom just off the kitchen.

Saturday morning I was awakened around 4:30 by shouting from Angelo and Alyce. At first I thought it was Mom and Dad at it again. When I shook the sleepiness away and finally realized where I was, I crept from my bed and sneaked into the kitchen. I stood at the bottom of the stairs so I could hear what they were saying.

"Where have you been until now, Angelo?"

"Out."

"What could you be doing all night?"

"I don't have to tell you anything. You just do what you're told and you'll have nothing to worry about."

As I listened to them, I realized they were not upstairs, but in the bathroom. Angelo's voice became louder, and I could hear something being dragged across the floor. He screamed, "Look in the mirror, Alyce. You're ugly."

Angelo opened the bathroom door as he knocked Alyce to the floor. I didn't have time to flee. I stood face to face with Angelo as he left the bathroom.

"Get back in bed," he shouted at me. "Don't ever sneak around here again, if you know what's good for you."

I peeked around him and saw Alyce use the sink to pull herself up. Her face was covered with a mixture of blood and tears. Frightened, I escaped to my bed, jumped in and covered my head with the blanket. I felt sick to my stomach when Alyce chased after Angelo saying, "I'm sorry I made you angry. I won't do it again."

Alyce dropped me off at home that Sunday afternoon. She didn't come into the house to see Mom. A bruise had formed near her nose and under her right eye. Alyce and I didn't talk about the bruise or what had happened that early Saturday morning in the bathroom. To me her silence meant she accepted her fate, while mine meant I didn't know what to say or do.

Mom was waiting at the door, her arms crossed just under her breasts. "How did everything go?" she asked.

"Fine," I answered as she made a space for me to pass. I headed for the chest of drawers to unpack my weekend clothes. Mom followed me.

"Why didn't Alyce come in for a while?"

I kept my back to her. "She and Angelo have somewhere to go," I lied. I didn't want to tell her what had happened because she wouldn't let me go back to the farm. I wanted to help Alyce, and selfishly I didn't want to give up TV and our "girls' night."

Mom placed her hands on my shoulders and turned me around to face her. "You're not trying to hide anything, are you? Remember we had an agreement. If anything happened at the farm, you'd tell me, right?"

I nodded and bit my tongue so I wouldn't blab something I didn't want Mom to know. I didn't want Alyce to be as angry with me as she was when I snitched about her being pregnant.

"I hope you're telling me the truth."

I could feel my eyes widen as I bit down harder on my tongue and nodded again. When I felt dizzy, I realized I was also holding my breath. After Mom took her hands off my shoulders and left, I let out such a sigh I sounded like some giant balloon releasing air. I suspected from Mom's persistent interrogation she was not persuaded that nothing was wrong at the farm.

Nevertheless, Mom did let me go back almost every day and on the weekends that whole summer. During that time, Angelo found work driving a cement truck and went out on Friday nights with his friend, Tommy, whom I had never seen.

Angelo worked long hours when the weather was good. He'd leave the house at five in the morning and wouldn't return until the sun had long set. There were fewer fights with Alyce because he was rarely home. But when the weather was bad, he spent his down time between the couch and the pool hall. During the down times he also became bored and easily agitated. During the down times, the fights increased.

Alyce picked me up as usual on the Friday of Labor Day weekend. Riding with the top down and my hair blowing in the last heat of the season, I lamented about how fast summer had gone by. Angelo was already home by the time we got to the farm. Alyce and I unloaded the groceries, while Angelo leaned against the car's trunk drinking a beer. He blocked Alyce as she lifted the last bag from the car. "What took you so long?" he asked.

"It's not late, Angelo." Her face was flushed from lugging heavy grocery bags.

He walked to the driver's side window, leaned in and checked the mileage. I held back a chuckle as his pants slid, exposing the top of his butt crack.

Alyce's face turned pale with fear. "Supper will only be a few minutes." She watched him from the corner of her eyes as she lumbered by him. Angelo raised, hoisting his pants up.

I carried Kyle from the car and opened the door to the kitchen for Alyce. Angelo walked through also, ignoring his son and me. The air that followed him as he passed by smelled of freshly applied Old Spice aftershave.

Once inside the kitchen, Angelo headed for the stairs. "I don't have time to eat," he said. "Tommy's waiting for me."

Alyce followed him. I stood at the bottom of the stairs holding Kyle in my arms, absentmindedly stroking his back. I listened to Alyce's footsteps travel the wood floor above as she pursued Angelo. Following those sounds, I looked from one spot to another on the ceiling. Kyle winced each time he heard his mother's loud voice. "Why are you going away this weekend?" she yelled. "You know your brother and his family are coming for a barbeque."

"I see Tony every week. Besides, I don't want to see you stuffing your fat face any more than I have to."

"I'm pregnant with your child, Angelo, not fat," she said, sounding hurt. "Can't you stay home this one time?"

I heard Angelo's saddlebags thump as he threw the rest of his gear into them. "We've had this trip planned for a long time. So quit your whining."

"You never told me about this trip."

"I don't have to tell you everything."

Alyce tugged at Angelo's arm as they came into view at the top of the stairs. "Please don't go. Not this time."

When Angelo shoved her hand away, Alyce lost her balance and fell down the stairs. Angelo quickly descended after her. Before I could put Kyle down to help, he lifted Alyce up and threw her onto a kitchen chair. "You need to be more careful." He heaved his saddle bags over his shoulder and left.

We listened to his motorcycle engine start and then fade as he rode up the steep hill of the driveway. I turned to Alyce, crumpled in the chair, and asked, "Are you all right? Can I do anything for you?"

Alyce placed her hand over her stomach and rose up from the chair. "I'm...." Blood covered the chair's seat and flowed from between her legs. "Oh God, I'm bleeding. Call my doctor. His number is on the pad next to the telephone."

Doctor Fields ordered an ambulance. I was left alone with Kyle. Since Mom didn't have a telephone, I called the Polish widows. As I waited for Mom to come to the phone, I passed time by counting the clicking sounds of the second hand on the kitchen clock. I counted 243 clicks by the time Mom came to the phone. I was crying uncontrollably, and through garbled sobs, I explained what had happened. Mom promised to walk to the farm as soon as we hung up. "You have to be strong, Tekkie. I'll be there as soon as possible. Ok?"

"Ok," I said through sobs. "But hurry."

I hung up the phone. I sat in the silent kitchen feeding Kyle, avoiding the bloodstained chair. I counted the minutes it would take for Mom to walk in the dark the five miles to the farm.

By the time Mom arrived, Kyle was asleep and I had put all the groceries away. It seemed a long time, maybe a day, since we had brought them home from the store. While I waited, many thoughts went through my head. Though

I felt such pain for my sister and her suffering, I was also angry with her for always giving into Angelo, for always taking the blame when she had done nothing wrong. In my eyes, Alyce had been stronger than that. As I was growing up, I had always admired her spunk, which I saw dwindling away in order to appease a mean, thoughtless man.

Doctor Fields called us late that evening asking where he could find Angelo. No one knew. He told Mom that Alyce had a miscarriage and had lost a great deal of blood. "She'll have to stay in the hospital for the weekend. Meanwhile, try to find her husband."

When Mom hung up, she turned to me. "What happened?"

I looked down at the darkened path worn into the linoleum floor by years of heavy farm boots. I slumped into a chair at the table. Defeated and overwhelmed, I started at the beginning—my first weekend at the farm.

Mom leaned against the old enamel kitchen sink the whole time I was giving my account. She wore the white terry cloth turban and her plaid house dress just as she had most of my life. Mom shook her head and raised her hand to her mouth when I described the arguments. I hadn't seen her look so sad since the day Alyce told her she was pregnant again.

"I'm sorry you didn't tell me sooner," she said. "You're lucky you didn't get hurt."

"But Alyce needs our help." I curled my foot around the leg of the chair and stroked the chrome that edged the Formica table top.

"She's made her bed and will have to lie in it. It's not our problem anymore." Mom stood over me twisting the towel she had taken from the hook near the sink.

I couldn't believe Mom was so uncaring, and I lashed out at her. I stood up from the table with such force, I knocked the chair over. "I hate you." I charged out the door and into the dark of the barn.

After a while, Mom found me sitting on the tractor. As she opened the old, weathered wood barn doors and stopped briefly in the entrance, her body cast an eerie larger-than-life shadow that engulfed me. She was framed by the yard light. The sight reminded me of a scene from a film noir. Her grotesque shadow grew larger and more contorted as she approached me. Seeing that ghostly figure, I was more apprehensive than comforted by her presence.

I had my arms tightly folded across my chest as though that inflexible action would protect me. Once Mom came closer and took on a more normal shape, I could see that she was wiping her hands on the kitchen towel, an everyday motion I had watched her do so many times before. My resistance weakened.

She put her hand on my right arm. At first I wanted to pull away from her to reinforce my independence and anger. But I gave in when she said, "I'm sorry, Tekkie. Of course we need to help Alyce if we can. I'm angry with Angelo, too, and sad for Alyce."

My body relaxed as I folded into hers. I desperately wanted her caress to erase my fear about Alyce's situation and the nightmare we were living.

"But there is so little we can do unless Alyce wants our help." She stuffed the towel into a pocket and put her arms around me. When I didn't answer, she added, "Do you understand?"

"Yes," I sniffled, the scent of her Ivory soap filling my nose. "But we need to be there for her, just in case."

CHAPTER NINE

Life is Just a Bowl of Cherries

Mom, Chuck and I moved into our new house in the fall two years after Dad died. The square, gray, asbestos-shingled house was one of five located on Cutler Street, a rural road lined with mature maple trees. Vast fields abundant with wild berries filled the vacant land stretching far into the horizon behind our house. There was one bathroom, a small living room and a kitchen with space in front of a window for the old Formica table. The two bedrooms at the rear of the house were separated from the kitchen and living room by a corridor where the bathroom and door to the basement were located. There were two outside doors. The one off the kitchen faced the Zewkowskis' house and the one off the living room faced a field. All the floors in the house were covered in red brick patterned linoleum. Though we still only bathed once a week, we took our baths in a real tub. The old laundry tub was now in the basement next to a ringer washing machine which Mom had bought at a second hand store.

Chuck had started his senior year in high school and I entered junior high. Seven hundred forty students attending seventh through twelfth grade shared the same old two-story brick building. Many students came from Catholic farm families with twelve to fifteen children in each, so I knew at least one kid from every family.

Since Mom had income again from Dad's railroad retirement benefits and legal settlement, she made sure I resumed the ballet lessons I had begun when I was five. Mom had visions of me dancing with the New York City Ballet. I, on the other hand, wanted to play baseball with the guys, a penchant I had inherited from Dad, to Mom's dismay.

Despite her desire for me to have a career in dance, Mom also never let

Chuck or me forget how important education was. "It will be your ticket out of poverty," she told us as she dished up our morning doses of oatmeal. I don't recall Mom saying gender would obstruct any goal I wanted to achieve.

Along with serving up a hearty breakfast, Mom made me wear brown oxford shoes. "They're to protect your feet for ballet," she told me.

I called them my Red Cross shoes. My friends called them barges.

"But Mom," I whined each time I laced the brown barges, "all the other girls wear saddle shoes or bucks."

Mom never budged from her decision. She'd tip my chin up with her hand so our eyes locked and say, "You don't want to be like everyone else, do you? Besides, you should learn to think and do for yourself." She'd turn back to the task at hand signaling the subject was closed.

At times Mom displayed moments of contradiction when it came to what our options were and how our world saw us. For instance, Alyce was born left-handed. Mom insisted she write with her right hand because she was afraid to raise a left-handed child, especially a girl, in a right-handed world. Knowing full well the 1950's expectations for a girl's destination—marriage, children and housework—Mom was determined that all barriers had to be removed to ensure our success. Consequently, Alyce learned to write right-handed but chose to do most everything else with her left.

Mom was also determined to take me as far away as she could from Dad's world of the railroad, bars and baseball. Her intent went beyond the opera and changing Alyce's handwriting. When I was in sixth grade, she enrolled me in ballroom dancing classes. Gary, a school friend, was my dance partner. He wanted to play golf, while I wanted to play baseball with the boys. So we often skipped dance class, a habit which became evident during our spring recital. Though I looked the part of a ballroom dancer in a lavender satin dress Mom made for me that was cinched at the waist with a large sash and bow, I'm sure the *Viennese Waltz* was not meant to be danced the way Gary and I did.

Gary's awkward six-foot body seemed to go in all directions, except the one, two, three-step-movement needed for the waltz. As though it would get us through the routine more quickly, he swung me around the floor at such a fast pace, we weren't in rhythm at all. I stumbled and tripped to keep up. Instead of being embarrassed, we giggled with unabashed pleasure at our unplanned scheme to mock refinement. Each time I stumbled, I heard the audience of mothers gasp. Each time Gary kept me from falling to the floor, they sighed with relief. Though there were nine other couples whirling gracefully around the gymnasium floor, all eyes were on us.

Mom stormed out of the gym at the end of our performance and walked home without me. When I got home, I tried to sneak into the house, but she was waiting at the door, hands on her hips and mouth in a frown, her lips pressed so hard together I could barely see a line. It reminded me of the time I brought her the bag of shoes from the green apartment.

"You made a fool of yourself today," she said. Mom grabbed my arm. Her hand tightened as she led me into the house. Trying to make me and my lavender dress disappear, I sank into the living room couch.

Mom paced the living room. When she stopped in front of me, I saw the hurt in her face. I wanted to crawl under the cushions. I hated disappointing her. But ballroom dancing? Ugh.

"No use trying to look sheepish," Mom said. "There is no excuse for what you did. How could you embarrass me like that?"

"In your own words, Mom, you gotta take the bitter with the better."

"Don't be such a smart-aleck." She half smiled. "I wish I weren't such a philosopher. It only gives you excuses."

"I just meant we can look on the positive side. I'm still taking ballet and I'm good at it."

Mom gave in after that ballroom dance performance. She let me get on with being a real teenager, dancing the jitterbug with Sue Zewkowski at the Friday night sock hops in the school gym, while Gary and the other guys watched from the sidelines.

For a while that year we moved into our new house, my life seemed to get back to normal. Once again, Mom occasionally greeted me after school as she had when I was younger and we lived on Kinne Street. Like those days she performed a Russian Cossack dance across our red brick linoleum floor. From a squatting position with her arms crossed over her full breasts and a butcher knife secured between her teeth, she'd kick her legs out from under her blue plaid house dress. Each time it was the same. When she'd finished kicking across the room to where I was standing, Mom would jump up, take the knife from her mouth and let out a glass-shattering laugh. She'd put on the recording of Benny Goodman's 1938 concert at Carnegie Hall and shimmy around me in a circle. Though swearing I'd never join her in that ritual, I always did. Eventually we'd jitterbug to our favorite Goodman piece, "Sing Sing Sing." When the piece ended we'd collapse onto the couch, out of breath and laughing.

She'd often stop in the middle of the shimmy and appear to be in a trance.

"You know I was a taxi dancer. But I had dreams of being on Broadway." She'd shake herself out of the daydream and resume the shimmy and shout above the Gene Krupa's drumming, "It'll be different for you."

Mom's daily attempts to keep her body trim by butt-walking across the same linoleum floor to the rhythms of the Big Bands were hindered by consuming the lemon meringue pies she'd make in ten-inch cast iron skillets. Lemon meringue was my brother's favorite pie and she would use every excuse to bake him one—birthdays, Christmas, Thanksgiving, graduation, baseball victories, baseball losses.

One time, she stopped in mid-butt-walk and looked up at me. "Maybe grandmothers shouldn't be too thin, do you think?" Before I could answer, she laughed. "Babies need some meat to cushion them when they're held." She patted her behind and continued butt-walking.

Though Mom was devoted to Benny Goodman, the opera, dancing and lemon meringue pie, housekeeping was her passion. With her head wrapped in that white terry cloth turban and armed with dust cloths, mops, Bon Ami and vinegar, she'd attack the house, singing, "Life is just a bowl of cherries. Don't take it serious. It's too mysterious. You live, you work, you worry so, but you can't take your dough when you go, go, go. So keep repeating it's the berries and live, love and laugh at it all." Sometimes she'd clean with manic energy while singing into the early morning hours.

Despite my mother's pursuit of cleanliness, my friends were never turned away from our door. Each day after school, we gathered around the TV to watch *The Mickey Mouse Club*. Chuck bought the televison for Mom with money he had saved during a summer camp counselor's job. All the girls fell in love with Spin and Marty and wanted to be Annette in spite of those absurd ears she wore. In winter while we watched TV, Mom made us cocoa in the old huge saucepan she used that last Christmas Eve when Dad was still alive. She'd scoop the drink into white crockery cups using a soup ladle. She'd serve us steaming cupfuls topped with marshmallows, but never scolded when the cocoa missed our mouths and landed on the floor.

Before she lost her hair, Mom had naturally wavy strawberry blond hair she often tucked under a chic hat that perched just above her large, sensitive blue eyes. Her high, elegant cheekbones and Romanesque nose were features models dreamed of. She held her 5'8" frame with dignity and wore clothes she had sewn herself that showed off her curvaceous figure without being provocative.

Although Mom was attractive, she was more striking than beautiful, and she had style. But beyond Mom's looks and skills, the most wonderful thing about her appearance was her smile. It lit up her face and intoxicated everyone in her presence—including once a real honest-to-goodness prince.

Mom had alluded to having known a prince, but she had never told me how she knew him. One day, following a jitterbug session and after much prodding from me—"Pleeeeease tell me about the prince"—Mom gave in. As we sat on the living room couch catching our breath, she told me what seemed more a fairytale than a true event.

"I met the prince while I was cleaning Mrs. Goodman's house. He was their guest."

"How would that stodgy woman know a prince?" I had met her only one time on a visit to New York City.

"Tekkie, don't be so cruel. She met the prince through her husband. He and the prince met in Europe at an auction."

"Umm, a prince." I jumped up from the couch and twirled around as if I was dancing with him.

"He often stood in the corner of the den while I cleaned," Mom continued as her eyes danced with me. "He never said a word. Just stood there and watched me."

"That seems odd," I said to the air as I stepped around.

"I thought so, too. Then one day he walked toward me, took my hand and brought it up to his mouth, but never took his eyes off my face. I was so stunned."

"Wow." I stopped twirling and smiled at Mom. "Just like the movies. What happened next?"

"He asked me to a party he said was in my honor. He said it was to celebrate my classic beauty and charm. Can you imagine?" She laughed and stood up to look in the mirror over the couch. While staring at her image, she caressed her face. She touched the turban. She turned toward me, giggled and posed like a model.

"What happened after the party?" I pried.

"I never went to the party."

"What! How could you not go to a party with a prince?" I bowed to her as though she were a princess.

Mom told me that she stood the prince up because her best friend, who was jealous of the invitation, pleaded with her not to desert her. "Besides, I was only sixteen. What did I know about princes?" she asked.

I had a strong sense Mom didn't feel she was good enough for such a man and used her friend and age as an excuse. One time after that day Mom revealed her true thoughts about passing up a prince and often told me, "I've learned a few things in my life, Tekkie. And one is that you can marry a rich man as easily as a poor one." She'd chuckle and add, "You may not be any happier, but you'll have more money to help with the sorrow."

Mom also kidded me when I complained about my big feet, a size eight when I was only eleven. She told me, "It's a sign of an aristocrat. All royals have big feet."

I believed her and often dreamed that I was a lost princess who would soon be found. Perhaps I had been influenced by the myths circulating about Anastasia. I secretly hoped Mom was Anastasia.

Every Sunday afternoon, as Mom had pledged, we visited Grandpa at the Onondaga County Poor House. He lived in a dorm with sixty other men. Their foot lockers and white metal hospital-style beds formed five perfect rows. Most of the men spoke Polish like Grandpa, making it easy for him to have friends. Each time I visited, he took my hand and carted me from one man to the other, smiling and pointing at me as he spoke.

As though nothing had changed, Grandpa and I walked together hand and hand across the acres of rolling hills. He wore the same hat and coat, patched many times by his friend Manny, a tailor from the old country who occupied the bed next to Grandpa. After our walk, we'd go to Grandpa's area, sit on his bed and open his foot locker, from which he'd take out a gift for me. The gifts were always fabricated from something he had found on his daily walks just as he did when he lived with us.

One day Grandpa introduced me to a woman he confessed was his girlfriend, Sophie. He met her in the cannery where they worked eight hours a day, five days a week except on holidays. She was thin and well-groomed, and was a fastidious dresser. She was also Polish and the absolute opposite of the woman, my grandmother, I saw in pictures. Unlike Grandpa's cheerful girlfriend, Grandma had been fat, stern-looking and ill-groomed. Sophie had more pizzazz. She wore colorful scarves to liven up even her dullest dress, while Grandma seemed to wear only black.

After working all week in the garden and cannery, Grandpa went to every Saturday night dance with Sophie until the day he died. I only could imagine these two young-at-heart souls dancing the polka until the midnight curfew. In my dreams they looked like Fred Astaire and Ginger Rogers. I wished Sophie was my grandmother.

Mom's meager beginnings and her lack of education and parental encouragement to go to school didn't stop her pursuit of knowledge. She and I went to the library each Saturday morning to exchange our books. She'd take out seven books and read one each night. These were not the dime store romance novels, but books like *The House of Seven Gables* and *Anna Karenina*. She also read every book she could find on world religions, psychology and philosophy. Every night we'd sit in the bed that once held Dad in his body cast, prop our pillows against the metal headboard and read our books while Chuck studied in his bedroom to make sure he won a college scholarship. I would fall asleep, but Mom would read on until she had finished the last page.

Mom also had an extraordinary vocabulary. She read the dictionary almost as much as she read the Bible. Though she often pronounced words incorrectly, she knew their meanings. Words such as sequacious and taciturn would sound like seequacheeose and taceeturn. She'd admonish me if I dared laugh at her pronunciation of the few words I recognized. Vicissitude was one word I did know. Mom used it to wiggle her way out of many situations or questions I had just like the day she told us we had to move from Kinne Street. She said, "It's just one of those vicissitudes of life." At least that was better than her telling me, "It's nothing you should know about."

Mom added another name to those we already called our cat, Tiger. One night she slapped a book closed and announced, "I'm changing Tiger's name to Yehudi."

I looked up from my Nancy Drew book and asked, "What's a Yehudi?"

"Yehudi Menuhin. He's a remarkable violinist. You should read this." She waved the volume at me. "It's his biography. He is a prodigy and is known throughout the world."

Tiger-Yehudi was stretched across the bottom of our bed. I leaned to pat him on the head. "You poor thing. Another name to put up with. Will you ever know your real identity?"

He purred and Mom laughed. "Tomorrow we'll play some of Yehudi's music on the record player. Even he," Mom pointed to the cat, "will appreciate his namesake's talents."

When Mom was forty and I was twelve, she took a test at Syracuse University and scored higher than anyone before in the areas of philosophy, religion and psychology. She was such a contrast to Dad and what he wanted from life. Yet in that era, the only acceptable force that could have separated them was Dad's death. If it was another time, I believed she would have left him. Fearing that inevitable state for all women, I thought about Alyce's question the day she ran away from us—"I'm destined for the same life as you, Mom. What woman isn't?"

As hard as I fought that idea, I prayed my destiny would not be the same as Mom and Alyce's. I wanted more from my life, even though I wasn't sure what that was. Except for the love they showed for their children, I just knew neither seemed happy in their roles.

After she took those university exams, I remember Mom opening the envelope holding the letter from Syracuse University congratulating her on her outstanding achievement. As she read the message to herself, Mom's mouth curved into a sad smile. She dropped the letter on the kitchen table and left the room. I hesitated for a moment before I picked up the letter to read it. I didn't what to snoop, but my curiosity got the better of me. Prepared for bad news, I was stunned when I read about Mom's test scores. I didn't understand how she could be depressed about such news.

After reading the two pages of accolades, I looked for Mom and found her sitting on her bed, hands resting in her lap. She looked up at me as I entered and patted the bed beside her.

"Sit," she said.

I did, but before I could ask her anything, she took both my hands in hers. "I want you to know how much education means if you put it to use." Her eyes fixed on mine. "It's too late for me." Her face was soft and showed no remorse.

"But Mom..."

She held her finger to her mouth to quiet me. "So although I've scored high on a few tests, I won't be able to do anything about it now."

Mom put her arm around me. "I don't want you to wait until it's too late for you. Get educated and do whatever you want. Never put it off."

"Why did you take those tests then?" I asked.

"To see what I taught myself."

I smiled at her, but wasn't sure I understood what she was saying or why she couldn't do something more. She patted my hand, stood up, and got her coat from the closet. "I'll be back in a while," she said as she shut the kitchen door and left the house.

I stood in the living room window and watched her walk down the street toward town. She didn't come home until the following morning. That was the beginning of her wanderings, and the first of many other nights she would leave me alone.

One day, Mom climbed on a stool and removed two large cardboard boxes from the top shelf of her closet. The contents of those boxes had always been a mystery to me. She carried them from the shelf and placed them side by side on the old Formica kitchen table. She motioned for me to sit next to her as she lifted the lids. Mom took out four huge photo albums from them and put them in front of me. "This is World War II," she said.

For several hours we sat together as she read page by page the articles from newspaper clippings that were browned and curled at the edges. Some had pulled away from the black triangle shape corner stick-ons. She pointed to photographs and read their captions. One picture showed several soldiers loaded down with gear wading through a large surf heading for a beach. The soldiers held their weapons high above their heads as gunfire exploded around them and bodies floated face-down in the water. She concentrated on the picture as I read and reread the caption, "Omaha Beach June 6, 1944." I turned to her and said, "June 6 is your birthday, Mom."

She answered without looking away from the picture, "Yes. It is."

We turned several more pages in silence. She fingered the pictures and articles as though her touch would bring the pages alive. Suddenly she took my hand and held it tight. "I don't want you to ever forget this war. I pray your generation will learn from its devastation."

Her voice was hoarse and shaky. Yet the determination I heard in her words told me I should absorb all I could from the history she laid out before me. That day was the first of many I spent with her and those albums. World War II became so vivid for me, it was my war too.

During one of our readings, Mom pointed to a picture of Andy, her sister Steffany's son and one of the boys she was raised with after Steffany died. Mom explained that Andy was more like a brother to her than her own siblings because they were closer in age. The picture was in shades of brown and looked old-fashioned to me. The information printed under the picture said Andy died a War Hero on Fiji. Mom stroked the picture for several minutes as her eyes became red and moist. She turned to me and said, "He was a hero. But that's not why he died. He couldn't take the war any more and killed himself."

I was thankful that we sat for several minutes without talking. It gave me time to process Andy's suffering, which was so horrid he took his own life. Mom closed the album, put it back on the shelf and left the room. While other mothers shared glamour magazines, recipes, and fashion with their daughters, Mom gave me World War II.

CHAPTER TEN

Changing

As I continued going to the farm to help Alyce, my tasks extended beyond cleaning and caring for Kyle, who was roaring through his terrible twos. I also worked in the small store that fronted Erie Boulevard where I sold the vegetables grown on the truck farm. Alyce and I became closer than usual sisters and more like best friends. During one "girls' night" she confided, "I'm pregnant again."

Though I was excited about the baby due in October, I was afraid the new arrival would draw her attentions away from me and more toward Angelo. Also when Alyce made her announcement, she sounded more tentative than happy for an expectant mother.

We all noticed Angelo had been more thoughtful during that pregnancy. He stayed closer to home and didn't ride motorcycles with Tommy as much. He often helped carry the groceries when Alyce brought them home. But he still kept his after-dinner habit, reclining on the couch. Mom and I, and Alyce especially, believed Angelo was changing.

Mom often walked to the farm when I was alone with Kyle. She never left home without carrying her white purse and wearing her wig, a white straw hat, her two-piece short-sleeved blue seersucker summer suit and white wedge sandals. People who saw her passing said, "Your mother always looks perfect." I had to chuckle when they added, "And her hair." They eyed her with admiration. "Never a strand out of place."

If there was enough money, Mom made one good outfit a season for herself. She wore it regularly and with panache. The blue seersucker was the one for that summer. Her physical appearance seemed important to her as though she thought that was all she had worth sharing with the world. I supposed she had forgotten about Syracuse University.

I once asked Mom, "Why don't you go to college now?"

She gave me a vague answer. "It's just too late for me." Mom followed that with a hug and quick smile and said, "Don't you worry about me. I know I'm smart and I can read any book I want. But you can be anything and do anything you want."

When not at the farm or home, Mom wandered off, taking long walks, her destinations unknown to us and perhaps even to her. Many days I waited at the window looking for her. She would be wearing her familiar two-piece seersucker or plum wool walking suit, depending on the season. Sometimes I stood with my head pressed against the window the whole night waiting for her, hopeful that every movement or shadow I saw was Mom coming home.

I also began cooking more of our meals and taking care of the house, though my cleaning, unlike Mom's, meant we could no longer eat off the floors if we chose. The first time I made dinner, I phoned Alyce at work and asked, "What's shortening?"

Alyce laughed so loud I had to hold the receiver away from my ear. "What's so funny?" I asked.

"Nothing. But I can see it's time I give you some cooking lessons when you're at the farm."

That first dinner—meatloaf, mashed potatoes and chocolate cake made with vinegar to sour the milk as Mom always did—never was eaten. Mom didn't come home.

As I took my station at the window, ever-vigilant as a prison guard, something horrible happened. Two cars collided head-on, throwing one driver across the road and decapitating the other. The head rolled down the street and stopped near the window where I stood. I was so frightened by what had happened, I couldn't move from that spot or stop staring at the head. When the police and the ambulance finally came and took the body and the head away, I vomited.

When Mom did get home, I was still sitting on the floor near the toilet. She scolded me for being up so late. After she saw the dinner I had made, waiting on the table and hardened into congealed mounds, she collapsed next to me. We held onto each other, sitting on the cold floor next to the toilet until dawn broke.

Chuck graduated from high school as the valedictorian and won a scholarship to Dartmouth. We all were proud, but also sad that even though it was Mom who encouraged school, Dad couldn't have been a part of his son's success. Dad, no doubt, would have been much happier if Chuck took the offer to play for the Dodgers. Chuck's decision not to play pro ball was partly based on a basketball injury which hindered his playing ability.

Chuck's nemesis, Ernie McBride, the sheriff's son, didn't win a scholarship. Though Ernie's relationship with Chuck had soured years earlier, a basketball game permanently ended it. During one of the first games in their senior year, Ernie wanted to get Chuck off the team. He knew Chuck was a better player, so when they jumped for the same ball, Ernie deliberately brought his elbow down hard into Chuck's right eye. Chuck fell to the floor as the spectators let out horrified gasps. Mom's voice could be heard over them all, "Oh no. No." She was held back by the spectators from running to his side until Chuck was carried from the floor on a stretcher and transported to the hospital. Though the game continued, no one cheered Ernie. Instead they booed him.

That injury almost cost Chuck his right eye. Visiting him in the hospital ward was just as startling as the first time I had seen Dad in the body cast. Chuck was hooked up to a metal apparatus that held his head perfectly still. He looked like something Doctor Frankenstein rigged up. If he moved his head even slightly, Chuck would have lost the sight in his eye. Fortunately his eye healed, but he had to wear glasses to correct the damaged vision.

After Chuck was released from the hospital, he returned to high school wearing a black patch over his eye. When he was benched for the rest of the playing season, Ernie thought he'd finally won. That was short-lived. The students honored Chuck during one half time. Ernie was enraged by the praise Chuck received that evening, but knew he had gone too far. Even Ernie's father, the sheriff, couldn't change that.

When Chuck left for Dartmouth at the end of August, I got to use his bedroom while he was at school. That year he seldom came home because of the distance and money, so I resented giving up the room when he did visit. On those occasions, mostly holidays, Chuck often wakened me by jerking me from under the covers and hauling me down the hallway to the kitchen. Standing over me like a huge shadow, he'd put his hands on his hips, deepen his voice and order, "Make me breakfast." He never did that when Mom was home, only those times she wandered away.

His behavior on those mornings wasn't as bad as the way he and Alyce had treated me when I was younger. Mom made them take me to their high school dances and games. I'm sure they were embarrassed to show up at the Friday dances in the high school gym with a snot-nosed seven-year-old. How cool would that look to whomever they had their eye on?

They'd park me on the bleachers and order me not to move. If they talked to me it was in pig Latin so I couldn't understand it while their friends snickered in approval. Alyce and Chuck threatened to leave me home alone If I dared complain to Mom about how they treated me. They even said they'd risk Mom's wrath if I exposed them.

One time at a dance they surrounded me. Alyce had her hands on her hips and looked like Mom while Chuck shook his finger in my face and asked, "Remember what she did to me the last time you squealed?" He crammed his stern face within inches of mine.

Feeling as small as an insect, I nodded at him and leaned as far back as I could without falling over as his six-foot athletic body towered over me. How well I remembered what happened when I snitched on Chuck. Sitting on the bleachers that night watching Chuck and Alyce jitterbug, I recalled one other gymnasium dance—or rather the day after. While Mom was gone and Dad was on the road, Chuck had shown me official-looking papers with my name typed on them. "You're adopted and if you make trouble," he said as he flaunted the papers in my face, "Mom will send you away."

I decided it was too exciting to be included in a teenage activity to complain and take a chance I'd be sent away. So I continued to sit in silence on the sidelines watching the older kids dance and tied and untied the sash wrapped around my waist. One night I had had enough of their pig Latin. The next day I decided to show Mom the papers that Chuck used to persuade me I was adopted and keep me silent. I was crying as I handed them to her. "Chuck says I'm adopted. He says these papers prove it."

Mom took the papers from me and hugged me in one motion. "He was just teasing you."

"But my name is on them."

"Of course it is. So are Chuck's and Alyce's. See?" She pointed to their names printed just as boldly as mine in the middle of the next page. "They're insurance papers."

I felt better about not being adopted, but I also wanted revenge for what Chuck put me through. I didn't have to wait long because Mom immediately stood up and yelled for him. She took the cat-of-nine-tails from a hook on the kitchen wall and met him as he flew into the room. As she hit him with the whip of nine leather thongs, she yelled, "Don't you ever do anything so cruel as that again."

Mom swung at him with such rapidity, her arms blurred in the motion and seemed not to be attached to her as the sound of leather meeting flesh was distinct. Mom's eyes were wild; her face crinkled into one that looked like a Halloween witch as she hovered closer to Chuck without stopping the thrashing. She was out of control and I was sure she didn't know why. I didn't recognize the woman reacting with such uncommon violence.

Chuck's face crumbled into a mixture of fear and hurt as he doubled up on the floor and covered his head. "What did I do?" His muffled sobs sounded like his head was in a hole in the ground.

Mom threw the papers at him. I crouched down beside him, screaming up at her, "I'm sorry. I didn't mean for you to hurt him."

Mom's mouth opened in horror at what she had done as she dropped the whip on the floor and walked out the kitchen door. Chuck and I clung to each other without talking for what seemed to be hours. I wanted to ask him what was happening to Mom, but was afraid to. She had never hit any of us before that day.

While making breakfast for Chuck was my least favorite activity, my most favorite was going to a Johnny Mathis concert as his date. That summer night made up for the pig Latin and adoption scam. I also felt Chuck had finally forgiven me for snitching on him to Mom.

To get me ready for my big date, Alyce outfitted me in one of her dresses, piled my hair into a well-lacquered French twist, and made up my face so I'd look much older than my twelve years. The top of the dress had long sleeves and was made from black eyelet, while the skirt was multi-tiered white organza. I had to stuff tissue in one of Alyce's bras to make the dress fit. When the make-over was completed, Chuck placed his fraternity pin above my left breast. Once disguised, I gave an Academy Award performance that fooled everyone at the night club. I felt like Eliza Doolittle from *My Fair Lady*. I too had been transformed from a scrawny, awkward young woman into a princess. Though my escort was just my brother, I reveled in the envious attention Chuck's classic Nordic good looks drew from the other young women at the club.

Alyce's second son, Todd, was born that following October. He was healthy and the delivery was normal. Angelo even gave up his last motorcycle trip for the season to be at the hospital. It was another signal to us that things could be getting better, or perhaps it was just as I had observed—Alyce was more obedient.

I was at the farm taking care of Kyle when Angelo brought Alyce home from the hospital. He carried her over the threshold as though she was a new bride. Wearing the muskrat coat he had given her on her graduation day, Alyce wrapped Todd in it and held him against her chest. Angelo put Alyce down on the living room couch and gave her a dozen red roses.

Before Alyce could introduce Kyle to Todd, Angelo took Todd from her and handed him to me. His large hand encircled Alyce's arm and he steered her upstairs to the bedroom.

Listening to the commotion from above, I held Todd in my lap with one arm and pulled Kyle close to me with the other. While Todd continued to sleep and hadn't noticed anything different, Kyle asked, "Where's Mommy going? I want Mommy."

I stroked his arm and said, "Mommy will be right back."

I felt abandoned and mentally questioned how the parents of a newborn could just up and leave as they did without any explanation. My first thought was that Angelo had suddenly become angry about something as he had so often in the past. So I expected to hear the usual scuffle. Instead the two appeared in about a half hour. Angelo was smiling. Alyce stared at the floor as she took both Todd and Kyle to the kitchen for something to eat without a word. Not wanting to remain in the room alone with him, I followed Alyce.

Though I still helped Alyce, I was concerned about leaving Mom by herself. She had begun talking more about religion and declaring she was going to hell. One day I mustered enough courage to ask her why she thought this. Fingering the Bible she held, Mom gave me one of those half-here smiles. "You'll see."

After another one of her destiny tirades, Mom stood up in mid-sentence and draped her coat over her shoulders. When she reached the door, she said, "I've got to go."

When my usual bedtime rolled around, I crawled under the covers and fell into a restless sleep. I had grown used to her night wanderings, but slept listening for the kitchen door to open.

She came home the following morning with a black Labrador retriever puppy. I was delighted, but she couldn't tell me where she had found him or where she had been. We named the Lab Tobias Tugmutton, Toby for short. Though Yehudi, a.k.a. Tiger, was not pleased about sharing his house with this foreigner, he eventually grew to tolerate Toby. In little time Toby was my constant companion and stood with me at the window to wait for Mom through those long nights. During all those hours of excruciating vigilance, it never occurred to Mom she was leaving me alone.

Mom almost sent Toby packing that following Christmas Eve when he took down our decorated tree with one powerful wag of his tail and dragged it across the living room. Mom had to laugh, though, when the more he tried to free himself from the tree, the more tangled he became. The more tangled he got, the more the ornaments spun off the tree, crashing and baffling Toby. The more he tried to shake himself loose, the harder we laughed. The harder we laughed, the more we couldn't move. Mom and I hadn't laughed together like that in months. If for no other reason than laughter, Toby was a good addition to our family.

Mom finally freed Toby, who fled from the room with his tail between his legs, yapping, and hid under the bed. He didn't come out until Christmas Day when Mom bribed him with turkey. Toby ate the turkey, but stayed clear of the tree.

On that Christmas morning, Chuck and I found Mom's beige cotton stockings left over from WWII stretched across the bottom of our beds. They were stuffed with oranges, apples, peanut brittle, ribbon candy and cream-filled chocolates made by a neighbor in his basement. Chuck and I gave Mom pink slippers and black, white and pink plaid flannel material so she could make herself a bathrobe.

Toby's behavior wasn't the only memorable part of that Christmas. Mom saved enough money to buy me my first real doll. I had admired her on our many trips to downtown Syracuse, but never dared to ask for something so expensive. I named her Ginger. She was a walking bride doll for whom Mom had also sewn three other outfits. I relegated Ginger to a place of honor in my (Chuck's) room and wouldn't let anyone play with her. It would have taken Mom two buses to get to Syracuse to buy the doll.

My trips to downtown with Mom usually meant I had to go to the dentist rather than shop. I was amazed and disappointed when Mom always found money to have our teeth cleaned and drilled. We boarded the Kinne Street bus near our house and rode it to James Street, where we transferred. James was lined with huge elm trees that formed a tunnel all the way to downtown. On those trips, Mom also managed to find enough money to treat me to hot chicken sandwiches, mashed potatoes, peas and hot fudge sundaes at Kresge's lunch counter. The special meal made it seem like a holiday celebration and helped me face the dentist.

Imagining what it took for Mom to save money and make that long bus trip, Ginger was even more special.

Alyce, Angelo and the boys came for Christmas dinner. For dessert, Mom made Chuck's favorite lemon meringue pies. I showed off Ginger and was careful to keep her far away from Kyle and Todd's curious hands. Though on the surface we were a happy family again, the cold silence between Angelo and Alyce said otherwise.

Alyce ate little and fidgeted through the whole Christmas feast, moving her food around the plate with a fork. I caught both Mom and Chuck checking Alyce with inquisitive eyes, but neither expressed their obvious concerns. I can't blame them. I didn't want this Christmas spoiled as it so easily would be if Mom started in on Alyce and her obvious lack of interest.

Kyle ignored all of us. He let nothing stand in his way to the food or racing through the house, playing army with Chuck. Thankfully he took our minds away from Alyce and Angelo's strife for the moment. Despite what I suspected we all felt about their again-deteriorating relationship, Mom, Chuck and I put on a happy face and enjoyed the day. We especially had a good time when Angelo left for a couple of hours to visit a friend. Even Alyce perked up a bit during his absence.

Mom and I were sad when January came and Chuck had to go back to Dartmouth. We knew it would be a long time before we'd see him again because he planned to work as a camp counselor on Cape Cod during the following summer.

The day Chuck left, Mom told him, "Don't worry about anything that might happen. Your only concern must be getting an education so you will have a healthy and happy life." She hugged him so hard he had to cough and she added, "Just remember, I've taken care of everything."

Chuck looked puzzled, but said, "Ok. Great."

When his ride honked the car horn, he gave her a quick kiss, rubbed my head and said, "So long, Chicklets," the nickname he had given me many years before.

Chuck bounded out the door. Mom didn't go to the window to wave good-bye. She picked up the Bible and closed herself into her bedroom.

When the car door slammed, I went to the living room window and wiped a circle in the frost to see out. As Chuck rode away I hugged my chest and felt overwhelmed with inexplicable fear and loneliness.

By the time the school year ended and Chuck went off to Cape Cod, I had forgotten those feelings. That summer I spent most days at the farm taking care of Kyle, almost four, and Todd, who was almost one. Mom walked to the farm to check on me and help out, especially since I had two boys and the farm store to tend to. I could see her proud stride coming for a quarter mile. Of course, as always, she wore the same two-piece seersucker suit.

On the evenings and weekends I stayed at the farm, Alyce taught me to drive the flat-bed farm truck so I could load the harvested vegetables and take them to the store. In the early evenings after my chores were finished, I'd often drive Kyle around the bumpy dirt roads and pretend we were on a ride at an amusement park. It was a delightful way to escape from the heat and share a special, private time with my nephew. Because I was only nine years older, he was becoming more like a younger brother.

Erie Boulevard, the road in front of the farm, was being widened, and most of the laborers were Italian immigrants who spoke with heavy accents. They always took time to talk with Mom and me, especially Giuseppi and Gigi, who often ate their lunches with me and the boys at the store. Giuseppi had just arrived in the United States and was in his mid-twenties, while Gigi was in his late forties. Gigi claimed to have lived in the States for several years. Giuseppi often talked about his family and showed me pictures of his two sons. Gigi never mentioned children. I felt uncomfortable when Gigi did talk tearfully about his sick wife. I was equally ill at ease when I caught him watching Mom through eyes that gleamed from under his sweat-discolored straw hat. His gaze followed her every move. Often the right side of his mouth curved upward when he let out a soft moan. While Mom never seemed to notice him, I thought he was a little odd.

I was approaching my thirteenth birthday when Mom decided we were going to go to New York City to visit what was left of her family. While making plans for this trip, Mom told me we might move there. That seemed the worst possible prospect of my life. I loved visiting Aunt Jean in Brooklyn, but I had no desire to live in a city of any kind, especially if my cousin Marty could get his hands on me again. My head actually ached with the thought.

Mom and I had many fights about her decision, which she defended by saying, "Your chances will be better. And we have family there."

I responded in my usual pubescent vocabulary, "I hate you," followed by, "You call Aunt Frances and Marty family?"

Mom shook her head. "You should be ashamed of yourself."

I wasn't ashamed. I was afraid. Things had changed too much for my liking already without moving to New York City. "Well, at least I can go to Coney Island," I whined.

"Why do you want to go there?" Mom asked.

"I can ride the carousel, get the brass ring and make a wish like you've always told me."

Mom smiled. "What will you wish?"

"To stay in East Syracuse."

Mom frowned. "You're impossible."

During that summer, when Alyce dropped me off after a day at the farm, I'd often find Mom, blank eyed, sitting in the dark. She had begun keeping the drapes closed all the time. She also had started smoking. I found her by following the spark from the lit cigarette and the repetitive motion of her hand lifting the cigarette to her mouth. The only sound I heard was her inhaling and exhaling the smoke.

One time she greeted me with the cat-of-nine-tails, which still held its threatening place on the kitchen wall. When I came through the door, Mom waved it in my face, yelling, "If you ever come home late again and I don't know where you are, I'll beat you to within an inch of your life."

I screamed, "I was next door. You knew that. You're losing your mind like Aunt Frances." I ran to my bedroom and tucked my face deep into my pillow. "What's happening?" I asked myself. Toby chased behind me and jumped onto the bed beside me. He nuzzled his head under my arm. Suddenly I had a dreadful thought—what would happen to Toby if we move?

When I told Alyce about Mom's behavior, I talked nonstop, almost manic. "Mom tells me she's going to hell. She's given up reading good books from the library for reading the Bible all day long. Many nights she takes off and doesn't come home until morning and I don't know where she is. And she sits in the dark day and night smoking, and sometimes chases me with the cat-of-nine-tails for no reason." When I stopped, my body was hot and my breathing was loud and quick.

Alyce chuckled. "I think you're exaggerating because you don't want to go to New York City."

I was devastated that Alyce didn't believe me. It was the first time I thought she hadn't taken me seriously since those days of pig Latin and the gym dances. I was hurt that she saw me only as a young, self-centered teenager looking for attention. On the other hand, Alyce seemed preoccupied, so I didn't press the issue. I also noticed the bruises around her right eye and upper arm again.

Staring at the bruises, I heard Mom's words reminding Chuck in January when he was going back to school. She told him that his only task at the moment was to get his degree. So I could never burden him with my fears and ask for his help. As young as I was, even I understood my role as a female in our family and in society as a whole. What was happening with Mom and Alyce were our problems to be solved.

CHAPTER ELEVEN

August 1956

Two days before we were to take the train to visit Aunt Jean in New York City, Mom paced the kitchen floor. Each time she reached one side of the room, she took a long, hard draw on a cigarette and then exhaled, making sounds like an iron lung. Mom stopped at the kitchen table where I was eating a bowl of oatmeal. She took several puffs on her cigarette. She squashed the cigarette out in her uneaten cereal and said, "You're not to come home alone tonight from the farm."

"What do you mean?" I asked, pausing with a spoonful of oatmeal at my mouth.

"I want to say good-bye to Alyce and the boys. That's all. So make sure Alyce comes with you." She put both her hands on my shoulders and shook me. "Do you understand?" she screamed.

The oatmeal flew off the spoon and landed on the floor. "I understand all right," I yelled back. "You're crazy. I hate you. And don't tell me this is another vi..."—I took a hard breath—"vicissitude of life. I've had enough." I threw the spoon down on the table and fled to the farm.

My chest felt like it would collapse from running all that way. Alyce didn't seem to notice my gasping for air or my tear-streaked face as I told her about Mom. She waved her hand through the air and said Mom was just having a difficult time because she was lonely. Alyce also told me she would have to pick up Angelo after work and handed Todd to me as she walked to the door. "I don't dare be late," she said.

When Alyce used the word dare, I knew things had worsened between her and Angelo.

Bewildered and angry because I felt abandoned by both Alyce and Mom,

I stood in the doorway for several minutes holding Todd in my arms. As we watched Alyce drive off, Kyle clutched the hem of my shirt and asked, "Where's Mommy going?"

"To work." *It's to early to pick Angelo up*, I told myself. I turned around and surveyed the kitchen, wondering what to do about Alyce and Mom. Though I accepted Alyce's observations that I was probably overreacting, I still believed there was something very wrong with Mom. There was no telling what Mom had up her sleeve, and I didn't want to face her by myself when I went home. I felt alone and afraid.

That evening as Alyce drove me home, she kept looking at her watch every few seconds. Any attempts I made during our ride to change her mind about staying with me and talking to Mom were overshadowed by demands Angelo had already made on her. She barely said good-bye when she dropped me off in front of our house and sped away to pick him up.

When I walked up the gravel driveway on the kitchen side of the house, Toby was in the yard howling. His head was bent back and his nose pointed to the sky like a wolf. It was not usual for Mom to leave him out in the heat. Remembering how she was that morning, I didn't think much more about it.

As I unhooked Toby's chain, he whined and shook as though he was cold. I hugged and petted him until he calmed down. "What's the matter, boy?" He nuzzled his nose into my arm.

I headed for the house and called, "Come on, boy."

I turned the knob on the kitchen door, but it was locked. "Mom sure is getting funny," I said to Toby and motioned him to follow me to the other side of the house. "She never locks the doors."

Toby stayed behind as I tried the living room door. It was locked, too. I pounded and shouted for Mom, but didn't get an answer. The house was silent.

My heartbeat quickened as I tore back to the kitchen door and retrieved the key from under the porch mat. I patted Toby. "Why isn't she answering?" Toby cocked his head and whined. "What's going on, boy?" I asked him and rubbed his ears.

I tried to steady my shaking hand as I slipped the key into the lock and wished I could be anywhere but there. Mom's words "Don't come home without Alyce tonight" resonated over and over in my head. Finally I steadied my hand and turned the key. When I pushed on the door, it wouldn't open all the way. The safety latch was hooked. I screamed, "MOM. Are you in there?" No answer.

Toby shadowed me as I searched the yard for a stick. When I found one the right size, I poked it through the small opening between the door and the jamb, lifting it until it unhooked the inside safety latch. When the door swung open, I was blasted by a surge of air as hot as steam spurting from a train engine. Toby howled again. The house was as still as a tomb.

Breakfast dishes rested in the drain. Everything else seemed in place, except Mom should have been in the kitchen cooking dinner. I walked through the kitchen into the living room. The shades were down, making it difficult for me to adjust my eyes to the dark. No sign of her lit cigarette.

"Mom?"

Nothing.

As I turned from the living room and made my way cautiously down the dark hallway, Yehudi curled back and forth around my ankles. I picked him up, rubbing his ears as I inched forward. Every few steps I called out in a low voice, "Mom?" And waited for an answer. There was none. All the doors were closed, also unusual. I checked each bedroom. No sign of Mom. The house was immaculate as always and painfully soundless.

When I reached the bathroom, I found a note tacked to the door in Mom's handwriting: *I am dead.*

The August heat couldn't warm me as I faced that note and read it over and over. I knew I had to open the bathroom door. It seemed a long time before I mustered the courage to do it. I turned the knob.

Mom wasn't there, but I saw blood in the sink and now could make out spots of it on the floor leading to the basement door where the dog was sniffing. "Oh Toby, you know something has happened, don't you, boy?"

From the top of the basement stairs, I pleaded, "Mom?" I heard only the sound of Toby's nose against the blood-streaked floor. When I took my first guarded step downwards, Toby let out a low, pained howl, which he kept up as I descended. I faced the wall at the bottom, terrified to turn around. Finally, my nerves on fire with fear, I compelled myself to look at the center of the room.

Mom was hanging by her neck from the rafters. Her head hung limply to the left. Her face was white and swollen. She wore her blue seersucker suit. I can't or maybe won't remember her eyes.

I ran from the basement, screaming. I remember little else after that until Sheriff McBride lowered Mom's body from the rafters and an ambulance took her away. As I waited for Alyce at Sue Zewkowski's house, the words, "I hate you," tumbled around and around in my head. I stared out the window at our house—the death house.

Suddenly it hit me. Mom took her life on August first, the same day Dad died. For days after I remained in a daze, remembering little except for unintelligible voices and mouths moving but soundless.

Chuck told us later that he'd been sitting in a restaurant on Cape Cod when the police tracked him down. He said he knew when they came through the door they were looking for him about Mom. That same day he had received a letter from her that made no sense because she repeated herself and dwelled on the importance of money. Chuck told us, "I should have known something like this was going to happen. When I went back to school after spring break she talked to me as if I had already graduated from college and was working."

His healthy tan belied the sadness that showed in his eyes. Chuck shook his head. "Mom talked about trying to blend the world she knew from the books she read—especially the ones on philosophy—with the religious world she sought." Chuck hung his head and cried, "Mom talked about religion in the letter, too."

He handed the letter to a stupefied Alyce. "Mom once told me," he continued, "that since she couldn't reconcile the differences between those two worlds, she'd find the only solution. I had no idea she meant suicide."

After reading, Alyce laid the letter down and consoled, "How could you know what Mom was going to do? This letter talks mostly about money." Alyce read part of the letter as proof:

Enclosed find scholarship papers. You must send back the blue card immediately. Since it is for $400.00 and the tuition per semester is $450.00. Maybe you better put down $50.00 to use from your loan for tuition. You'd better read those papers over thoroughly. <u>Because I was wrong when I said money is not important, IT IS.</u> You cannot do what you please without it. And when you are being helped through college you have to obey their rules. And <u>that is</u> what I meant by it's <u>being hard for you right now.</u> Because you may have to give up the idea of a car and other pleasures right now, and leave them for the future when you are through with school. Right now, you have to concentrate on your school work. You do not get anything for nothing in this world, in one way or another you have to pay for everything. Even rich sons have to work though they usually have a job in their father's business. You have not, so the most important thing for you to do is think about a future job *and train yourself for it. Because that <u>for you</u> is the <u>important</u> thing. It will be your <u>bread and butter and car.</u> You <u>will not</u> get those things from baseball if baseball is to be your profession, nor will a car now help you in the future. All good things have to be worked for and waited for.*

All of us smiled a little acknowledging Mom's constant worry about money. I could hear her voice clearly in the words she wrote. I could also envision her sitting at the kitchen table penning each thought after a careful analysis. Perhaps she had even shooed me away as she had done many times, telling me not to disturb her because she was writing something important.

A tear slid from Alyce's eye when she read:

I don't care what other people say. So many different churches and ways of teaching religion confuse people and make them unbelievers. But believe me, what religion teaches is true. There is one God and 10 Commandments to obey and no other way to happiness.

As I listened to Alyce and Chuck talk about Mom's obsession with money and hatred of Dad's ball playing, visions appeared of those lonely nights lying awake in my bed listening to angry words. Watching Alyce's and Chuck's mouths move in sorrowful rather than angry motions, I still wanted to poke my fingers in my ears to block the sounds.

Then as though Alyce knew she had to lighten the moment a little, she said, "This really sounds like our Mom." She choked back her grief and read the end of Mom's letter. "You'll have to excuse this messy letter. I'm writing it with Tekkie's pen, the only one I could find and it's terrible."

We all forced acknowledging chuckles at Mom's other obsession—neatness. Yet knowing what she was planning next—to kill herself—I found it difficult to understand Mom's practicality throughout her written chronicle and apologetic closing. On the other hand it was so like Mom to think of her children before all else and to worry even then about money.

As Chuck recounted the details of Mom's talk with him, I saw the young boy leave and a man take his place, and I observed my sister's true strength arise. As the head of our family she had to fill the mother role.

I didn't tell either Alyce or Chuck how scared I was. My whole world had fallen apart, had ended. But their lives were never going to be the same either. I'm glad I said little, because even without hearing my despair, Chuck wasn't ready to forgive Mom for committing suicide and leaving us, especially me. He made it clear to us that day after we read Mom's letter that he believed taking her own life was a selfish act rather than a sacrificing one.

CHAPTER TWELVE

Crazy

After the news was out about Mom's suicide, my schoolmates called me "crazy." They avoided me as though I had a contagious disease. Some threw stones at me as they yelled out, "Crazy! Crazy!"

Even my friend, Sue, crossed to the other side of the street when she saw me coming. Sue's mother had ordered her to stay away from me. Their behavior suited their small-town mentality. Almost everyone I knew was born, raised and would probably die in that town. Though I was born in East Syracuse, it wasn't the same to them. My parents and siblings were outsiders.

When the townspeople diagnosed Mom's children as crazy because they thought she was, I was sure they felt righteous about not accepting newcomers. "They're just not like us," one person would say to another, who nodded his head in agreement and added, "The Dennisons have brought shame to the whole town."

Others said, "It's a sin, you know, even if Marion wasn't quite right in the head."

"She'll surely go to hell and take her kids with her."

No one tried to hide their comments from me. In fact I thought they talked louder to be sure I heard them. They never said "suicide." They only talked around it.

I didn't want to feel the shame they foisted on me. Though I wasn't sure about Mom's sanity and whether it was contagious like they said, I knew suicide didn't happen in normal or good families. I was hurt that even my life-long friends couldn't trust me anymore. I was traumatized by their heckling.

In the eyes of the town's Catholics, who made up the majority of the population, Mom had committed a sin that sent her to hell. By the way the pious citizens treated me, I was headed there too. I was guilty by birth. Everyone thought I was just like Mom, so I was convinced. I had to be crazy too. Besides, hadn't I called her crazy? Didn't I already know?

No one ever talked about Mom's depression or the reasons for her feelings of hopelessness. Though they thought she committed suicide because of grief, they could not pardon her actions. While listening to all those conversations, I wondered why Ernie, the sheriff's son, hadn't brought shame to the town when he deliberately elbowed Chuck in the eye during that fateful basketball game.

Mom's funeral didn't have the fanfare that Dad's did. The meager group of mourners that attended were mostly relatives and only a handful of them. Except for Dad's three railroad friends who built our house and Sheriff McBride, the townspeople stayed away. That didn't surprise me.

When I saw Mom for the first time at the funeral home, she looked like she had fallen asleep and happened to pick a coffin to do it in. She was dressed in her blue seersucker suit, which the mortician apparently had cleaned. He also bought a blouse that had a high neck trimmed in ruffles. The ruffles were supposed to hide the swelling and bruises around her neck. Since Mom never wore ruffles, the mortician's efforts drew everyone's eyes to that area.

The funeral home scent of wilting carnations and lilies made me dizzy as Alyce, Chuck and I led the mourners past Mom's casket. Alyce propped me up against her just as I was about to keel over.

Mom looked more like an angel to me than a crazy woman. I wanted to tell her that I loved her and didn't mean what I said about her being crazy. I leaned close to her ear and said, "I'm not ashamed of you because you did this."

I turned to Alyce and asked, "How could anyone like my Mom go to hell? How could Mom go to hell when she never hurt anyone when she was alive?"

She answered with a head shake and tears.

I couldn't get the carnation smell out of my nose for the rest of the day.

We found we had been left in the dark about Mom's condition just as we had with Dad's fatal illness. Mom had sought counsel with Father Absent, the Episcopalian priest, several weeks before her suicide. He told us she was confused and depressed. "Your mother couldn't forgive herself for not grieving over your father's death," he said.

Apparently she felt guilty about never crying over Dad and repeatedly told Father Absent that she was destined for hell. Mom, Father Absent told us, was confused about her feelings of sadness for the loss of someone she had lived with for so many years while at the same time she rejoiced in her freedom.

"Your mother had been angry with your father for most of their marriage," Father Absent added in a quiet voice, "because she felt oppressed and betrayed. Because she was poor. Your mother surrendered to her guilt by ending her life."

I asked Father Absent about Mom's senseless death. I asked him why she was unable to forgive herself and live the life she had always wanted. I asked him, "Why couldn't she go to college?"

The only explanation he gave was, "God acts in mysterious ways. We must trust him."

Not believing Father Absent, I heard Mom's answer as clearly as though she had leaned over and whispered in my ear. "Tekkie, it's a vicissitude of life," she said.

I knew Father Absent meant well. After all, he visited Dad in the hospital every day even though Dad never went to any church. The answer he gave about Mom was not good enough for me. And neither was the one I heard in my head from Mom. I had a hard time trusting anyone, especially a God who saw fit to take Mom. After that I began my estrangement from organized religion.

Father Absent presided over Mom's funeral service and eulogized her as a generous, compassionate, intelligent woman. "Her loss," he said, "is not just for her children but the world." That didn't answer my questions either about why God took such a remarkable woman from us.

When Mom's casket was lowered into the ground next to Dad's grave, I felt panicked and couldn't catch my breath. I threw the handful of dirt I held at her casket and screamed, "I never really knew you."

I ran from the grave mumbling, "What did you really think about? Why didn't you try to live? What will we do now?"

Alyce chased after me, but even her arms holding me close couldn't console me as she said, "We'll probably never know why Mom did this, but you must remember, she always loved us."

I backed away from Alyce and pounded my clenched fists up and down into the air. "I don't understand any of this. Why didn't you believe me? Why didn't you see she needed help?"

Alyce reached for me as I leaped into the mortuary car and slammed the door. She opened the door and climbed in beside me. "Tekkie, you are too young to understand about marriage. And I have been blinded by my own situation. But no matter what I did or did not do, I don't think anyone could have stopped Mom."

Mom was secretive, so Alyce's explanation should have made sense. Yet at that moment I only knew I never said good-bye to Mom or told her that I loved her or begged for her forgiveness for calling her crazy. And the real reason for her death was buried with her.

That night the nightmares began. I dreamed I was being buried alive under mounds of black dirt and that there were holes in my arms where maggots made their home. Sometimes I dreamed that I was walking down a street and disappeared into a deep, dark hole in the earth. As I struggled to climb out of the hole, nuns watched and glided over me, covering my face with the skirts of their black habits. They refused to help me as I reached the surface, extending a hand to them. When no hand reached for mine, I would descend back into the hole.

I woke up most nights moaning, sweating and terrorized. I was more frightened by the guilt I felt than the actual nightmares. I was convinced the nightmares were penance for my sins, particularly those regretted spoken words, "I hate you. You're crazy." I felt those words pushed my mother over the edge.

The attitude of the townspeople convinced me I too would commit suicide by the time I was forty-one. I was told over and over, "You're just like your mother."

I started counting the months and years, apprehensive about my forty-first birthday. I also spent many hours in front of a mirror amazed at my image. I even looked like Mom.

Gigi, the Italian construction worker at the farm, came to Mom's funeral, which seemed normal to me since he had been considerate of our well being in the past. He wore the same wide-brimmed straw-hat that he did at the construction site and a navy blue suit threadbare at the knees and seat. When he saw me, he took his hat off and held it in both hands at his waist like a peasant. I could see the sweat-darkened area of the band where the hat nestled against his head. It was the first time I had studied his eyes. They were encircled with lines from squinting in the sun. His eyes were cold and held no laughter.

While offering his condolences, Gigi invited me to his house to visit with him and his wife. In my sorrow, I had forgotten the way he leered at Mom so I agreed, but asked, "Can my friend, Sue, come, too?"

He smiled and said, "Of course." When his large full lips parted into a wide smile, exposing moist and swollen brown gums, I regretted accepting his invitation.

Sue convinced me to go the very next day, thinking it would help me grieve. Those gums were all I could think about.

Sue's mom had relented before other townfolk. She let Sue stay friends with me despite Mrs. Zewkowski's superstitions surrounding Mom's death. Sue managed to convince Mrs. Zewkowski I didn't inherit Mom's suicidal ailment. So the day after Mom's funeral Sue and I took two buses and walked the last mile to Gigi's duplex. Though we wore our usual summer outfits—clamdigger pants that stopped at mid-calf and sleeveless shirts, hanging loosely around our hips—we wilted in the steamy August weather.

I knocked at the front door to Gigi's house. When there was no answer, I leaned my head against the screen and cupped my hands around my face so I could see inside. A cloud of dust burst forth. Undeterred, I inspected the interior. Most of the furniture was covered with sheets and there were no sounds coming through the screen door. My heart raced as my stomach filled with that weightless sensation of dropping a hundred feet on the Cyclone roller coaster at Coney Island.

Sue and I had just agreed to get out of there when Gigi flung the door open and smiled, revealing those horrific gums. Staring into Gigi's unsmiling eyes, I wondered if he had been watching us the whole time. I sensed something was terribly wrong and we shouldn't have been there.

The house smelled like damp dirt. Cobwebs hung in most ceiling corners and dust balls gathered under the sheeted furniture. Though pictures of a woman and children lined the walls, fireplace mantle and table tops, the house seemed uninhabited.

I took slow, cautious steps toward the fireplace and asked Gigi, "Where's your wife and who are the people in the pictures?" I pointed at the dusty row of faces peering back at me.

Gigi looked as though he was caught off guard. He was about to answer when Sue interrupted saying she had to use the bathroom. When she left the room, I asked again about the pictures. Gigi didn't answer me. Before I knew what was happening, he threw his arms around me and kissed my mouth. I was frightened and disgusted that those repulsive gums touched me.

I screamed, "What are you doing?" I pushed his arms away.

Sue came back into the room and I yelled, "Run."

We didn't stop running until we got to the bus stop a mile away and collapsed to the ground. My heart pounded so hard I could feel it pulsating into the grass under me.

We couldn't get on the bus fast enough. We sat in the rear so we could look out the back window. We expected to see Gigi chasing us. After a while I rested my head against the seat back. Everything spun. The dizziness made me nauseous. I stayed that way hoping that sensation would go away and waited for my heartbeat to go back to normal.

I'm not sure Sue knew what happened. I believed we both sensed we did something wrong. She never asked and I never told her or anyone else.

While resting on the ride home, I had the first of many flashbacks to one day when Dad was still alive. Dad wore his back brace and appeared drunk. He and Margaret Thorpe stood in a corner of Thorpe's living room at DeRuyter Lake. Leaving Mom in the yard, I had just come into the house from feeding the rabbits and caught them. Dad was embracing and kissing Margaret. I had never seen him do that to Mom. After that, I watched my parents' arguments become more regular and violent until they stopped speaking to each other altogether.

On August 8, the week after Mom's funeral, I celebrated my thirteenth birthday by sitting in a swing located on the playground at Park Hill Elementary School. For well over an hour, I glided back and forth in the swing, scraping my feet through the sand as I tried to make sense of Mom's suicide. I went over and over my last words to her, "You're crazy. I hate you." I regretted each word. I wanted to turn back the clock to tell her I loved her. I wanted to thank her for all the wonderful things she gave to me—the love of ballet, opera, books—and for letting me play baseball.

I sang Mom's song: "Life is just a bowl of cherries. Don't take it serious. Live and laugh at it all."

I stopped gliding and asked, "Did you really believe that about life, Mom?" An image of Mom cleaning our house plagued me that day. I felt she was trying to cleanse herself as well.

To understand Mom's suicide, I needed to make an inventory of her life, but I knew so little about her. I felt so guilty for surviving when she died, I didn't have the courage to ask anyone about Mom's life. I didn't have the courage to find out that maybe I was partly to blame for her death.

"Mom," I yelled out to the blue sky above. "Don't tell me this is just one of those vicissitudes of life because that's too easy." I kicked the sand.

Feeling lonely and scared, I was fast losing any confidence Mom had built in me. And I dreaded going to New York City with Aunt Jean. Mom had left an unwitnessed will stating I was to be put in a boarding school and spend holidays with Aunt Jean. Mom believed Dad's Social Security and pension payments would cover the cost of the school. Her bank was supposed to act as my guardian and dole out the meager funds. I couldn't believe Mom would do this to me unless she was trying to get back at me for my insolence.

The next day I boarded the train with my aunt. The night before a tearful Alyce held my head against her shoulder and stroked my hair. "I'm going to court, Tekkie," she said between sniffles, "and I'm going to fight for your custody." She lifted my face in her hands and turned it up to face her sad eyes. "You'll be home soon."

Though I was positive Alyce was sincere, I believed I was leaving Toby, Yehudi and my home forever. I hadn't realized Alyce was taking her first steps toward becoming a mother to me.

As the train pulled out of the station, I pressed my face against the window and whispered, "I don't blame you, Alyce. Please take me back."

When we passed the scene of Dad's accident, I cried. I cried for eight hours, all the way to New York City's Grand Central Station. When the train conductor called out the stops at Poughkeepsie and Tarrytown, the places Dad promised to take me, I cried harder.

During the long train ride, Aunt Jean tried to console me and even bribed me with shopping trips, plays and the ballet. All I heard was the clacking of the train wheels against the tracks repeating over and over *I'm alone, nobody wants me, I'm alone, nobody wants me, I'm alone, nobody wants me.*

I just wanted to go home and have everything back the same.

CHAPTER THIRTEEN

New York, New York

The only way to evade the notorious New York City heat was by sitting on the fire escape outside the kitchen window of Aunt Jean's seven-flight walk-up. I spent most days reading there. I sat on a pillow to cushion the hard metal grate and used another pillow to lean against. Reading wasn't at all the same without Mom. I longed to talk with her about the books I was reading. She had often influenced my choices but never belittled the books I picked that she felt weren't good quality. That summer, I only read Gothic romances by Daphne du Maurier: *Rebecca*, *My Cousin Rachel*, *The Scapegoat*, *The House on Strand* and *Jamaica Inn*. As I let each book carry me away from New York City and East Syracuse, I wondered if Mom would have approved. Even in those moments I wanted to please her.

Usually I was able to block out the noises of the city: the honking horns, mothers calling their children, a fight in the alley below, the rumble of a passing subway. No matter how engrossed I was in any story, I couldn't block out the sirens. Every time I heard one, I was back at the scene watching Sheriff McBride lower Mom's body from the rafters and carry her to the waiting ambulance.

The laundry hanging on lines between the apartment buildings also reminded me of Mom. She loved the smell of a wash dried in the fresh air. But there wasn't much fresh air in Brooklyn.

No matter how many times my reading was interrupted, the stories allowed me to avoid the reality that I was a permanent resident of New York City. When I immersed myself in a fantasy world, I forgot I was an orphan. Instead I pretended I was being held in the arms of the handsome Maxim de Winter, master of Manderly Estate in *Rebecca*.

Aunt Jean's son, Guy, a college student, worked and was rarely home, so we had the apartment and days to ourselves. Given Guy's wildness and constant arguments with his mother when he was younger, I thought it was a miracle he was still alive.

The apartment was long and narrow like a train car. One room followed the other, starting with the entry into the kitchen and ending with the living room, which faced the street. Two bedrooms were sandwiched between. The only windows were those in the living room and the one in the kitchen, which opened onto the fire escape and overlooked the alley and neighboring apartment. When the living room window was open, I could hear people's laughter and passing footsteps. I was never sure whether the opened window let more hot air in or out. The heavy, damp air seemed only to circulate from the living room to the kitchen window and back, depending on the direction of the wind.

The bedrooms were dark, but also cooler than the rest of the house. There was no shower and the bathtub was in the kitchen. When the tub wasn't being used, it was covered with a board and served as part of the kitchen counter top. The only sink in the house was also in the kitchen. The toilet was in a tiny enclosed cubicle near the tub. It had a door with a transom at the top for ventilation. We flushed the toilet by pulling a long chain attached to a tank near the ceiling above the toilet.

Although the apartment was modest, it was better than living in the garage. It also held many delights. Aunt Jean stored wonderful surprises under every piece of furniture and on every shelf that lined the apartment's walls. She was like a magician pulling items from the storage boxes. She showed me beautiful cloth—plaid wools, cottons in many colors and patterns, and linen— from which we planned my school clothes. From a wooden chest Aunt Jean retrieved embroidered linen handkerchiefs, a music box and fine bone china from Europe that once belonged to her mother, Steffany.

In many boxes she also stored the items she had purchased on sale especially from Macy's bargain basement. Aunt Jean later would use those sale items for gifts. "Never pass up a good deal," she once told me. I used to look forward to receiving her Christmas box filled with these treasures. I remembered once fighting with Chuck and Alyce over who would be the lucky person to open her package.

All the storage containers smelled like moth balls. The clothes she made for me from the material and the gifts stored in the boxes often held that scent for months.

Each morning as I struggled to do something with my limp hair, Aunt Jean shared her wisdom about styling. "Just let it go where it wants. Trust me, it's easier than fighting with it."

She pinned her hair every night and wrapped a scarf around it to hold the pins in place. In the morning she'd take the bobby-pins out and comb her hair without any thought to styling and kept the mass of curls in place with one of several colorful head bands she kept in a drawer of her vanity. Unlike her mass of curls, my hair was totally under the control of the humidity. It usually stuck flat to my head.

Aunt Jean took leave from her seamstress job. We went shopping as she promised, but it was in Greenpoint, Brooklyn, not Manhattan. She was 4'11" tall with a six-foot attitude. She attacked every shopping expedition as though we were in a marathon. Her shortness didn't stop her from out-pacing me or any jogger I knew, even though she only wore wedge shoes.

Aunt Jean demonstrated her skill to me when she insisted we walk the two miles to Greenpoint. In the middle of a New York summer, that was no easy task. But when she took me to Radio City Music Hall for a movie and a performance by the Rockettes, we took the subway. Its rocking motion and flickering lights proved to be therapeutic for me as the train lulled me into a hypnotic state. The clicking of the wheels against the tracks and the screeching sound of metal against metal as the subway cars careened around corners in the dark underground tunnel was oddly comforting. Mom and I had shared such rides many times.

Remembering how much I enjoyed the beach, Aunt Jean also took me to Coney Island. Splashing out of the ocean, I stopped midway through my run for our blanket. Mom wasn't sitting next to Aunt Jean. My heart felt like ice. My throat tightened. After several moments I sat down on the blanket and said, "I want to ride the merry-go-round."

"Aren't you a little old for that?" Aunt Jean asked as she rubbed a towel over my back.

"Mom said that we were never too old."

I rode on Mom's favorite white horse on the outer circle of the carousel's platform. I reached as far as I could for the brass ring. On my second time round, I caught it. Holding it tight in my hand I made a wish, "I want to go home."

Aunt Jean fed me warmed-up pizza for breakfast and shrimp cocktail for dinner, thinking all teenagers ate like that. I didn't eat most of the time because of the heat and the grieving. Other times, when my imagination roared into fifth gear and I believed Mom was still alive and I was just visiting Aunt Jean, I had a voracious appetite. One time, I even tried to call Mom through the Zekowskis to tell her what I had bought on one of our shopping expeditions. I dropped the telephone receiver when I realized she would never answer.

There was one telephone in the hall on each floor of the apartment building. That phone was used by the occupants of the six apartments on each floor. Just before I was supposed to go to boarding school, Aunt Jean's neighbor came to the door and told her she had a long-distance call. Though Aunt Jean smiled at the neighbor, when she looked at me, her lined forehead had become a web of suspicion. She told me to wait in the apartment.

Aunt Jean disappeared into the dim corridor while I stood in the doorway trying to hear her whispers. Several times she glanced at me. Mostly she faced the wall and cupped her hand over the receiver and her mouth so I could not understand what she said. The longer she talked, the more I imagined something tragic had happened again. Perhaps something had happened to Alyce.

When Aunt Jean hung up the phone and walked toward me, I rubbed my hands together as though I had soap on them. Anticipating bad news, I bit my lower lip so hard it bled.

The troubled look on Aunt Jean's face brought on a second wave of anxiety. A cool, clammy sensation pulsated through my body. When she reached me, I attacked her with questions. She responded coldly, "You're going home."

The following week Aunt Jean loaded me on the train with a warning: "I'm not happy about sending you back there. If there's any trouble, I want to know immediately." She sounded like Mom when she warned me about being at the farm.

She stood on tiptoe to hug me and whispered, "Take care of yourself." I had to bend to embrace her.

"What could possibly go wrong?" I asked. Yet, I wasn't all that positive about Angelo.

Aunt Jean's hand brushed my cheek. "Don't be afraid to get in touch with me if you need my help." Trying to cheer me up, she said, "Besides, I'll miss shopping with you." She nudged me toward the train steps.

I was too excited to think about what she said. I was going home. Alyce had kept her promise; she had fought for and won my custody. Aunt Jean was worried for nothing. I couldn't think of anything that could be better than going back to East Syracuse.

Alyce, Kyle and Todd met me at the depot in downtown Syracuse. I leaped from the train before it came to a full stop as the conductor cursed at me. The four of us huddled together in a mass of encircling arms. Fearing I was only dreaming, I was afraid to let them go.

All three appeared delighted I had come home. Both Alyce and Kyle looked like they had lost weight. Kyle wasn't the roly-poly kid I had left, and although Alyce kept up with the fashionable dress of the day, she looked haggard. Engrossed in my own fervor about being home, I let those thoughts slip away. I decided their changed appearances were due to the passing of time rather than any specific circumstances.

As we drove to the farm with the top down on Angelo's convertible, Alyce, her hair held in place by a green gauze scarf, chattered on. "We'll stay at the farm until two more bedrooms are added to Mom's house," she said and smiled at me. "As soon as that's done we're moving there."

I felt sick to my stomach.

"Meanwhile," she continued, "I'll drive you to school, but you'll have to walk home."

"I don't ever want to go back to Mom's house," I said. "How could you?"

Alyce let out a nervous laugh. She sounded like Mom when she said, "It'll be ok. You'll see."

When Alyce parked the car, Angelo walked toward it and checked the mileage as he had done so many times in the past. "What took you so long this time, Red? I've been waiting for supper."

That was the first time I'd heard him call Alyce "Red."

"The train was late," Alyce answered. Her eyes saddened as she gestured in my direction and continued, "Say hello to Tekkie."

"I'll talk with her in a minute. Get out of the car and make supper."

Alyce took Kyle's hand and I carried Todd. We decided to get my luggage and unpack after we ate. When I walked through the door, Toby jumped on me, almost knocking Todd and me over. I put Todd down and hugged Toby. "I've missed you so, boy." He licked my face in response. "Where's Yehudi?" I asked.

Alyce looked away. I repeated the question as I scratched Toby's ears. "Where's Yehudi?"

Angelo followed us into the kitchen and told me, "Leave Toby alone and sit down." Unlike his wife and son, he had gained several pounds. I took delight in seeing his hairline receding and hoped that would make him less arrogant.

Alyce finally said, "We don't know where he is. We brought Yehudi here, but he ran back to Mom's. We brought him back. He ran away again."

Saddened by Yehudi's reaction, all I could say was, "Oh."

As ordered by Angelo, I sat at the kitchen table—in the same chair I'd used the night Alyce miscarried and was rushed to the hospital. Standing over me like a giant black cloud, Angelo laid down the rules. I had to come right home from school and prepare dinner. I had to help clean the house, do the laundry, make everyone's lunches and take care of the boys. Under no circumstances was I allowed to go out after dinner or stay at school for any activities. "As long as I allow you to live with us, your responsibilities are to me and the family," he ordered. "Nothing frivolous, nothing else."

He smirked at Alyce. "Red bitches enough about all the work she has to do, so now she has the help she wants."

He turned back to me. "Understood?"

I nodded. I understood all right. But I wasn't happy about being a charwoman. Angelo was happy, though. He had everyone at his beck and call.

That night while I was supposed to be asleep, I heard Alyce and Angelo arguing. She tried to convince him I needed to do more than go to school and be a slave. I heard a loud slap followed by Angelo telling Alyce, "Tekkie's lucky anyone will take her."

Maybe I was lucky that they took me. Alyce had told me that no one contested her fight for my guardianship, not even Aunt Jean or the Thorpes. We hadn't seen Bill and Margaret Thorpe since Dad's funeral.

Angelo added, "Besides, we can use her Social Security money."

"That's not right, Angelo," Alyce said. "That money is for Tekkie's support and help toward college."

Angelo let out a dark, guttural laugh and said, "College? She doesn't need to go to college to be a secretary and have kids. You didn't. I'll spend that money as I see fit as long as she's here. And remember, I can change my mind about where she lives."

After I heard the door slam shut and Angelo's motorcycle leaving, I inched my way to the kitchen. I found Alyce standing near the sink wearing her bathrobe and loafers. She didn't see me. The left side of her face was flushed where Angelo had slapped her and she was crying. She was also loading a shotgun. Once finished she headed out the door. I yelled after her, "Where're you going?"

"After Angelo." She sounded angry and determined. The door banged behind her.

Fortunately, Kyle and Todd slept through the whole quarrel. Perhaps they had become so accustomed to such arguments they didn't hear them anymore.

For over an hour I crouched in the corner, facing the door and waited for Alyce to come back. Toby kept a vigil at my side just like the days we had waited for Mom. It wasn't the homecoming I had dreamed about. When I finally heard the farm truck, I hurried outside. Toby followed me.

Alyce parked the truck and stepped from the cab holding the gun. "The damn thing won't fire," she shrieked. Looking like a shrew, she threw the gun into the barn.

Though not sure how to react, I decided to hug her and asked, "What would we do if the gun did work?"

"I would have killed Angelo." She sounded just as determined as when she left earlier. She didn't sound like my compassionate sister.

Though I wanted to do away with Angelo as much as she seemed to, I didn't want my sister to go to prison. I placed my hands on her shoulders and stared into her dazed, hazel eyes and said, "I'm glad you didn't kill him, even if he does deserve it. The boys and I need you here with us, not in jail."

Alyce gave me a half smile. She looked away and said, "This is jail."

A few days later, Alyce dropped me off at East Syracuse High School. It was my first day back. I stood across the street, ignoring the tardy bell. I watched from behind a tree as the excited students, many once my friends, shouted to one another and bounded through the doors. When the last student disappeared, I walked to Park Hill Elementary School and sat on a swing.

I was afraid to go to school. I didn't want to be called crazy and be shunned again. It was bad enough no one but Alyce wanted me around. I sat in the swing until children came screaming out of the school's doors for morning recess and stampeded onto the playground. An hour later I stood in the principal's office at the high school getting a tongue-lashing for my tardiness. As he scolded, "Not a good way to start your first day," he gave me a pass to my class.

Miss Gifford, the history teacher, snapped at me when I interrupted her lesson, "Who are you?"

"Tekla Dennison," I mumbled as the other students snickered. Miss Gifford slammed a ruler against her desk. The class fell silent.

Miss Gifford's manner of teaching never varied. She believed in rote learning. It didn't matter if you understood any of the dates or the people attached to them. Her goal was to make sure every student passed the year-end Board of Regents exams administered by New York State. She'd stand before the class, all five feet and 90 pounds of her, slamming her right fist into the bony palm of her left hand as we stated in unison facts we had to commit to memory. "George Washington was the first president of the United States, " she'd say as she pounded that fist. "Who was the first president of the United States?"

We'd shout as though a chorus, "George Washington."

"The Constitution of the United States was signed in Philadelphia on September 17, 1787. When was the constitution of the United States signed?" She'd ask as she walked between the rows of wooden desks.

"September 17, 1787."

"Abraham Lincoln was the twelfth President of the United States. Who was the twelfth president of the united states?"

"Abraham Lincoln."

Once at the front of the room she'd point her finger as bony as a witch's at us and say, "They'll ask you every time on the test." There went the hand again into her fist. "When did Cuba become a mandate of the United States? The answer is, Cuba never became a mandate of the United States."

And so it went. She only stopped to adjust her glasses when they had slipped down her narrow nose or to return a piece of errant gray hair to the bun at the nape of her neck. If we dared to speak out of turn or not pay attention, she'd clench our arms with such intensity we'd be bruised for weeks.

Miss Gifford never missed a school function or a chance to show support to the students. She also was one of the few teachers I ever knew who could control an unruly football player by jumping up to reach his ear and twist it. That gesture brought any burly brute to his knees, a comfortable level for Miss Gifford to lecture him. For me, Miss Gifford was a blessing on that first day. No one cared if I was crazy or not. They didn't want any more bruises.

By the end of that day, I had made a few new friends who didn't know my history, while a few of my old friends including Kay, my friend from the Kinne Street duplex, braved ridicule and ate lunch with me on the bleachers in the gym. There was no cafeteria. By the end of the week, I was diagnosed as normal and began to be treated like the rest of the girls, including having my locker slammed shut by boys just as I took my hand away.

Angelo decided Mom's house was a nicer place to live than the old farm home. So the week before Thanksgiving, we moved to Mom's house. Dreading that first step inside 105 Cutler Street, I delayed packing and loading the last box as long as I could. I pleaded with God to let Mom still be there waiting for me, even if she greeted me with the cat-of-nine-tails.

Angelo yelled at me to get a move on and called me lazy. The hate reflected in my face must have caught him off guard, because he stumbled and dropped the box he carried.

Tommy, Angelo's motorcycle buddy I had heard so much about, helped us move. For every box he loaded into the truck, he drank a beer. That was enough for me to know I didn't like him even before he started leering at me like Gigi ogled Mom. Tommy was about Angelo's age, twenty-eight. Unlike Angelo, Tommy was edgy as though he had drunk too much coffee. His sandy brown hair was cut in a flattop, making his gaunt, pale face and owl eyes stand out more than they should. He rolled the sleeves of his white T-shirt up to expose his upper arms and tucked a pack of Lucky Strikes into the left cuff at the shoulder. With a two-pack-a-day habit, his teeth matched the brown stains on his fingers. Tommy walked like he had six-shooters strapped on his hips—even before he finished two six-packs of beer.

Tommy and Angelo moved Alyce's piano into the house first. I was glad they did that while Tommy was still sober. I was also glad Alyce carted that piano with her even though she rarely played it any longer. After Mom and she patched up their differences, Mom told Alyce she could have the piano, which had been stored at the Thorpes' house. Before she eloped, Alyce played the piano every day. I remembered how she breezed through the difficult "Hungarian Rhapsodies." Mom had dreamed Alyce would become a concert pianist just as she dreamed of me becoming a ballerina.

Before I knew it, the farmhouse was empty and locked, and we were sitting in the driveway of Mom's house. I was the last to get out of the truck and remained cemented in the driveway, staring at the kitchen door. Angelo grabbed my arm and propelled me toward the door. "Get inside and help unpack," he roared like a drill sergeant.

I told him, "NO! I'm not ready."

He ignored me, yanked me inside and pushed me toward Alyce. "Put her to work."

Alyce held me in her arms as I cried, "I don't know if I can do this."

"We'll go slowly. What do you want to do first?" She patted my hair like the fur of a frightened dog. Her steadiness surprised me.

"Walk through the house," I whispered.

I tried to call Toby to me, but he wouldn't come any farther than the kitchen and hid under the Formica table. "He feels the way I do," I told Alyce as I went with her down the hall.

My steps repeated those I took the day I found Mom in the basement. By the time I reached the bathroom, I was sick. Even though the linoleum had been replaced, I could still see blood.

I vomited.

Alyce quickly cleaned up the vomit before Angelo saw it. I slid to the floor and laid my head on my knees. Kyle waddled to me with Toby in tow, both curious about my behavior. Though Kyle offered me his glass of juice for comfort, it was his smile and Toby's perked ears, cocked head and outstretched paw that made me laugh. The two of them helped me cope with the rest of the day as they trailed behind me.

Grandpa's mahogany rocker was still at the side of Mom's bed, and Grandma's cedar hope chest was at the foot. Those and the World War II scrapbooks were the only tangible things left of Mom, her only history. Despite that emptiness, Mom was everywhere, even her Ivory soap scent.

When Alyce opened the chest, neither one of us said anything. On top was a framed picture of Grandpa, Grandma and Mom. Stern-faced and wearing black, Grandma sat in the oak rocker and Grandpa stood behind with his left hand on her shoulder. In contrast, Mom, who appeared to be about ten years old, stood in front between them. She wore a white lace dress and white stockings and shoes. Her hair was held in place by a large satin bow. As I examined the picture I realized I had never known Mom with hair.

Neither Alyce nor I had the strength to look at the rest of the contents. So we closed the lid. That night I awoke, screaming and sweating from my usual nightmares. I had also added a new one. I was being buried alive under the cement in the basement floor.

CHAPTER FOURTEEN

Life With Angelo

As weeks turned into months, it became less of a punishment and more a reward to be shut away in my room each evening. Angelo sent me there after I had completed chores. At least in my room, I could read and study without being ridiculed or interrupted by Angelo asking, "Where's my beer?" Or "Did you make the lunches?" Or "You may be fat like your sister, but she doesn't have fat ankles like you. What man would want you?"

His words haunted me. I began to see myself as a fat, studious person with thick ankles. School was my solace.

I didn't mind doing most of the chores Angelo directed me to do. They kept my mind off what was really happening in our house. I especially liked hanging out the laundry because the fresh scent reminded me of Mom. Dancing in and out of the sheets, I saw Mom taking each one down, folding it carefully and placing it into the wicker basket. I pretended she was there scolding me, "Be careful, Tekkie. Don't drag that sheet on the ground."

Listening to her caution me, I'd fold each sheet just as she did and place it into the same basket.

Despite our home life, Alyce tried to be a mother to me. Even in those early days, I recognized Alyce's need to nurture me. She and I both were also acutely aware that no one could replace Mom, and though I welcomed her mothering, we also didn't want to give up the powerful friendship we developed as sisters.

In her new role Alyce helped ease my grieving by letting me decorate my room. Under the guidance of Alyce's more adept artistic sense, I chose a black, white and pink theme with gray accents, colors which were considered quite sophisticated. There were no pictures on the wall or frills. Every line was crisp, clean and uncluttered, the way I wanted my life.

Alyce also set about redecorating the rest of the house in an attempt to erase any negative memories of Mom and to make the house hers. Our living room was transformed into the latest of what *Good Housekeeping* had to offer for shoe-string interior design. Alyce painted three walls green and papered the fourth wall in a green and tangerine floral pattern against a black background. Two tangerine-colored vinyl club chairs with blond wood spindle legs sat in front of the papered wall and were separated by a matching blond wood two-tier table. Our telephone though a party line was my first and sat on the table.

When Angelo sent me to my room, I lay on my bed for hours with Toby nuzzled in one of my arms. I often imagined what my life would be like without Angelo. Sometimes I even plotted his murder. I visualized twisting a knife round and round in his fat stomach or cutting out his tongue. This vivid plotting made me wonder what I had become.

Many nights I sat on my bed counting the tiles in the floor. First I counted the gray ones, then the white, and then pink. When I reached the black ones, I pretended I was Sheriff McBride interrogating Angelo. We were in a ten-by-ten gray cinder block room. Angelo sat in the center of the room on a wooden chair. A single light bulb hung over his head. I'd place a chair in the center of my bedroom and walk around it as though Angelo sat in it. I'd ask him one question after another and laugh ghoulishly every time he answered. In my made-up story, Angelo was charged with murder and sent away forever.

Other nights, especially when I couldn't sleep, I'd use my bedpost as a barre and spend hours practicing ballet routines. I studied my movements in the mirror hanging over the dresser, which limited my view to the position of my back, head and arms. I was grateful I wouldn't have to expose myself wearing a leotard and tights. Large thighs and fat ankles were not exactly qualifying assets for a ballerina. But neither was my blonde hair. All ballerinas seemed to be brunette. On those occasions I even longed to be back in ballroom dance classes.

Alyce inherited Mom's sewing skills. Using Mom's old Singer treadmill machine, she made me new clothes. "No more hand-me-downs if I can help it," she said as she showed me her first. It was a long-sleeved, pink organdy dress with tiny blue and white flowers, a full circle skirt, tiny buttons down the bodice and at the cuffs, and a large bow tied at the neck. To go with the dress, she also made a pink corduroy full circle coat that was lined with the dress material. I looked as though I had stepped out of *Seventeen Magazine*.

When I wore the outfit for the first time on Easter Sunday, I felt special and so feminine, I wished Mom could have seen me. She would have been pleased to know I would wear something other than clamdiggers or cutoffs and men's shirts. Mom would also have been happy to learn that her sewing lessons weren't for naught. Alyce sewed as well as Mom had. Not I though. I never got the hang of that skill.

Before we went to church that Easter, Alyce made Kyle, Todd and me hunt for our Easter baskets. "I'm too old for that," I whined. But when Alyce put her hands on her hips, a vision of Mom took her place. I nodded toward the boys and did what Alyce said.

The boys shouted, giggled and raced through the house in search of their treasure. I chased after them as we looked under and behind every piece of furniture until we found our prizes. Alyce had filled huge multi-colored straw Easter baskets purchased at Kresge's with jelly beans, marshmallow eggs and bunnies. A foot-high solid chocolate bunny filled the center. We both laughed when I told her, "Mom would never allow me to have this much chocolate in a year." It was a poignant moment, but it didn't stop me from gobbling the treats.

Angelo rarely departed from his usual after-dinner ritual of sprawling on the living room couch and watching Mom's TV. Night after night, he lay in the same place barking out orders to Alyce and me. Over time, I realized how he had changed physically. His stomach fell over the top of his pants, which lowered them precariously downward, often exposing his unappealing butt crack. His receding hair exposed a gleaming forehead where drops of perspiration formed each time he moved. The couch strained from the weight of his enormous body, which shifted the springs to within inches of the floor.

During commercials Angelo ordered Alyce to serve him snacks, which she carried to him as though she was a slave, her head lowered, and never speaking. He'd point to the floor where she'd sit within reach of Angelo's groping hands. Ignoring the boys and me, he often fondled her. Alyce seemed to grow smaller with each touch. She wouldn't look at me. At those times I was grateful for the solitude of my room, the one sanctuary where my imagination let me shut out the world.

I wasn't able to shut out that world for long. I always had to face the next day and Angelo chiding Alyce. One morning he yelled at her, "Why didn't you iron my shirt?" He rammed his blue work shirt in her face. "You are so damn lazy."

Alyce hung her head and mumbled, "I didn't have time to iron it. You wanted me to watch TV with you." She lifted her head to look at him through watery eyes.

"You should've ironed it after."

"When am I supposed to sleep?"

Angelo shrugged. "You need to plan your time better."

"I'll iron it," I said as I reached for the shirt.

Angelo blocked my hand with his. "It's not your job. It's my wife's." He waved the shirt in front of her face. "Don't make me late for work," he spit.

I wanted to hit him with the iron. I froze to my spot as though Angelo had cemented my feet with concrete he had poured from his truck. If I made any sudden move, Alyce would pay for it.

Even his sons were cautious around Angelo. Often the boys had to play in their bedroom so Angelo could watch TV without interruption. If they made too much noise, Angelo spanked them with his belt. Kyle and Todd would stare up at him through eyes brimming with tears. Their little mouths quivered as they sought his sympathy. When that didn't come, they'd hide behind Alyce or me. As they twisted our skirts in their small hands, they'd sneak a peek from their asylum, peering around our legs to see if Angelo had left. If he had, they'd tiptoe out.

Angelo never allowed us to vary from our weekly menu. On Sundays, we had pasta with red sauce, sausage and chicken left over from Saturday night's dinner. Fridays we had pizza, Mondays we had hot dogs and beans, and so forth. Each meal was always accompanied by Kool-Aid and a salad made with iceberg lettuce, tomatoes and onions floating in a vinegar and oil dressing poured from separate carafes. I was thankful that we had food at all, but on the rare occasion Angelo allowed, it was a delight to eat pirogis and kielbasa with the Zewkowskis. It brought memories of holidays with Mom when such food was a special treat.

Preparations for those holiday meals would begin days before the event. It was one of the few times Mom let me help her cook. All hands were needed to prepare and fill the pirogi dough with sauerkraut, or cheese, or onions and potatoes. My favorite, though, were angel wings, which were crisp pastries sprinkled with powdered sugar. I ached for those days.

Tommy, Angelo's friend, came for dinner every Sunday. When the weather was warm, he and Angelo went for a motorcycle ride. Angelo usually insisted Alyce go with him because he didn't like leaving her unsupervised. Tommy also became more at ease with me at Angelo's urging. So when a sitter was available for the boys, Angelo insisted I ride with Tommy.

Having to hold onto Tommy as I rode behind him made me nauseous. Tommy thought fondling me was his right in return for me being a passenger on his new Indian motorcycle. When I protested he laughed, "You going to tell your sister, or maybe Angelo?" He pointed to Alyce being dragged away by Angelo, while she struggled to watch Tommy's next move. "You're lucky I like you at all." His hand swept my breast and lowered to rest on my butt.

When Chuck came home for Christmas that year, it was the first time I didn't have to give up my room. In honor of his homecoming, I baked a lemon meringue pie like Mom would have. My offering of a burnt crust, watery filling and seared meringue made him laugh so hard tears came to his eyes. Or perhaps he was crying.

That Christmas, Chuck's presence inspired Angelo into a really good mood. I had to admit that when Angelo was in a good mood, his humor could not be surpassed and we all partied hard. We celebrated Christmas Eve with Angelo's whole family at his brother's home. We ate from early evening until after the midnight service. Tables laden with spaghetti, Italian breads and cookies, ham, turkey, eggplant specialties, sweetened garbanzos, chocolates and pies took over the whole house. We went home to sleep for a few hours, but even Angelo wanted to be up early enough to watch Kyle and Todd's reactions to this abundant Christmas.

The little boys entered the living room dressed in matching green and red plaid bathrobes. Their new brushcuts emphasized their excited eyes. They surveyed the magical scene before them and screeched at the sight of wrapped gifts heaped around the tree and spilling into the middle of the room. While the boys danced in delight, a new Lionel train circled the tree. The only time I'd seen so many gifts amassed in such splendor was in the windows of Flah's Department Store in downtown Syracuse.

In minutes, the room overflowed with shredded paper and ribbons. By mid-morning the boys ignored their bounty and charged through the pieces of wrappings, throwing them into the air as though they were tossing autumn leaves.

Though the shouts and laughter of my nephews were the best part of that Christmas day, we relished opening Aunt Jean's Christmas box. We never knew what unusual surprises we would find. I was honored with the task of baring the carton's contents. I slowly retrieved the unaddressed, individually wrapped items from the package and passed them to the eagerly waiting hands. One by one we uncovered goods, happily astonished by what we found. Chuck unveiled a tin pretzel container filled with empty jars that once held jam, peanut butter and pickles, while Alyce uncovered a box from Macy's that held recycled all-occasion cards and an envelope filled with postage stamps. Kyle's choice was a large frying pan which still had leftover food stuck to it. I, however, got the prize—the doohickey. That was the best title we could come up with for the wooden thing I turned over and over in my hands, puzzled by its irregular shape and pattern of holes. It wasn't square, oblong or circular. It was sort of all three. Each of us took it in our hands, turning it around and around and over and over. None of us could come up with anything better to call it than the doohickey.

During the Christmas festivities, Alyce sat near the tree, sipping eggnog. With her hair pulled back in a ponytail like a teenager, her eyes fully revealed their sparkle like the tree lights. A soft, hopeful smile formed across her freckled, makeup-free face. Alyce set the eggnog down and joined Angelo, who was draping ribbons over his and the boys' heads.

We all danced to records we played on the new portable record player which Angelo gave Chuck as though trying to bribe my brother's favor. Despite that possible overtone, Chuck and I took full advantage of Angelo's good humor and jitterbugged. Aside from my solitary practice sessions in the bedroom, dancing with Chuck that day was the closest I had gotten to any dance form since Angelo had laid down his rules when I returned from New York. It brought back sweet memories.

When Chuck was still in high school, most nights he'd come home from his summer job, turn on Mom's record player, pull one of her Benny Goodman LPs from its jacket and place it on the turntable. He'd move the living room furniture to the side, circle his arm around my waist and we'd jitterbug. Our movements were so coordinated, Chuck and I could easily have passed as dancers from a USO scene in one of those 1940's war movies. One time, Chuck brought home an LP of Latin American music and taught me how to samba, cha-cha and rumba. Like the night he took me to see Johnny Mathis I felt I was no longer just his tag-along kid sister. I was becoming a real person.

While I danced with Chuck on that Christmas day I could hear Mom laughing and telling us, "Your dancing is far better than the two of you bowling with Coke bottles and tennis balls in the hallway." She'd grab one of us and dance too.

We ended Christmas day with hours of playing Monopoly and eating a turkey dinner preceded by a hors d'oeuvre plate that rivaled any five-star restaurant. We were stuffed, happy and hopeful our lives were on the mend.

Angelo's cheerfulness was short-lived. By spring, I had devised a method of sneaking out of the house without being noticed. After dinner, Angelo would eventually fall asleep on the couch and not care where I was. Perhaps he felt I was too afraid of him to disobey his orders. That contemptuous self-assuredness ended up being his weak spot and my salvation.

Angelo had sealed my bedroom window shut the day we moved in. After working for several days, I pried open the window with a screwdriver. When the weather turned warm, I'd crawl out the window and run through the fields behind our house. I'd climb the largest maple tree and hide among the branches. I'd wait there until I was sure I had not been seen. Sometimes I'd sit in that tree for a couple of hours squinting through the leaves like lace curtains at our house. If I stayed there long enough maybe Angelo would go away and Mom would come back.

When I was certain I was safe, I climbed down the tree. I crept through the bushes to rendezvous with Gary, Sue or my new friend, Tasha. I never told them about my home life in its entirety because when I was with them, I just wanted to be a normal teenager. I wanted to talk about baseball, about who was going steady with whom, about Jimmy Dean, Marlon Brando and Elvis.

Sometimes I chose to stay in the maple tree, pretending I lived in another country and was the kidnapped daughter of an aristocrat. Once rescued, I would be taken home to the arms of my tearful mother. I'm sure part of this daydream stemmed from Mom telling me, "Your feet aren't big. They are long and narrow, a sure sign of an aristocrat's."

Sometimes I dreamed I was a cloud and could drift away any time I wanted. As a cloud person, I could change the world to suit my longings. Mom would be making cocoa. Dad would be in our back yard drinking beer with the guys. I would be pestering Mom to let me go with Alyce and Chuck wherever they were going even though they didn't want me.

My new friend Tasha and I were among the smartest in our class. We prided ourselves on being different. Most of the girls wore poodle skirts and sweater sets with rabbit fur tie-on collars, while we experimented with the beatnik look: black turtleneck sweaters, black skirts, black tights and black flats. Tasha even dared to paint her lips white. We were scorned by the "in group." Their arrogance, I believe, gave us more strength and determination to stand apart. Mom's words came back, too, the day she lectured me about the brown oxfords. "Do you want to be like everyone else?"

Tasha, more than I, was able to deliver that beatnik style with grace. I often surrendered to a less groundbreaking approach to dressing and spent hours soaking three to four crinolines in a bathtub of starch so I could wear them under a poodle skirt like the other girls.

Tasha came from a large Polish-Catholic family. Her mother dutifully produced six children while her father drank. Being novel was a way for Tasha to have an identity and get out of the rut her siblings found themselves in—marriage, the church, raising children, and drinking on Saturday nights at the VFW Hall on Manlius Street. Her three older sisters, like her mother, suffered abusive relationships in silence. Tasha's existence reminded me of my own, which was probably not unlike most my friends, except Tasha and I wanted our futures to be different.

For a while, we thought Tasha's sister, Anita, was one of the few lucky girls in our town. In her senior year in high school she met Rich, an attractive, meticulous and generous man. He lived and worked in Liverpool, a nearby town. Rich lavished Anita with gifts, including the largest diamond ring we had ever seen. They married right after Anita graduated. As with most weddings in town, the reception, part of a three-day Polish style celebration, was held at the VFW hall. As the last car pulled out of the parking lot, Rich, enraged by a sudden attack of jealousy, initiated a fist fight with Leo, Anita's former boyfriend and a local football hero. It was the first time we had seen Rich angry or raise his voice. Anita said, "He's had too much to drink and is exhausted from all the celebrating."

We all nodded in unsure agreement.

On their honeymoon in the Catskill Mountains, Rich fatally stabbed Anita. When they found her body, the diamond ring was missing. The monster we saw at the wedding had been the real Rich. Tasha told me later when Rich was arrested that her mom found out he had been suspected in another assault on his first wife, whom no one knew about. After that, I was never surprised by anything Angelo did. After that I became more distrustful and vigilant of him.

Stunned by the murder of her sister, Tasha was never quite the same. She was aloof toward everyone but me and was often the brunt of ridicule because of it. To our knowledge she never dated. The only thing that seemed to keep her going was her dream of getting out of East Syracuse and not being caught in any permanent relationship like her sister's.

Tasha and I spent all our free time together. Our classmates nicknamed her Skin and me Chub. I was named Chub because I was so much larger, not fatter, than Tasha. But, like Angelo calling me fat, the image that Chub created stayed with me, and I envied Tasha her slight build. She was the only friend in whom I confided. She knew everything about me, including what had happened that day with Gigi. I never had anyone I could talk to like her. She helped me get through some difficult times. We supported each other's dreams and never made fun of each other's fantasies. We'd huddle together at her second floor bedroom window looking out over the train tracks glittering like rivulets of water in the moonlight. Inhaling the ever-present smoke-laden air, we resolved we'd get out of East Syracuse. Even the frogs' croaking in the nearby swamp seemed to say, "Get out, get out, get out."

CHAPTER FIFTEEN

Into the Sun

One night, Angelo broke his ritual and didn't turn on the TV. After dinner, he sent me to my room with Kyle, Todd and Toby. He locked us in. I pressed my ear to the door as the boys sat in fearful silence on my bed. I heard Angelo accusing Alyce of seeing another man, which I knew was ridiculous because she had no free time to do that. When Alyce wasn't working, she was at home or with Angelo.

Alyce screamed, "Let go of my hair, Angelo, you're hurting me."

Kyle cried out, "Mommy," and pounded the closed door.

I clutched his hands to my chest and whispered, "Sshh."

Whimpering and resolved, Kyle rested his head against me.

"I saw you today with that man. You can't deny it, Red. Who was he and what are you up to?"

Alyce gasped and breathed heavily when she responded, "What man? What are you talking about?"

"At lunch, you whore."

Whore wasn't a word I heard a lot, and I winced at the insult.

"God, Angelo, he's my boss. He was just taking me out for lunch."

"I don't want you to go to lunch with him or any man. Is that clear?"

"You want me to lose my job? He's my boss."

I heard crashing, more screaming, and then silence. While we listened to the scuffle, I was aware for the first time of the fear etched on Kyle's face. I'm sure the fear had been there for months, especially when his father was around, but I hadn't paid attention. I had been too absorbed in my own world. I held Kyle close to me and remembered the many days he'd hidden in his bedroom after being hit with Angelo's belt.

The thrashings were for everything Kyle did "wrong," from not responding to Angelo's call to dinner within some irrational time, to laughing with his brother while Angelo watched TV. Relishing Kyle's wild-eyed fear, Angelo would slowly remove his belt from his waist. Dad doing the same thing suddenly flashed into my mind. I could see him removing his belt, but I recalled nothing else.

With Angelo, Kyle's tears formed long before the belt ever stung his small body. Alyce and I ran interference and occasionally felt the belt's burning contact. It was about the third time I came between the belt and Kyle that I saw the apprehensive look on Angelo's face. He was afraid to hit me. I was not his possession and he didn't know how to deal with that. I didn't know what that meant. However, I would soon find out.

After several of those beatings, Kyle stopped talking and withdrew to his room at the first sound of Angelo's car or motorcycle. I'd find him there, wide, glazed eyes filling his ashen face, staring at nothing and shaking. Kyle should have been a robust four-year-old. Instead he was timid and silent.

A few days after Angelo's accusations, Alyce told me to pack a few things. "We're getting out of here, now, before Angelo gets back from Tommy's." She threw clothes into a suitcase. "A cab will be here in a few minutes. We don't have any time to waste."

Before I knew what was happening, Sue took my dog, Toby, to her house, and we were headed for the airport. Despite Alyce's emphasis on the urgency of our departure, she made sure we dressed in our best outfits, the flying protocol for the 1950's—suits, heels, hats, and gloves.

I learned on the way to the airport that we were going to Las Vegas to live while Alyce got a divorce. She also told me, "I had lunch with my boss the other day. He helped me set everything up in Las Vegas, including job interviews."

"Where's Las Vegas?" I asked. "Does anyone really live there?"

Alyce laughed, "It's in the Nevada desert and, yes, people live there." She looked excited. "We'll be safe and can start a new life."

When the engines of the TWA Constellation rumbled to a start and we bumped down the runway, I wasn't sure we'd make it to Las Vegas. It was the first time I had seen a plane up close. I was so uneasy about the flight, I squeezed Todd to me throughout the whole trip and peered out the window to the darkness below.

Alyce filled some of the time on the long journey answering my question, "How can we afford this?"

"Angelo sold the truck farm to Tony," Alyce said. "Since Angelo bought a new car with some of the money, I feel justified in spending the rest." The window reflected her pensiveness as she gazed into the darkness and added, "Especially if it means a happier life for all of us. He owes us that."

I agreed that he owed us that, but I also harbored thoughts of Angelo's wild temper. He wasn't going to let Alyce get away with stealing money from him and fleeing with his sons.

All the stewardesses were willowy brunettes. They were approximately the same height and looked like Miss America. They dressed in identical navy blue suits, white blouses, navy shoes, pillbox hats decorated with silver wings, and white gloves. They wore deep red lipstick and no jewelry and looked like they had come off an assembly line that made the all-American girl. A horrified reality hit me as I watched the stewardess' mechanical movements. Ballerinas were also brunette, but anorexic rather than willowy. Blondes were considered sirens, sex symbols like Marilyn Monroe and Jane Mansfield. Where would I fit in the scheme of things?

We landed at McCarren Airport as dawn broke in Las Vegas. Once the rolling stairs were pressed securely against the plane's exit, a stewardess flung the door open. As we descended the stairs, we were met by the chill of a desert winter morning and the oranges and reds of the sunrise. A man holding a sign with "Alyce" scrawled across it stood by the waiting area door. His eyes assessed each passenger as they passed him. Alyce, who carried Todd, walked quickly toward him. I followed, holding Kyle's hand securely in mine. Alyce waved and called out, "Mr. Pruitt." The man with the sign turned toward us, reached out and shook Alyce's hand. She turned to me. "This is my attorney."

Mr. Pruitt, a short, bald-headed man, dangling a cigar from his mouth, whisked us out of the airport. It was about ten in the morning and the temperature soared into the 80's. We were sweltering in our wool suits and coats. If I hadn't just left Syracuse, I'd never have known it was February.

As we drove from the airport to our house, I kept looking for Las Vegas. All I could see was miles of desert scrub, beige earth and mountains in the distance. Mr. Pruitt drove us down The Strip, explaining why it was a phenomenon. "It's the gambling Mecca," he said as he puffed on a cigar and gestured with his arm out the window, pointing to each wonder.

Struggling to recognize these marvels, I pressed my nose against the car window. But all I saw was sand as Mr. Pruitt winked into the rear view mirror and said, "The Strip's transformed the desert."

A desert as described to me or as I had seen in books was devoid of life, a forsaken place. How did Alyce think we would find a new life in an area that by definition was unoccupied? From my view point The Strip was barely a step up from a dirt road and lined with low-profile gambling casinos with names like The Sands, The Flamingo, The Dunes, The Sahara and The Desert Inn.

I had never seen or heard of stucco until I saw our two-bedroom house. Located ten miles north of downtown Las Vegas in a rural undeveloped area, the house was about the same size as ours in New York, but seemed dwarfed by the endless parched landscape that surrounded it. The house was white, trimmed in blue, and was long, rather than square. Like our New York house, there was no garage. The sidewalk to the front door and driveway to the side of the house was made from compacted sand rather than from concrete or gravel. Sand and a few tumble weeds replaced the lush green fields and maple trees of East Syracuse and the rolling hills and lakes of upstate New York. Nothing stopped the panoramic view but the sky and the Spring Mountains to the west. The vastness went on forever. I felt as though we were the only people alive.

I soon learned why our closest neighbors, about a mile away, told us to keep all our food in the refrigerator or in tightly-sealed containers. One night I got out of bed and when I turned on the kitchen light, the floor and counter tops undulated in a massive brown motion. Cockroaches. As the light hit them, they scurried in all directions until they were hidden in the cabinets, in cracks, and under the moldings. I was amazed how quickly they disappeared. When I searched for a sign of them behind cabinet doors, they couldn't be found. I shivered. The cockroaches lurked nearby whether I could see them or not. They probably watched me race from one cabinet to another in pursuit. To do what? I didn't know. I'm positive those cockroaches admired their own cleverness and cheered when I gave up the chase.

I never went barefoot again in that house and I dreaded getting up in the dark. After that night, I lived in fear of cockroaches, especially when I discovered how difficult it was to exterminate them. I believed the chemicals used to destroy them only made them more reproductive. I suspected that like rats, cockroaches would live when everything else died.

Cockroaches weren't the only creatures I was introduced to. Much to my surprise, the desert was not uninhabited, as I had thought. It was common to share our house with tarantulas, lizards, snakes and salamanders. I discovered there are over 3000 species of lizards in the world and I believed they all lived in our Las Vegas house. Shaking out our bedding each night and our clothing each morning was routine. Still, I often awakened in the night, swatting at imaginary critters creeping in my bed. Or at least I hoped they were imaginary. While living in Las Vegas, I never got over the sensation that something was crawling over my body or the suspicion something might jump into my food.

These new roommates were nasty enough to contend with, until we met our first sandstorm, which welcomed us only a week after our arrival. The wind howled with such fury it reminded me of the hurricane that hit East Syracuse. Those hurricane winds in New York reached ninety miles an hour and took the roof off a house across the street from us.

In the Las Vegas storm, sand swirled, drifted and flew for two blinding days. Gale-force winds hurled sand like gunshot, leaving pit marks on every exposed surface. Our rented car and windshield looked like Swiss cheese. Sand made its way through the tiniest crevices into the house, coating the floors with grit. Miniature dunes appeared in every corner. Sand even permeated all the drawers and closets, leaving layers of tan dust on all our clothing.

Schools and businesses were closed. If I dared go outside, I had to tie a scarf around my face just below my eyes like a bandit. I walked with my eyes shielded or closed, making the venture hopeless. Even if I could see, the sand pelting me stung like a thousand needles. Eating was also dreadful. For each bite of food I took, it felt like I was swallowing enough sand to cover the beach at Coney Island.

When the wind died, we spent nearly a week carrying furniture, drapes and clothes outside to shake or beat free of the sand. We had to wash every dish, pot, pan and utensil and clean out all the closets and cupboards. Most of the unrefrigerated food had to be thrown away. But no matter how diligently we cleaned, for weeks I found sand concealed in the creases of my clothes or dislodged from its hiding place in cabinet corners or door jambs. We were exhausted, disheartened and ready to retreat back to New York until we compared the horror we were used to—Angelo—to the one we didn't understand—the Nevada weather. We decided we'd rather go through another sandstorm. So we stayed.

The week we arrived, Alyce started her job as a secretary at the *Las Vegas Sun* newspaper. When Mr. Annenberg interviewed her, he asked, "Are you pregnant?" Since she wasn't and he also shared her Irish heritage, he hired her. During the first week of her job, he took her to a newly opened country club where she met Nevada's Lieutenant Governor. Things appeared to be looking up.

I was happily enrolled at Rancho High School. My peers accepted me. But this wasn't unusual. I discovered that in Las Vegas, almost everyone was welcomed. I may have been considered different, but being odd to them didn't mean I didn't belong.

My teachers thought I was a whiz kid after they saw my first homework assignments, legibly written in ink and completed on time. That was something they were not used to. In fact, that adult play land wasn't used to teenagers at all.

Mr. Sidwell, my history teacher, paraded me in front of the class, telling them, "I've finally met an 'A' student." I could feel the heat in my face. Embarrassed, I believed he ruined any chance I had of being approved by my classmates. What an outsider I must have looked in a red plaid pleated wool skirt, white sweater set and knee highs. I looked like I should be attending a Catholic school while my friends dressed in feminine pastel dresses with matching sweaters. I was also certain the students considered me a nerd and a brown nose. But to my surprise, instead of being ridiculed for Mr. Sidwell's compliment, I was held in high esteem. The other students admired my academic skills. Suddenly I found myself to be almost as important as the homecoming queen.

While Alyce waited for her divorce to be final, our lives settled into a safe routine. I went to school, Kyle and Todd went to day care, and Alyce worked. We enjoyed family meals and outings to the Strip and Fremont Street, marveling at the lights. Fremont Street was dominated by a giant, mechanized neon cowboy beckoning vulnerable gamblers to risk their life savings in the casinos. The enormous cowboy had help with his job of enticement—the other lighted buildings that lined the path ensured that darkness never fell on the busy thoroughfare. The atmosphere there was what I envisioned summers in Alaska were like, twenty-four hours of light and little sleep.

Though bouncers prevented me from entering the make-believe worlds of the casino floors, each time a door opened I caught a glimpse of the chaotic milieu along with a douse of refreshing coolness from air conditioning. I heard coins clattering against metal pockets as someone won at the slot machine. It was like being on another planet.

We often ate in one of the many coffee shops and restaurants which fought for space with the casinos. Along with a sandwich and coffee, a patron could play Keno at every table. Many of our new friends designated a portion of their weekly paychecks to that game. Many others abandoned their entire wages to Keno. As I watched them lose money that should have gone for food and bills, I thought of Dad drinking with his friends and Mom's worried tirades. I vowed never to gamble.

I also vowed I would never be one of the girls who cruised Fremont Street on Friday nights looking for who-knows-what. I envisioned those girls aging into older women, thirty-plus, strolling up and down Fremont in short-shorts and white vinyl boots.

I looked forward to our Sunday drives into the Spring Mountains. These forested mountains, hemmed in by the desert, formed a unique island towering over Las Vegas. They let me feel more at home than I did anywhere in the arid surroundings. These mountains were a cool, green retreat enriched with white fir, mountain mahogany and Ponderosa and Bristlecone pines. The Sundays we drove forty minutes to the mountains, we also packed picnic lunches. As we ate from a perfect vantage point above the desert floor, I could watch the heat rising in waves, distorting commonplace buildings and roads below into a dreamlike quality. From there, the heat's haze melted into the horizon taking with it the turmoil in our lives.

Many other afternoons we spent watching the Thunderbirds, a precision flying team based at Nellis Air Base. The expert pilots performed their routines in the skies over our house. The jets spiraled skyward and dipped suddenly toward the ground. Sometimes they'd soar upwards as though a single unit and split apart like fireworks. Breathlessly, Kyle, Todd and I followed their every move. Each time they flew precariously close to each other, we oohed and aahed. Sometimes I covered my eyes, expecting a collision. Our heads moved in unison with each stunt while my stomach went up, down and sideways with the graceful movements of the planes. The whole time we watched, we munched hamburgers or hot dogs, eating fast then slow, in precise rhythm with the acrobats above.

Kyle and Todd spent their days tumbling through the house and into the yard, shouting and laughing. At last Kyle talked and asked questions nonstop. Without Angelo's punishing vigilance, both boys thrived in the desert sun. They even liked those loathsome crawling critters. I often found spiders and lizards captured by the two great hunters stored in mayonnaise and pickle jars throughout the house. Kyle and Todd had become ordinary boys.

One night Alyce had to work late, so I was the only one home with the boys. After we ate, we sat on our front porch and watched the sun set behind the mountains. The darkness introduced a cacophony of desert night sounds.

I was sure I could hear even the smallest spider crawling through the dry scrub. Though I had read tarantulas slept at night, I wasn't convinced, especially after the cockroach episode.

I was so absorbed with the deep purples, reds and pinks of the desert sunset, I barely registered the car passing in front of the house. It was rare to see any traffic on that road at any time of day. The car slowed a short distance down the street, turned around and drove by our house again. The driver braked briefly in front of us. There was something sinister about the glow from the tail lights. It could have been someone lost, but with an odd foreboding, I ordered the kids into the house. I followed them and locked the doors. I called Alyce. The car had looked too much like Angelo's convertible.

The sheriff showed up at our house as Alyce pulled into the driveway. She had asked him to meet her there. When I told them about the car, the sheriff confessed he had given a man directions to our home after hearing over the radio that a mother, two boys and a teenage girl were missing. The man, matching Angelo's description, had asked the sheriff if he had seen these people.

"He's looking for you, ma'am," the sheriff said as he handed Alyce a picture of us. "That's you and the kids, ain't it?"

Alyce took the picture from him. While inspecting the photo, her breathing grew more rapid.

"He's been following leads clear across country. Says he's lost weight and almost died looking for you and the kids here." The sheriff nodded toward Kyle, Todd and me huddling in the corner of the living room.

"You told him where I lived without checking with me first?" Alyce screamed. She chewed her lower lip and rubbed her forehead as she listened to the sheriff.

"He seemed nice enough. Besides, you shouldn't run off the way you did." He tipped his hat and waddled off. He reminded me of Sheriff McBride.

"How'd you know where we lived?" Alyce's voice raised to a frenzied pitch.

The sheriff stopped beside his car and rocked back onto his heels. "I make it my business to find out about people who are in the reports that come across my desk." He smiled a crooked, mean smile. "This town ain't all that big, and red hair ain't all that common, like blonde is." He nodded at me. "Besides, your husband called me after he discovered you were in Las Vegas. Seems like your girlfriend is on your husband's side, too. She told him where you lived." He tipped his hat and forced his body behind the steering wheel and drove off.

Josie squealed on us. I felt betrayed, but Alyce didn't ask any more questions or mention Josie. She ran inside the house to the phone. Her eyes looked wild as she dialed a number. She twisted the phone cord in her left hand as she spoke with Mr. Pruitt. When she hung up, she told me to pack enough things for a few days. The boys approached the move like a familiar game, a game of running away like the Lone Ranger and Tanto.

Within minutes we fled the house. Mr. Pruitt met us in front of a small hotel on Fremont Street just down from the *Las Vegas Sun*. As he whisked us inside, I looked over my shoulder to check the street. I saw the car. "Wait!" I yelled. "Angelo's followed us."

Mr. Pruitt looked out the door. He turned to us with arms opened wide and herded us toward the elevator. He gave us instructions not to answer the door or telephone. As we got on the elevator, Mr. Pruitt gave us his guarantee he'd return the next morning to take us to work or school.

Chewing her lower lip, Alyce paced the hotel room most of the night as the boys slept seemingly without a care. I tossed and turned and jumped up each time I heard voices in the hall. With daylight, I was awakened by a low knock at the door. The fear I felt immobilized me until I heard Alyce speaking to the hotel employee delivering our breakfast. Alyce, dressed in a work suit, had already showered and ordered breakfast through room service. We ate, dressed, and waited for Mr. Pruitt. When it was time for us to go, he hadn't shown. Alyce decided we should leave without him because she didn't want to risk being late and losing her job.

After we got off the elevator, Alyce sent me ahead to search the lobby and the street outside while she held the boys' hands tightly in hers. She huddled close to the wall as though trying to make them disappear into the hotel wallpaper.

I reported back to her, "I don't see Angelo lurking anywhere."

"Let's go," Alyce said. We headed out the front door. We walked cautiously toward the *Las Vegas Sun* building, inspecting every face which passed or was camouflaged in doorways. Even though it was early morning, the streets were already alive with hopeful gamblers and leftover late-night revelers. Angelo could easily hide in such a crowd.

We had just reached the entrance to the *Sun* when Angelo jumped from behind a parked car, snatched Kyle from me and broke for his convertible parked across the street. Kyle's weight slowed Angelo's stride, so when I sprinted toward the car, I beat him to it. Alyce was carrying Todd but chased after Angelo, too. Before either reached the car I managed to lift its hood, pull off the distributor cab and dash inside the *Las Vegas Sun* building. While I stood panting in the lobby, watching the tumult, I thanked Chuck for teaching me something about cars.

Meanwhile, a reporter from the *Sun*, alerted to the commotion we'd caused, strutted toward the car followed by a photographer snapping countless pictures.

Alyce kicked, clawed and screamed at Angelo, "Let Kyle go."

Kyle was wailing, "Mommy, Mommy!"

A crowd formed as Mr. Pruitt arrived, yelling, "Sorry I'm late. My car wouldn't start." He turned to Angelo. "You'd better let the boy go. You don't want to go to jail, do you?"

Angelo laughed. "These are my kids and wife. They'd never send me away for wanting them to be with me."

When I saw Mr. Pruitt, chewing on his cigar like a pacifier, I walked outside to join the crowd. As I waited for Angelo's next move, I noted he hadn't lost any weight like the sheriff said. It was just another one of his tricks. Angelo was the undisputed master of deception and charm. He came to collect what he thought he owned—Alyce and the boys.

"Let him go," Mr. Pruitt begged Angelo.

The lawyer turned to Alyce, pleading, "And let's see if we can't work things out."

Alyce collapsed to the ground in tears. Folded into a ball in the middle of Fremont Street, my sister clutched Todd beneath her as though protecting him from unspeakable evil. She looked ten years older than her actual twenty-four.

Mr. Pruitt circled his arms around her and lifted Alyce to her feet. She leaned heavily against him, putting him off balance. She spoke between her teeth, "I'll go to your office to talk things over."

For a brief time we were a better show than at the casinos. But as Mr. Pruitt was helping Alyce up, her boss, Mr. Annenberg, made his way through the gawking crowd. He nodded toward Angelo when he spoke to Alyce. "Don't report to work until you have your life straightened out," he said. "We like the news, but we don't want to be the subject."

I knew we'd be going back to New York.

A few days later, Alyce, the boys and I flew home, while Angelo drove. On that flight, Alyce admitted she had to go back for the kids' sake. "They need a father."

They may have needed a father, but not the likes of Angelo. Even at fourteen I was sure of that.

"He said he was so sick without us, he thought he was going to die." Alyce seemed to be trying to convince herself she had made the right decision.

She looked at me. Her eyes were drained. "He said he can't work." By that time she had chewed her lower lip raw. "He swore to me things would be better."

Alyce leaned her head against the seat. The gray circles around her sad eyes made her look like a medicated, insane person.

Though I didn't believe Angelo would keep his word, perhaps Alyce felt guilty. "And you believed him?" I wailed. "Mom always told us only the good die young. Angelo's too evil to die. He'll just slowly torture us to death."

She didn't respond. Her face said everything. Alyce was scared. I was scared, too. I knew once Angelo had found us he wouldn't let go. Watching the white clouds pass by the plane window, I also wondered whether Angelo would ever forgive Alyce.

Las Vegas, the town that devoured the wanna-be millionaires, sentenced us back to hell in New York.

CHAPTER SIXTEEN

Sweet Fifteen

It seemed we had lived in Las Vegas forever. Yet we were there less than two months. By the time I got back to East Syracuse High, I had fallen behind in my school work. So I was tutored every day after school by teachers, including Miss Gifford, determined I would be ready to take the Regents exams that June. Each grueling day I sat alone after class in the study hall in a one-piece wooden desk and chair. Each day a different teacher lectured at me as though I deliberately had not learned about the Pythagorean theorem or the Civil War or English conjugations. They seemed to have forgotten I had been in a geological and academic desert and not by choice. Their cajoling did little to help me memorize two months of class work, while heat from an unusually hot, early spring poured through open windows to torment me.

Despite the tutors' lack of compassion, I preferred Miss Gifford's bruising hand-holds to going home each day. The longer I stayed after school to study, the less time I spent at 105 Cutler Street. There, silence was broken only when Angelo gave orders. Kyle hid in his room and rarely talked or ventured out to play with Todd. I would have moved back to Las Vegas at any price, even to face the cockroaches, just to see the boys racing again in the desert sand and sun, collecting lizards and snakes.

I was, however, happy to be with my old friends, Sue, Tasha and Gary. I was content doing Gary's math homework for him while he caddied or golfed. One day, our cover was blown in algebra class. Mr. Smallwood, our math teacher, shook Gary awake and asked him to do one of the complicated homework problems on the board. After several moments of Gary's blank reaction, Mr. Smallwood turned to me. His scorching gaze nearly burnt holes in his glasses. "I'm sure Gary appreciates your contribution to his education," he said, "but I don't."

Though we never discovered how Mr. Smallwood figured out our game, I didn't do Gary's homework after that. In the end, it didn't matter. Gary passed the class anyway without further help from me.

After that, I decided math was not for me. Unlike Alyce and Chuck, both math wizards who loved anything to do with numbers, I found it boring. My decision to scratch math from any future course study didn't deter Mr. Smallwood from expecting me to perform like Chuck and Alyce. In fact, all my teachers at East Syracuse High expected I would be just like my sister and brother, graduating as the salutatorian or the valedictorian. The more they assumed the similarity, the more they pushed me to perform. The more I was pushed, the more unequal I felt. It was a vicious and tiring circle which left me insecure about my own abilities.

"You should be more like your brother," Mr. Smallwood often said.

Miss Gifford sneered at me when I didn't know the date of the Marshall Plan. "You should be more like your sister," she scolded.

I responded to their demands with cold, blank eyes as I twisted a braid in my hand.

After Dad died, Mr. Smallwood had taken Chuck under his wing. Mr. Smallwood was a kind, soft-spoken, gentle man who often could be heard telling his students, "Have the courage of your convictions." He not only encouraged Chuck academically, but was his mentor, friend and surrogate father.

Though Mr. Smallwood's expectations scared me away from any mathematical pursuit, he also convinced me to give up the idea of being an engineer. Though I had already ignored the math requirement for that profession, Mr. Smallwood went a step further. "No woman can do that," he told me one day. So I figured his inspirational lectures were meant for the boys and not the girls. Nevertheless, I relied on his persuasion to have the courage of my convictions. I stored that phrase in the back of my mind and dredged it up when I needed it to get me through bad times.

My teachers' expectations were not as threatening as the uncertainty of summer vacation on Cutler Street. I didn't know what it was going to be like with Angelo. I much preferred the heat from the tutors' stares than Angelo's off-again-on-again rage. So unlike Gary, Tasha and Sue, who looked forward to summer and hitchhiking to Green Lake, I wished school would go on forever.

In spring, I passed the Regents exams, and Chuck graduated from

Dartmouth. Alyce, Angelo, Kyle, Todd and I trekked up to New Hampshire for the ceremony. Angelo put the car top down and we sang songs, mostly "100 Bottles of Beer on the Wall." When we weren't singing, we played games like who could be the first to guess the state on a license plate, Hang Man and Truth or Consequence.

While we waited for the ferry to take us across Lake Champlain into Vermont, Angelo treated us to hamburgers and shakes at a dockside diner. He and the boys skipped stones across the water like they were father and sons on a Sunday picnic. The boys shrieked at the longest skips. Where the stones landed, tiny ripples formed one after another and disappeared into the quiet, deeper water like the stone had never existed. I felt there were times in my life that I was like that stone being dragged down by a relentless weight into an unknown condition.

When the ferry arrived, we piled into the car and drove onto it. I got out of the car and stood on the bow, letting the breeze carry my hair like a mermaid's spreading out in the water. I pretended I was that princess again escaping from my captor. The sensation of the air blowing through my hair gave me a sense of freedom.

Angelo seemed to be trying to make things right for us. Although we had fun on that trip to Dartmouth, I never totally relaxed. I still couldn't forgive Angelo for hitting Alyce and the boys or enslaving me. I also had grown suspicious of his positive behavior changes. In the past they hadn't lasted for long. I kept waiting for Mr. Hyde to reappear and spoil everything as he always had.

Chuck was drafted into the army right after his graduation and only spent a few days with us, just long enough to go to Grandpa's funeral. Alyce, Chuck and I were the only ones at the service and grave site. Though one of Grandpa's sons, a doctor and relative I had never known, had sent money to help support him, none of Grandpa's children came to say good-bye. Social security gave Alyce $250 to bury him, hardly enough for a pine box. So Alyce's old boss, who helped with our temporary Las Vegas asylum, paid for the funeral, which was held at Bordinsky's, the best mortuary in Syracuse. Grandpa was laid next to Mom and Dad.

I placed a few of the treasures Grandpa made for me on top of his casket. "To remember me and keep you company, Grandpa," I said.

I was growing weary of burying the people I loved. I wasn't sure I could face any more deaths. Watching Grandpa's casket lower into the waiting hole, I became overwhelmed with terror. I saw my face in that hole.

After the funeral, our only contacts with Chuck for weeks were his long and funny letters from boot camp at Fort Benning, Georgia. In one letter he sarcastically wrote, "The weather here is getting better, too; the afternoons often gets as low as 95 degrees." In that same letter he mused, "I have come to the profound conclusion that the army is an organization of the unwilling, led by the incompetent to do the unnecessary, inefficiently."

One letter I kept under my pillow and read it when I needed special comforting. Chuck said, "In the Army you either laugh or cry. I choose to laugh."

I needed to laugh more.

During the year following Chuck's graduation, Angelo became more lenient about my "after chores were done" activities. With all that free time, I found my first love. Rocky Wojack, a football hero, was the same age as I. He wore his sandy blond hair in the fifties flattop and had a smile that broke every girl's heart. The dimples in his cheeks were enough to make any girl melt.

Rocky spent every summer day in football practice, while I took care of Kyle, Todd and the house. At night, he jogged to my house and we'd sit for hours on the steps outside the living room snuggling, rarely talking and occasionally sneaking a kiss. When it was time for him to go, he jogged home while I timed him. It was part of his football fitness program. If the party line was free, I telephoned him after the agreed-upon length of time it should take him to get home. We spent another hour saying good night.

I was happy that on the nights Angelo didn't work late, he and Tommy went for rides on their motorcycles and left us to ourselves. Tommy appeared to have recovered from whatever fascination he had for me. As long as Rocky was around, neither Tommy nor Angelo paid any attention to me. Perhaps it was because Rocky was as big as Angelo and twice as strong. Because he also seemed to have a male sense about Tommy's motives, Rocky kept his arm around my shoulders or waist and followed Tommy's every move, intimidating him with his gaze and possessiveness.

On Saturday afternoons, Rocky and I met at the Pit. Like all the other young lovers, we sat in the back row and snuggled. If we dared kiss, the kids who saw us risked getting thrown out of the movie when they stomped their feet loudly on the floor to signal they'd seen us. Others screamed, "Shut up! We can't hear." That goaded all of us into a popcorn fight. If the manager evicted us, we'd sit on the curb outside the movie house and watch the fights at the pool hall.

On Sundays, Rocky and I met on the corner across from St. Matthew's Catholic Church where he attended Mass. We walked hand and hand to Temple's Dairy on Manlius Street, a block from the Pit. We perched on the red vinyl-top, chrome stools and ate hot fudge sundaes. After each mouthful of ice cream, we spun on the stools. We chatted with the other kids who also gathered there before we headed home for our respective Sunday dinners.

Father Kelly tried to persuade Mrs. Wojack to stop Rocky from seeing me. "He should date a nice Catholic girl," he told her.

Father Kelly's talks with Mrs. Wojack didn't work. Nothing separated us until Carolyn Mason moved into town. She not only was the nice Catholic girl, she became Rocky's new steady. Perhaps Rocky was intimidated by Angelo and Tommy, or perhaps he was giving into Father Kelly's guilt trip. I didn't want to think it had anything directly to do with me. Rocky represented a boy like Chuck—handsome, athletic, intelligent and respectful to girls— and I didn't want to give up that kind of security. He had none of the negative characteristics of the other men in my life except that he appeared fickle and easily had his head turned by a new blond in town.

Father Kelly discovered I was a leader among my peers. He noticed few of the teens did anything unless I was involved. I don't remember how I became a leader unless it was my obstinate curiosity which gave me the appearance of being a confident and daring person. I often wondered if I had become a curiosity or someone to fear because of Mom. Whatever it was, I had the other teens' ears.

Being a feisty person, I also felt an obligation of sorts to be a thorn in Father Kelly's side after the way he treated Mom. One day he stopped me as I passed the Catholic school and asked if I would attend the Catholic Youth Organization (CYO) dances so the other kids would go. His request made me feel heady, triumphant and important.

When I told Alyce about Father Kelly's plea, we laughed. "You are a Pied Piper," she said as she ruffled my hair.

She wrinkled her nose and said, "I have a little secret to tell you about how I tricked Father Kelly." For that moment she was my sister and friend more than a mother.

"Knowing you," I said, pointing my finger at her, "you probably persuaded him to give you half the money from Sunday's collection plate."

"Not quite, but it's almost that good," she said as she sat down on the front steps to our house. We watched Kyle and Todd ride their tricycles up and down the street, Toby barking as he followed.

"Every week Mom sent Chuck and me to Sunday School with ten cents each," she began. "The money was supposed to be for the collection plate," Alyce giggled. "But I never liked Sunday school, so I took Chuck to the drugstore instead."

"That's not such a big deal unless Mom caught you," I challenged, yet relished that private moment with her.

"Wait, I'm not finished. I spent the money on comic books that Chuck and I read in the alley behind the drugstore. After we finished reading the comic books, we threw them away and went home. Mom never caught on." Alyce lifted her hand to her mouth as she tried to hide a victorious smile.

"One time, though, Father Kelly tried to get the truth from me during Confession. He asked me if I ever missed Sunday school, and I told him no. He asked me if I ever lied, and I told him yes."

I laughed before she had a chance to finish. I knew what was coming next. Alyce laughed, too, as she pulled her hair up, cooling her neck, and went on with her secret. "I knew that not going to church was a mortal sin while lying was just a minor one."

Sitting with her like we were just two friends sharing our thoughts on a warm afternoon felt ordinary and easy. It was always too short and we soon had to face our real lives.

Her story didn't surprise me and only reminded me that Alyce usually understood how to get the best from any situation and how to circumvent the system. With all her moxie, I had a hard time comprehending why she remained stuck in a marriage with Angelo.

When Angelo went out on Fridays, my life was easier. But that was not true for Alyce. Several times she waited for him to ride out the driveway and then followed him. She'd return an hour or so later alone and in tears. On one Friday when she returned she told me, "Angelo's seeing other women." She cried, "And I don't know what to do. I thought coming back here..."

I finished the statement she couldn't: "...Was the right thing because of the kids."

Watching her brought back the memory of years earlier when she ran after Angelo with the shotgun. I was happy we didn't own a shotgun anymore. "I think we should consider leaving again," I said and quickly added, "but not Las Vegas."

She didn't need to answer. She raised her eyebrows in surprise and was pensive, rubbing her foot back and forth across the kitchen floor. She seemed to be thinking about it, too.

Late one night, Alyce stopped Angelo in the driveway after he came home from a rendezvous. I watched their confrontation from behind the kitchen curtains.

I moved into the living room when Alyce blocked the kitchen door, bracing each hand on a jamb. "I know where you've been, Angelo," she said, her voice seething. "Who is she?"

Though Alyce was tall, Angelo's shadow swallowed her. She formed her right hand into a fist, raised it into the air and brought it down like a hammer and shrieked, "Who is she and how many others are there?"

Angelo ignored her. He shoved her aside and entered the house. He stopped halfway down the hallway, turned around and walked back to Alyce. He wrapped his arm tightly around her shoulders to restrict her movement, steered her into their bedroom and kicked the door closed. The sounds coming from other side of the door told the rest of the story.

"Get off me," Alyce yelled. "You're hurting me."

I stood motionless at the door as Kyle and Todd hid behind me—an all-too-familiar refuge for him. Kyle squeezed my shirt. I heard muffled sounds from Alyce as though Angelo held his hand over her mouth. After several minutes it was quiet. The bedroom door opened and Angelo walked past me hoisting up his pants. Alyce was sprawled across the bed naked from the waist down.

In the morning we went about our routine as though nothing had happened. Alyce bore no bruises, but her gaunt and sallow face looked tired and old. The voluptuous body I once envied had disappeared and had been replaced with an unfamiliar skeleton. Alyce had stopped styling her hair long before. She had pulled it away from her face in a shapeless ponytail caught in a rubber band. That morning when she spoke, her vacant eyes told me my sister's true spirit was far away from our house on Cutler Street.

For a while I had to set aside any notion Alyce would give me guidance. Though I believed she wanted the best for all of us, Alyce at that moment was lucky to get through the day. Most of the time her maternal, nurturing ways were overshadowed by Angelo's bullying.

Many days I found myself sitting in the trusted maple tree talking to Mom. I wanted her to tell me what I should do. "How can I help?" I asked her spirit that I had to believe hovered nearby. "I feel so alone, so powerless, Mom." Sniffling, I'd add, "And though Alyce made her bed like you said, there has to be something I can do to shake her up, to get us out of here."

That summer Angelo, befitting his roller coaster personality, told me I could have a fifteenth birthday party. "Invite all your friends," he encouraged. Though leery of his motive for the sudden outburst of generosity, I was delighted at the prospect. Tasha, Sue and I planned every detail.

On the day of the event we trimmed the yard with pink, purple and white crepe paper and balloons. When we had hung the paper, Alyce drove me to the A&P to pick up my first bakery cake decorated with chocolate frosting and pink roses. Bouncing up and down on the car seat like Kyle and Todd would, I could hardly contain my excitement at having a real birthday party with all my friends.

Finished with the preparations, Sue, Tasha and I retreated to our homes to spend many hours preening—only to be defeated by the oppressive August humidity. My hair straightened, while Sue and Tasha's hair frizzed. Any makeup we dared to wear ended in blurred, colorful smudges on our faces.

The partygoers danced and ate. After I opened gifts, several boys filled balloons with water. Suffering from an overabundance of testosterone, they projected their maleness by heaving balloons at unsuspecting targets. When a balloon exploded in a girl's face, she would look shocked, then pleased. She secretly thanked Cupid for being a chosen one. Just as the last candle was lit on my cake, I made a silent wish: Don't let this night be a dream. As I bent over to blow out the candles, Gary lobbed the final water-filled balloon into the center of my cake.

While we ate the soggy cake, I heard motorcycles pull up the driveway and realized Angelo had been absent the entire evening. He and Tommy swaggered into the back yard wearing leather jackets and hats copied from the one Marlon Brando wore in the movie *The Wild Ones*. They stuffed cake into their mouths and wished me a happy birthday through chocolate frosting and pink, rose-covered lips. The party was over.

After everyone left, and happily exhausted from the festivities, I chastised myself for fearing Angelo's motives for the party, his absence and untimely appearance with Tommy. Once everything was cleaned up, I went to my room and fell asleep almost as soon as I laid my head down.

Well past midnight, I was awakened. I thought I was having one of my nightmares. My body rolled toward a depression on the edge of the bed. I shuddered into consciousness and bolted upright. When my head cleared, I faced Tommy, who was sitting on the bed reaching for me. "Happy birthday," he sneered.

I opened my mouth to scream, but he slapped his hand across it and grinned at me. "Even if you scream, no one will come." Tommy slowly removed his hand and grasped my arm so hard I winced. He raised his eyebrows, acknowledging his strength. I couldn't imagine anyone sleeping through Toby's howls unless they were deliberately ignoring his warning.

Except for his whining outside my closed bedroom door, the rest of that night has been blocked from my memory. Like the incident with Gigi, I never wanted to admit what happened. Unlike that day with Gigi, the truth of that night with Tommy was so unbearable I blanked out the details. So even if I wanted to let someone know about what he did, it became a ghostly image that stayed tucked far into the back of my mind and never shared or fully remembered.

It had also come to mind that keeping secrets was part of my family legacy—Alyce never spoke about her relationship with Angelo, Dad hid his other family from us, Mom roamed the streets to unknown places and sought counseling behind our backs. Now I must stay quiet about Tommy as I had about Gigi. If we didn't hide these truths, we would risk being called trouble makers, not right or crazy.

Though I was well aware that the events of the unspeakable night with Tommy would forever affect me, I didn't know when or how much. As time went on, my anger festered and crept in my day-to-day life like a cat sneaking up on a field mouse. I had always been spirited, but I wasn't prepared for that liveliness to manifest in violent outbursts. One time I clobbered a neighborhood boy for not letting me have a turn at bat as a way to prevent me, the only girl, from playing baseball. Another time I pummeled a boy to the ground for trying to kiss me. Any sudden touch by a boy, no matter how innocent, sent me into a rage. I found socializing with girls more appealing and safe.

In the morning, Tommy was gone and Alyce was in the kitchen doing the final clean-up of the party. She was wearing the pink and black plaid bathrobe Mom had made from the cloth Chuck and I gave her that Christmas which seemed a century before. Alyce handed me a glass of juice as she said, "Great party, eh?" She sounded as though she was trying to convince both of us.

I struggled to answer her, but couldn't goad the words past the lump in my throat. Alyce faced me. She looked as though she hadn't slept. Her face was gnarled with worry. "What's the sad face for?" she asked. "Didn't you have a good time at your party?" Her eyes had the same emptiness I saw in them the night Angelo had forced her into their bed.

I nodded my head. I wanted to tell her about what had happened. But what should I tell her? Something in her voice said she already knew. How could I add any more to the problems she faced every day? Besides, I must have done something to provoke Tommy, just as I must have with Gigi. I felt certain I was to blame. I felt so dirty.

I set the untouched juice down on the kitchen table. "I'm leaving," I said. "I'm taking Kyle and Todd with me if you won't get out of here."

"What's gotten into you?" She swept back a piece of her uncombed hair. "Things are better, and you had a wonderful party." Though Alyce smiled, her voice conveyed no emotion.

"I know I had a great party, but things aren't great, and if you can't get out, I will."

"It's hard for us sometimes, I know, but..."

"But what? We should stay in hell? You've given up."

Alyce turned away from me. She braced herself against the sink as her whole body shuddered. "I don't expect you to understand. My only goal right now is to get eight hours of sleep each night so I can face the next day."

Tears welled up in my eyes. "It can't be this hopeless."

I left the house as Alyce called after me, "Tekkie, wait."

I didn't stop until I reached the maple tree. I climbed as high as I could and sat in it for hours staring at our house. There was nowhere else for me to go. Who in that town would care about Alyce and her situation other than her former boss? And he was getting fed up with the whole mess. They would probably say the same thing Mom told me in the barn the night Alyce miscarried: "She's made her bed and must sleep in it." I was also sure no one would listen to me about what had happened during the night with Tommy. Yet I was positive whatever did happen with him was a warning of what lay ahead.

In the end, I climbed down the tree and went home.

Facing the next day for Alyce meant working fourteen hours in what was her first business venture. After we returned from Las Vegas, Alyce and another woman became partners in the Meals Away Restaurant. It was located two doors from the Eastwood A&P where we had always grocery shopped. Their specialties were homemade ravioli and sauce. People drove from all over the county to eat at the restaurant or to carry the food out.

Alyce introduced Syracuse to the innovation of the Western Burger, which we had fallen in love with in Las Vegas. The only hamburger New Yorkers ate was a ground beef patty on a bare bun. The Western Burger had the works: a hamburger, cheese, lettuce, tomatoes, and pickles on a toasted bun.

After school each day I worked in the restaurant. That job was short-lived because I screwed up every order and had a tendency to spill sauce and coffee on the good-looking male schoolmates on whom I had crushes. Perhaps it was for the best. I didn't waste any future education pursuing a career in restaurant management.

Though the earnings from the restaurant weren't as great as the efforts, Alyce looked on the positive side. "There's always a meal for our family." Indeed there was. Angelo, the boys and I ate there almost every day. We also ate the day-old doughnuts many mornings for breakfast.

When the demand grew for the sauce, Alyce and her partner froze it. They tried to market the frozen sauce to local stores. It was the first frozen sauce in the area, and like any new product, Alyce had a difficult time convincing market owners to try it. Unfortunately, despite their efforts, she and her partner couldn't pay the bills and filed for bankruptcy.

Shortly after they closed the restaurant, a local supermarket chain tried to place a huge order. If she had known business protocol then, she would have taken that order to a bank for financing and reopened the business. Instead she gave me a hopeless smiled and said, "Like Mom always told us, 'you got to take the bitter with the better.'"

From what Alyce had been through, I felt she actually believed that.

CHAPTER SEVENTEEN

The Knife

Angelo was laid off for the winter, as usual. Concrete wasn't poured in cold weather. Each day he carted Todd to the pool hall on Manlius Street, while Alyce went back to work as an executive secretary for a new employer, the owner of Cain and Recorder. He was so forgetful, one of Alyce's duties was to place cards in his hat to remind him where he was going and for what reason.

Kyle and I went to school, while three-year-old Todd spent his days perched on a stool eating junk food as his father and other unemployed men knocked balls around a green felt table top. When not in the pool hall, Angelo lay on the living room couch and watched TV, leaving Todd to fend for himself. When I got home from school, I often found Angelo asleep on the couch, dirty dishes strewn around the floor, Toby wandering the yard and Todd in soiled clothes and underpants playing with his truck, pushing it around as he said, "Zoom, zoom." When the truck didn't go in the direction he wished, Todd said without anger, "Oh hell," a curse he most likely heard each of us use one time or another.

Though Todd appeared undisturbed by his condition, the first order of business for me was to change and wash Todd. Then I'd give him a snack. After that I cleaned up the dishes, fed Toby and started supper. Sometimes Angelo pretended to sleep through the whole ritual. Other times, he moved enough to change the TV channel. But he hardly moved until Alyce walked through the door, tired from a day at work yet ready to face Angelo's demands.

One night in late spring before I retreated to my room to study for the Regents exams, I stood in the doorway between the kitchen and living room drying a carving knife we'd used at dinner. I studied Angelo as he finished his first after-dinner snack, a salad prepared by Alyce. His white, sleeveless T-shirt was dribbled with oil and vinegar dressing, the only kind he ate. Without taking his eyes off the TV, Angelo placed the empty salad bowl on the floor beside the couch, wiped his oily mouth with the back of his hand, belched and lay down on the couch. As I watched him, I twisted the carving knife in the dish towel and thought about ways I could kill him.

Kyle and Todd played with toy cars in the middle of the floor. They giggled and shrieked when the cars crashed and argued over who controlled the black Corvette. Though Kyle was three years older than Todd, he didn't always win the arguments. Amazed at their resilience to our tenuous environment, I chuckled with pleasure hearing their laughter.

"Red! Shut these two kids up. I'm trying to watch Ed Sullivan."

Angelo's voice unnerved me. My resentment of him filled my veins. I squeezed the handle of the knife and raised it to chest level. All those nights in my bedroom planning to kill Angelo could pay off tonight. He suspects nothing. Just throw the knife. Would anyone miss him? Would anyone blame me?

Angelo's hollering alarmed Kyle and Todd. They stopped playing to look at him as Alyce passed by me walking from the kitchen, wiping her hands on her faded blue plaid apron. A wisp of curly red hair hung over her right eye, partially hiding an amber bruise. As she approached the boys, her eyes shifted from Angelo to her sons as though she was not only frightened but searching for a way out. Her voice was tired and hardly audible as she spoke to the boys, "You two keep quiet. Your father is watching TV. Maybe you should play in your bedroom."

The boys stopped rolling their cars and Kyle pleaded, "Please let us stay. We'll be quiet, Mommy." Alyce's eyes softened as she patted Kyle's head. Ed Sullivan's voice droned on. Alyce returned to the kitchen to finish cleaning up. I didn't move. The knife felt heavy in my hands. I wiped the blade over and over.

After a few minutes, Kyle and Todd resumed their game. Their voices grew louder each time a car spun out of control and collided with another. Angelo raised his head and yelled with such fury the blood vessels on his forehead and throat bulged. "Red! I told you to shut these kids up. Can't you do anything?"

Alyce rushed back to the living room in time to watch Angelo lift his great form from the couch and lunge at Kyle. Before either of us realized what was about to happen, Angelo held Kyle by his right arm and threw him across the room, screaming, "Shut up! Shut up!"

Alyce's face filled with rage as she watched Kyle's expression change from shock to terror when his head hit the edge of the TV cabinet. Blood spurted from the cut on his forehead. She hurried to Kyle who held his arms out and screamed, "Mommy, Mommy!"

Todd crawled to them and cried too, more out of confusion than hurt. As Angelo towered over the huddled group, Alyce embraced both her sons and rocked them until their cries became quieted sniffles. She looked up at Angelo. "You could've killed him." The hate I saw in her face reminded me of the look she gave me when I told Mom she was pregnant.

Angelo glared at the three of them. He turned away, hiked up his pants and strutted back to the couch. "Quit your whining and get me a beer, Red." His uncaring tone sickened me. I wanted him dead. That's what he deserved.

When Angelo faced me as he sat on the couch, I threw the knife at him. He ducked as it whizzed past his head and quivered to rest in the wall above him. His eyes jutted out wildly from his face. He whipped his head up to look at me. I could feel the satisfying grin on my face while I punctuated each word through clenched teeth: "Next time I won't miss."

Angelo jumped up from the couch and vaulted toward me with arms raised for assault. He stopped within inches and just as fast turned toward Toby, who was snuggled next to Kyle. Within a flash he jerked Toby by the neck, making the dog yelp from the sudden pain. I lunged after Angelo, tugging at his arms and screaming, "Don't, please don't. He's not to blame."

Toby's expression pleaded with me for help, but I could not stop Angelo. He threw Toby down the basement steps and strolled back to the couch. I flew down the stairs. But I was too late. Toby was dead.

I held and rocked Toby. "Please forgive me, Toby. Please forgive me. Please, please, please."

Alyce slowly descended the steps and sat by me. She tried to persuade me to come upstairs. Toby's fur was soaked with my tears as I wept for him, for Alyce, for the boys, for Mom and for me. "I let all of you down. I am so sorry the knife missed."

"Don't be foolish, Tekkie. What do you think Sheriff McBride would do with you?" She held me close to her and stroked my hair over and over as I rested my head against her shoulder.

"I don't care."

Alyce didn't cry that evening. She had nothing left inside her to come out, but she stayed by me until the boys called to her. "I've got to get them to sleep if I can, Tekkie," she said. "Please come upstairs. We'll take care of Toby in the morning. I swear to you that this will never happen again."

I shook my head. "I won't leave him here." I spent the night in the basement wishing I had killed Angelo. Toby would be alive and we would be free. I never saw Angelo as a human being, so why would I consider that murdering him was immoral or a crime?

That night was the first time I had been in the basement since Mom's suicide. I saw her hanging from the rafters. Gigi cut her down and pressed his swollen gums against the dark line cutting into her neck, and Tommy, devil's horns protruding from his flat forehead, road his motorcycle through the air, petting my head as he flew by and laughed at my fat ankles. After that, I never wanted to live in another house with a basement.

I buried Toby the next morning under my maple tree behind the house. As I caressed the mound of dirt covering his beautiful, silent body, I pledged, "One day I will make Angelo pay for killing you, boy."

I didn't get that chance, though. Within a few weeks, one morning before the boys were awake, Angelo and Tommy left for a weekend motorcycle rally in New Hampshire. Alyce begged off the trip, pretending she and the boys were too sick for her to go. "The flu, I think," she told him.

After the episode with Kyle and Toby, Angelo believed we were all too afraid to do anything that might make him angry, so he had no reason not to believe her. Angelo now felt in enough control to leave Alyce at home. She gave an Oscar-winning performance as a loving wife when she told Angelo how much she was going to miss him and the trip. She even had me fooled until Angelo sped away on his new BMW. As soon as he was out of sight, Alyce dashed into the house and said, "We have very little time to get the car packed and leave. I want to be out of here in an hour." The sun was just breaking over the crest of the eastern hills.

"Where're we going?" I was puzzled and excited. "Do I have time to tell Sue or call Tasha or Gary?" I thought about leaving Toby's body alone under the maple.

"We can't tell anyone," Alyce said as she threw clothes into a suitcase. "No one can know where we are. Angelo can't find out or we're doomed."

"That didn't work the last time. He found us in Las Vegas, didn't he?"

She turned to me and placed her hands on my shoulders. "We're driving as far as we can today and not stopping until we get at least a thousand miles away. Hopefully that will give us enough lead time."

We stuffed toys, clothes, Mom's TV and a cooler into the red Mercury station wagon that had replaced the convertible. I also packed my doll, Ginger, into my suitcase. But when I saw Alyce throw the muskrat coat into the back of the car, I had to question her sanity. "Why are you taking this?" I picked up the coat. "You never wear it, and it will always remind you of Angelo."

"It's the only decent thing he ever gave me. Besides, it might come in handy one day."

"Yeah, like how?" I wished I hadn't sounded like that thirteen-year-old who told Mom I hated her.

Alyce ignored my question.

We went to the boys' bedroom and lifted them from their beds. We carried their tired and unsuspecting bodies, heads draped over our shoulders, arms dangling like rag dolls. We put them in the back of the station wagon on blankets and the muskrat coat Alyce had laid out. The sun was completely up by the time she locked the house. As we sped west on the New York State Thruway, I asked, "Where are we going anyway?"

"California."

CHAPTER EIGHTEEN

On the Road Again

Chuck charged into the coffee shop near the Fort Niagra Army Base. As he came through the door, Kyle and Todd raced to him yelling, "Uncle Truck, Uncle Truck." That caught all of us off guard and we had to laugh at their mis-pronunciation of Chuck's name.

Chuck gave both rambunctious boys a big hug. "You two sure are growing like weeds," he said. They giggled. Each took one of his hands and pulled Chuck toward Alyce and me. He looked so handsome in his army uniform, I almost forgot why we were there.

While the boys tugged at him, Chuck's forehead wrinkled into a worried, questioning frown. He took off his hat and asked, "What's the matter? Why are you here?" He looked as though he was expecting the kind of news that was delivered to him by the Cape Cod Police when Mom died. Alyce brought bad news, but not at quite the level of Mom's suicide.

The boys enjoyed hot chocolate and we drank coffee while Alyce told Chuck our plans. She finished her tale with, "You and my friend Josie are the only two people who know where we are going."

"Jesus, Alyce, I had no idea things were this bad." He put his arm around her shoulder.

"How could you?" Alyce said as she nuzzled against him accepting his comfort. "Besides, it's not your problem and there is little you can do but wish us luck."

Chuck confessed that he could offer little help because of his obligation to the Army. He put his cup down and fiddled with the salt and pepper shakers. We sat in silence until he reached for both our hands. "I love you both. You're all I have. Please be careful."

Alyce's face brightened as though she wanted to assure him we were going to make it. "I have everything planned. It will be a wonderful new beginning for us." She stood up. "We've got to go." She searched the area before heading to the door.

After we hugged each other good-bye, Chuck stood outside the restaurant as we climbed back into our car. His face looked like it hung down to his collar. I waved continuously out the window until I couldn't see him any longer. I swallowed hard and slumped into the car seat. Alyce looked straight ahead as if that would block the pain of our separation.

We were not just headed for California, we were headed to San Francisco, a city whose name I barely recognized. Alyce reassured me that town bordered the ocean and was definitely far from the desert. But before we reached the waterfront, two days after we left the lush, green rolling hills and rich, blue lakes of New York, we made a memorable stop in a small town in the middle of Nebraska. Nebraska was so flat and treeless, I believed we could see all the state's borders from that town. It was 102 degrees with a humidity to match when Alyce pulled the station wagon into the parking lot of the only restaurant in the area, Betty's Home Cooking. We ordered lunch—tuna salad sandwiches and lemonade—while suffocating under fans circulating hot air. As we ate, we listened to country and western music coming from a radio perched on the counter next to the cash register.

I was familiar with country and western music. My father's nephews had a band, The Ely Boys. They played during the summer months at Suburban Park outside Syracuse. The Ely Boys also tossed the idea of family relationships into the wind and tried to seduce Alyce every chance they got.

A song playing on the radio at Betty's seemed to have been requested just for us and directed at Angelo: "You're gonna look out across the highway to a two-car garage and one of those two cars will be gone."

By the time we were halfway through our sandwiches, the entire town had showed up, about 50 people, to see who the New Yorkers were. Our cautious answers to their questions seemed to make them suspicious of us.

"Where ya from in New York?" one man asked. His face was perfectly divided. The lower two thirds of it was bright red, while the forehead which had been covered with a baseball hat was creamy white and protected from the harsh sun.

"Upstate," Alyce answered.

"Where you and those kids headed?"

"West," she said as she pointed at the vast prairie.

"You city folk aren't much on talkin,' are ya?" a man in denim overalls and a straw hat asked. "You city folk are all the same—secretive. What ya got to hide?"

He obviously thought all New Yorkers lived in the city and that there was no countryside in that state. We didn't let on we were from a rural area. We didn't want any leads left for Angelo like the last time.

In an attempt at being friendly in case we might need their help, I asked the overalls man, "Where are all the trees in this state?"

He took off his hat, scratched his head, showing a white band of flesh, and opened his mouth without saying anything. He put his hat back on and left.

Alyce leaned over to me laughing. "That may not have been the right question to start a conversation."

I shrugged, tugged at my shorts trying to expose less leg and finished off my lunch. The lemonade was cold and the tuna sandwich filled me up, but I was glad to get back on the road so the wind blowing through the open car windows could cool me off. I stuck my arm out the window and let the fast-moving air carry it up and down like a wave.

Before we got twenty-five miles from that town, Alyce was sweating and shaking at the same time. Suddenly she veered from the road onto the shoulder, opened her door, and threw up. She restarted the car and drove on. I hadn't turned sixteen yet, could hardly drive and had no license, but after she almost hit the only tree in Nebraska, I took over at the wheel.

"Move over and give me the keys," I told her.

"You don't know how to drive," she said as she stopped the car, handed me the keys and threw up again.

I turned the car around and went back to Betty's to get help. While I struggled to keep the station wagon in the correct lane, I decided it wasn't as easy as driving Angelo's old farm flat-bed truck. Thankful for being in a place with few people and cars, I couldn't possibly hit anyone or thing. I kept my head by pretending the line dividing the lanes was the yellow brick road and if I followed it, we would get to the Land of Oz and our wishes would be granted.

I sang in a determined low voice, "We're off to see the wizard," but the road took us back to Betty's and not Oz. Betty didn't look like the good witch, either. She was definitely Nebraska farm stock in a blue floral house dress filled quite respectably with her abundance. Her robust complexion, no-nonsense shoes like the oxfords Mom made me wear, and a net securing her hair in place finished off the look. Yet Betty was quite an entrepreneur. She also owned the only motel in town, which was next door to her restaurant. She put us up and called the doctor, who traveled fifty miles to treat Alyce. The doctor diagnosed her with a severe case of flu and ordered her to bed for the next two days.

For me, those days were spent hauling food from Betty's Home Cooking and entertaining my nephews. The latter wasn't easy in that one-block town where all the major activities took place at Betty's or Hank's Gas Station, which was also the post office, and both of them closed at 5 P.M. The grocery store was in the town fifty miles away where the doctor lived. It was too hot to play outside and there was no TV. Those were two hard and long days playing hide and seek, kick the can and Simon Says.

The day we finally got back on the road, Betty packed us a lunch for free and told us, "Come back any time." For a fleeting moment, and despite Betty's kindness, I actually thought living with Angelo would be a better option than in the middle of Nebraska.

We were all secured in the station wagon and Betty leaned in the driver's side window. She put her hand on Alyce's shoulder and said, "You take care of yourself." The way she said that I was sure she knew we were running away. I prayed she'd keep her mouth shut if Angelo talked to her.

When we reached the four-corner stop sign in town, a familiar-looking convertible passed us. Neither Alyce nor I wanted to look directly at the car for fear it was Angelo hunting us again. A large icy hand squeezed my heart to stop its beating, while Alyce froze in place until the driver behind us grew impatient and honked his truck horn.

Alyce chuckled, "We've both forgotten that Angelo doesn't have the convertible and we're driving the only car." She put the car in gear and sped away. I don't believe she stopped looking in the rearview mirror until we reached San Francisco.

In the next town, I got sick and discovered that my wisdom teeth were coming in. So for the next 1500 miles I suffered with pain and a fever. I held a melting ice pack against my jaw and wished I could die. This was especially true when we reached Laramie, Wyoming, during their rodeo days. I felt we had arrived in a stagecoach followed by drunken wranglers shooting their guns into the air. With all the commotion, sleep was not a possibility, nor was getting food without waiting hours in line. I don't know where all those cowboys slept, maybe on their bed rolls with their horses under the sky. Fortunately for us, they weren't in the motels, because we easily found a room.

Alyce, always looking on the bright side, said, "Let's look for an amusement park."

I rolled my eyes at her and slurred, ice pack firmly pressed against my jaw, "What for?"

"Laramie," she said, waving her arm wide in front of her and yelling through the shouting cowboys, "looks like a great spot to unwind for a day or two and allow Todd and Kyle to let loose of some of their pent-up energy."

Though I dropped my chin to my chest and muttered, "Oh no," I had to agree. Playing in the back of the station wagon for five days and two days at Betty's had done nothing to quell my nephews' exuberance. So we embarked on a mission to find an amusement park.

After asking several people in town, we were directed to a softball game, Laramie's idea of an amusement park. At least it was cooler than Nebraska and we feasted on hot dogs and popcorn.

On our way back to the motel after watching the game, we drove on unlit country roads and met one of those dips that cross the road to allow high water to flow after storms. Both boys flew forward and Kyle cut his lip. He screamed. I grabbed a cloth and held it to his lip.

"What happened?" I asked.

We got out to inspect the scene and discovered the car hit the dip head on, damaging the frame. The car was not driveable. "God," Alyce whimpered, "what next?" She kicked the flat tire.

We packed up what we could, locked the doors and carted the kids to our motel. It seemed everyone was still on Laramie's main street hooping and hollering, including all the mechanics. After walking a couple of miles back to the motel, we were too exhausted to care or do anything but collapse into bed.

The following morning, the bad news was delivered to Alyce at the Lunch Box Café while we ate breakfast. We would be visiting Laramie for a while until our car could be repaired. Faced with two more days of Rodeo Days, we joined in the festivities. Alyce offered up the tired and true cliché: "If you can't beat 'em, join 'em."

I curled my lip and answered, "Ugh."

We ventured to our first rodeo and decided it would be our last one. Too much blood. And we both felt sorry for the animals. We did enjoy the street cookout, chuck wagon style, the Old West parade and another softball game. The competing teams couldn't hold a candle to our old town team.

When the mechanic handed Alyce the repair bill, she screamed, "This is highway robbery. What did you do, build a new car?"

"Take it or leave it, lady," he smirked and wiped the sweat from his forehead with a greasy red rag. "I'm not the one traveling across country." He turned his head and spit out a dark, gooey liquid.

Alyce paid the bill, knowing we had no other choice. That mechanic saw an easy mark when the New York car was brought into the station. He took full advantage of it.

After three days, we were back on the road west with a lot less money in our pockets and anxious to get this trip over. "We'll have to be careful how we spend our money," Alyce said. "There's not much left."

The next day was a blur. I was tired and the toothache worsened. I perked up when I saw Salt Lake, not the city, but the lake. I was so intrigued by its vast saltwater body that the sight of real mountains played a minor role. That, however, would soon change, but not before we faced the barren and desolate lands of northern Nevada. After living in Las Vegas, I didn't want anything to do with another desert.

"Is California like this?" I asked as I scrunched up my face with disapproval.

Alyce pointed to the mountains looming in the distance. "No. That's California."

My mouth dropped open as I eyed the towering rock formations ahead of me. I swallowed hard to keep my breakfast from rising into my throat. That sight temporarily made me forget about my wisdom teeth.

Our next stop was outside Reno, Nevada, another small gambling town, though more folksy than Las Vegas. I was glad we stayed there only long enough to sleep, shower and eat. But the road out through the mountains to Lake Tahoe almost persuaded us to retreat back to Reno.

Tahoe's beauty was overshadowed by our first encounter with mountain driving. We pulled off the narrow highway more often than we drove forward, to allow the cars lined up behind us to pass. Alyce's cautious five-mile-an-hour speed did nothing to endear us to the drivers who passed us. They often yelled, "Get off the road, lady, and go back to New York." Some made obscene gestures. Her slow driving also obligated us to endure an eternity in switchback hell.

Once I sighted Lake Tahoe, I believed the mountain drive was worth it. We spent the night in Tahoe exploring the area, which was in two states. The half in Nevada had casinos and reminded me of an upscale Las Vegas, which did not appeal to me. The other half in California was more inviting because it was committed to the outdoors and related sports, especially snow and water skiing. We learned that Tahoe is the largest alpine lake in North America, nestled in the mountains at 6223 feet above sea level, and is 22 miles long and 12 miles wide. Tahoe's water was so clear we could see down forever. We were told we probably could see as far as 75 feet.

I could smell the pines everywhere. I lay in the grass near the lake and let the scent engulf me. That majestic Alpine wonderland was as different from the flat lands of Nebraska as the desert was from the Atlantic Ocean. It would have been easy for me to take up residence there.

The next morning Alyce had an interview for an executive secretary at Harrah's Club on the south shore in Nevada. Though the area was inviting and the job challenging, she decided the pay wouldn't be enough to support the four of us in that resort and gambling Mecca. So it was back into the mountains and on to San Francisco.

On the road out I asked, "Why'd we stop there anyway? I thought we were headed to San Francisco."

"We are, but while researching places to live, I found a job opening here," Alyce said with more confidence than I had heard in a long time. "I didn't want to pass up any opportunities."

Alyce, I discovered, had done months of research before deciding to leave Angelo. As a result, she found job openings in Lake Tahoe and San Francisco and scheduled appointments for interviews. She admitted, "I'd rather live in California. Though divorces are easy to get in both western states, California is more woman-friendly." She smiled, raised her eyebrows and added, "The wages are better in California, too, and college tuition is next to nothing in the state schools."

I should have known Alyce would never skip out of town without a well-thought-out plan. As we increased the distance from Angelo, the old Alyce returned. The Alyce who took us across country reminded me of the person who had indulged in many daring and often mischievous exploits like the time when she was eight. She skipped school, taking Chuck's kindergarten class with her to a Syracuse Chiefs baseball game. She was caught and spanked in front of that class, but that didn't stop her from being truant again to see another home game.

By the time we reached San Francisco, I was delighted that my obstinate, impish sister had returned. She laughed with ease, she gained back some of the weight she had lost and her complexion reclaimed its radiance. Even her hair became a deeper, more lustrous copper red, its brilliance challenging the sun's rays. It seemed there was nothing that could stand in our way. Except my teeth.

Though San Francisco must have been a breathtaking sight, all I remember are the hills and how terrified we were that the car brakes would fail. Riding the streets in a cable car, however, provided us with the amusement park thrill we missed in Laramie. The old-fashioned red cars reminded me of the ones Mom had told me she used to ride when she was a little girl in New York City. I taught Kyle and Todd the words to the song that Mom had often sung to me: "Clang, clang, clang went the trolley." So as the cable car carried us over the steep San Francisco hills, we sang it smiling and waving to people strolling on the sidewalks. They and the other passengers rolled their eyes at us, nodded their heads to each other and mumbled, "Tourists." I also admired the many riders who could jump onto the platform of a moving trolley and hang onto an exterior handle as the trolley sped up and down the hills. I believed those maneuvers are what set them apart from the tourists.

Whether we rode in the cable car or the station wagon, reaching the pinnacle of a hill and seeing nothing but sky before me sent my stomach to my throat. When our station wagon crested the hump and plundered down the other side, I felt like we were dumped from the hundred-foot drop of the Cyclone roller coaster. I held onto the dashboard praying, while Kyle and Todd cheered and Alyce fixed her vision straight ahead. She squeezed the steering wheel until her knuckles turned white and shouted as though the hill prevented us from hearing her, "This is worse than the mountains." At that point my stomach went from my throat to its regular spot and back to my throat until the car came to rest at the bottom. Each time we made the descent safely, Alyce sighed, "I'm glad that's over."

Within a few days, Alyce found the perfect job as an executive secretary with an oil company. Unfortunately, housing was scarce and expensive. The one place within our budget was a small and charming beach house 45 minutes from her downtown office. We had small-town vision and thought 45 minutes was too far. We knew little about California's freeways, the local love of cars, and the distance people traveled to work.

Discouraged, we left San Francisco and headed for Los Angeles. When the Golden Gate Bridge vanished from our view, I considered the possibility that if Los Angeles didn't work, there was always Mexico.

CHAPTER NINETEEN

California Here We Are

Driving the magnificent California coast was a haze, either because I had a teenager's dim appreciation of nature or my aching wisdom teeth clouded the experience. By the time we headed south alongside the Pacific, we had been traveling for two weeks and were suffering from being in the car too long. We were anxious to get settled in one place.

Alyce only had $60 left after the Laramie accident took a huge chunk of our funds. She wired Aunt Jean for money so we'd have enough for a deposit on our first apartment. It had to be difficult to seek Aunt Jean's help because she would be another person who knew where we were. Even knowing that risk, it was clear Alyce had decided we were going no farther than Los Angeles.

Our spirits were high when we arrived in L.A. As we came into town, we sang along with Bobbie Darren's "Mack the Knife" on the radio. Dinah Washington belted out "Don't You Know" as we passed Angel's Flight, a one block cable-car which hauled people up the steep incline of Hill Street. Always the optimist and a die-hard Dodger fan, Alyce said, "We'll tell everyone we left New York and moved to L.A. because the Dodgers did."

"Your baseball fanaticism almost matches your guts," I laughed. "Hopefully neither will get us in any trouble."

The day we arrived Alyce picked up the loan from Aunt Jean at a Western Union office. Combined with the other sixty dollars, our meager funds landed us in a one-bedroom apartment in East L.A., a predominantly Mexican area. Our housing complex was located in a rough neighborhood and was a typical Californian one-story, flat-roofed, cream-colored stucco with all the front doors lined up around a courtyard entry. It was difficult not to see the comings and goings of every tenant. It was equally difficult not to hear our neighbors' business and arguments, many involving knife fights. Even so, most of the tenants were hard-working people who had learned little English and spoke mostly in Spanish, the first language other than Polish and English I had heard.

Our one-bedroom apartment was unfurnished. For tables and chairs we used orange crates which we got from neighbors who picked fruit at orchards over fifty miles away. The pickers were selected daily from a rag-tag group of men who congregated at a nearby corner. If selected by the driver they were taken to the orchards in the bed of a truck. The sight of them being carted off reminded me of the pictures I had seen in *Life* magazine of the Depression.

Kyle and Todd slept in the only bedroom on the muskrat coat. In fact, they had napped on that coat all the way across country. It seemed natural now. Alyce and I shared the murphy bed that pulled out of the living room wall. We had enough money left from the deposit and first month's rent to buy staples, allowing us to eat fried potatoes and pancakes most days. It was just like the last few months Dad was alive except our home in California had partitions, tiled counter tops, hardwood floors, and no cockroaches like Las Vegas.

Our immediate neighbors, the Garcias, were young parents with one child, a daughter named Esperanza. She was six years old, the same age as Kyle. The Garcia family could speak a little English and had arrived in L.A. only a few months earlier to live with Mr. Garcia's brother. By the time we rented the apartment, Mr. Garcia's brother was in the L.A. County Jail. He did not have the gentle and religious temperament of Mr. Garcia and had knifed one of the other neighbors during an argument over a loud radio.

Alyce searched for a job every day, pledging to get us out of that neighborhood before school started in less than two months. We had no telephone so it was difficult for any prospective employer to reach her, but fortunately for us, she found a job and Gene Stanton in the first week.

When Alyce followed up on the interview with Mr. Stanton, she was told by the personnel manager that she should not get her hopes up since the position was promised to a family member. Undaunted, Alyce called again in a few days and was told the same thing. She really wanted the position as his executive secretary and felt depressed about not getting it. So on the following day when a telegram arrived, we suspected bad news from the only people who knew where we were, Chuck, Aunt Jean or Alyce's best friend, Josie. To our surprise, the telegram was from Gene Stanton offering her the job.

Mr. Stanton hired Alyce not only because he was impressed by her secretarial skills, but because she wore a hat and gloves to the interview. It was an image he had left behind in his native Midwest and surely never saw in casual Los Angeles. The first day on the job he told Alyce, "You'll probably not stay here longer than a year. You're smarter than the job needs."

She told me she was amazed and flattered by his praise. Alyce had rarely heard such accolades from a man other than Chuck and Dad.

Though he never discussed our situation with Alyce, Gene contributed to our well-being from behind the scenes. The first such demonstration of his kindness and concern came during Alyce's first week on the job. She found a large box of candy and tickets to Disneyland on her desk with a note: "Welcome to Los Angeles."

Each day I learned more about Mr. Stanton from Alyce and decided he was as colorful a personality as any I had read about. Sharing his personal history and family with us made our relocation a lot easier. As I became more acquainted with Mr. Stanton, I believed he and Alyce shared similar venturesome attitudes. For instance, Gene Stanton was raised in Detroit and worked his way through high school and college as a bootlegger for the notorious Purple Gang. After graduating from college, he and a friend conceived the first door-to-door cosmetic company called Beauty Counselors. That venture, similar to Avon, came to an end when he entered the Army and was assigned to intelligence during WWII. He met his wife, Carmella, at a USO Club in California.

Fortunately for Alyce, the Stantons remained in California, where he became a prominent businessman. Despite his stint with the Purple Gang, Gene Stanton was a conservative who thought slumming it was when he wore a hounds tooth jacket, a cotton shirt without a tie and khaki slacks.

Though I envied the Stanton's *Leave It to Beaver*-type family life, I had difficulty envisioning anyone living other than the way I did, without parents and on the run. Despite my envy, I was happy for the bit of sanity and stability the Stanton family gave us.

Although Gene tried to break the chauvinistic mold from which he was created, and therefore was a leader in that arena, he often found himself caught in a *faux pas*. For instance, Alyce's duties went beyond her secretarial role to taking over many office manager and administrative assistant tasks. Though Gene recognized her talents and put them to use, he once introduced her at an all-male meeting with "I want you to meet our top girl."

Men-only clubs were socially accepted, and Gene belonged to one of the most prestigious in L.A., The Jonathan Club. When Alyce met him for lunch, she had to ride the "Women's Elevator." If that wasn't bad enough, women were overly judged by the way they looked and dressed rather than by their intelligence. Gene was no exception and didn't mince any words when it came to his likes and dislikes. When he disapproved of what Alyce wore, he'd tell her, "Your sister obviously got up before you and beat you to the clothes." Or he'd invite her to sit in on an important meeting, "but put on some lipstick first."

Gene Stanton treated Alyce as an oldest daughter who had brains, but needed refinement. "She's just a country girl so I had to fix her up," he told colleagues and friends. But he also knew her abilities and was instrumental in pushing her to a much higher career goal.

While Alyce worked, I took care of the boys and the apartment and cooked. Having confidence in Alyce, Gene, a generous man, gave her a salary advance so she could buy decent food.

I sat on the apartment stoop most days and nights as our neighbors did to cope with the heat, while Kyle and Todd charged up and down the courtyard playing with the other children. Few of them had any toys to speak of, so they fashioned guns from sticks and pretended they were the Lone Ranger and Tanto or Roy Rogers and Dale Evans. The Mexican children weren't sure who these heroes were, but they had been convinced by Kyle's enthusiastic explanations these Americans were special.

Esperanza Garcia visited us daily. After befriending her parents, I realized how lucky I was. As impossible as it seemed, they had far less than we and lived on what Mr. Garcia could earn as an orange picker. Mrs. Garcia told me once, "We're very happy for whatever we get. In Mexico we lived in a cardboard shelter and rummaged through garbage heaps for food."

We often shared our evening meals with the Garcias, who always came with an offering. Mrs. Garcia introduced me to my first tortillas and refried beans.

Esperanza eyed my doll, Ginger, the first day she came to our apartment. I kept Ginger, my one connection to Mom, close by me. That doll was the only personal item I packed other than clothes. Like her parents, Esperanza could speak only a little English, but I knew by her bright, wide eyes and the joyous look on her face she had never seen anything quite like Ginger. The day I caught Esperanza gently touching Ginger's dress and hair, I scolded, "Don't touch her."

Esperanza retreated from our house in tears. I felt terrible about making her cry, so the next day I let her hold Ginger. I heard Mom's voice, "Give Ginger to Esperanza. You have so much more and will get more from life than she."

As I handed Ginger to Esperanza for keeps, I hoped Mom was right. Except for my Susan Hayworth paper dolls, Ginger was the only toy I can remember from my childhood.

Esperanza held the doll to her chest as she danced around our living room. She banged out the door, shouting in Spanish, "Mom, Mom. Look at me," alarming the whole complex. Everyone was relieved to see she was unharmed and the proud owner of her first store-bought toy, a walking bride doll.

Alyce never missed breakfast or dinner with us until she decided to take a second job as a cocktail waitress. "We need the money," she said, "so we can move to a better place."

For Kyle, Todd and me, the days were long and lonely. We looked forward to Alyce's days off, which were spent at the beach where we cooked our meals, even breakfast, on a portable grill.

Our first trip to the beach flooded me with memories of Mom and me at Coney Island, especially the smell of the ocean carried onto the shore by the cool, salty breeze. The sound of the waves crashing against the sand gave me goose bumps from my feet to my head as I stood in awe of the Pacific's beauty, power and vastness, larger than the two Great Lakes I had seen, Erie and Ontario, put together. It seemed bigger than the Atlantic and there were fewer people on the beach. I dreamed of living in the noble, waterfront Victorian house near our favorite little-used sandy knoll. The house had braved contractors' bulldozers and survived despite the apartments rising around it. I could relate to its courageous stance, though surely faced with eventual extinction.

We ended that first day at the beach at the Santa Monica Pier. It was like a miniature carnival midway. We threw darts, fished for prizes in a tank and ate candy apples, cotton candy and my favorite, hot dogs on a stick. Leaving the Pier, I heard the music from a carousel and said, "Let's ride the merry-go-round."

My nephews didn't need much persuasion as each grabbed one of Alyce's hands and dragged her in the direction of the music. All four of us mounted the platform. Kyle and I took moving horses and Alyce rode in the sleigh with Todd. My horse was on the outer rim. As the carousel picked up speed, I heard Mom saying, "Grab the ring and make a wish."

155

On my third try, I got the brass ring. Squeezing it in my hand I said to myself, "I think Mom followed us to California." My hair flying and me waving the ring at the onlookers, I made a wish. "Please let us always be this happy and free."

One day while we were finishing up our grilled hot dogs, Alyce announced, "We're going to Disneyland for Tekkie's sixteenth birthday. Mr. Stanton has given us the tickets."

I responded with all the dignity of a teenager, "I don't want to go to some dumb amusement park."

Todd and Kyle chanted, "Mickey, Mickey." They bounced up and down as they circled the picnic table.

My scornful look didn't stop them from that sing-song yelling. I guessed they wanted a diversion from our beach ritual.

Alyce chimed in, "You'll love it, Tekkie. You'll see."

She sounded more and more like Mom. In fact, she was becoming Mom, at least the good parts I remembered.

No description or advertising brochures of the newly-built Disneyland could persuade me that it was anything but some dumb amusement park. It may be better than Laramie, but as a soon-to-be sixteen-year-old, I surely was above such childish entertainment. When I walked through the gates of the Magic Kingdom and into an extraordinary fantasy, it was difficult to keep up my teenager's "I know everything" image.

Though Dumbo and the Mad Hatter's Tea Cup rides were Kyle and Todd's favorite, I much preferred the rollicking trip on the Matterhorn and the dreaminess of the train going through the replica of the Grand Canyon. "One day we're going there," Alyce said as we passed the miniature display. Knowing what she had already brought us through, I believed her.

Alyce attacked the day as she did any event. Determined to miss nothing, Alyce wanted to do everything there was to do and reveled in the laughter of her three charges. When we slowed, she dragged us to the next attraction. Though exhausted, we stayed until fire works filled the sky and the park closed. Excited by the day's adventure, we planned our next trip to the Magic Kingdom.

Although Disneyland was spectacular, Chuck's birthday letter to me outshone it and brought me to tears. In part it read:

I see that you have turned your talents back to the artistic and creative. Good! You should keep up the ballet. I may not be very

156

old, Tek, but one thing I have learned in my lifetime is that the beautiful is necessary and important. Be aesthetic and look for the beautiful. It is there in everything, even in the lowest and dirtiest thing in the world. Look for it and you will find it; finding it will help you ease over the rough spots in life. Life is good. Live it as it comes—do your absolute best to help others and to be sincere in your dealings with others. Keep in mind that education is important. Don't throw your chances away by something foolish. Think about how you can make the bad a little better and more pleasant. Be thankful for what you have—and we in the family have plenty.

I marveled at Chuck's tenderness, optimism and concern even though he had lost his parents and had no money. His letter helped me get through that first year in L.A. Though none of us knew what still lay ahead, Chuck was right about one thing: I was lucky to have Alyce and him. Besides Kyle and Todd, they were the only family that I had left. Though at times I fought off feelings of aloneness, because of my brother and sister, I always knew I was loved and wanted.

On our way to Disneyland for my birthday, I saw the mountains to the east of L.A. for the first time and thought we were lost. Alyce eased my panic when she reported that unlike that day, the San Bernardino Mountains were often obscured by fog and something new to me—smog. I soon learned I didn't mind the fog as much as I did living with my eyes stinging from dirty air.

That summer the mountains hadn't been the only new discovery. I also found out that Caucasians weren't the only inhabitants of the United States. Though I knew about the Onondaga Indians because I had seen them at the New York State Fair and read about them in history texts, I never thought about them as citizens actually living in our country. When I encountered African-Americans and the Mexicans who were my neighbors, my narrow, sheltered world was altered forever.

On our first shopping expedition to downtown L.A., I was introduced to even more diverse cultures. I saw a man in woman's clothing and a braless woman wearing a see-through blouse—white organdy with a lace collar that formed a V ending at the wearer's waist. I will never forget how she was dressed. The blouse had long sleeves cuffed in lace and was tucked into incredibly brief red shorts cinched at the waist with a three-inch black elastic belt. The outfit was set off with white patent leather go-go boots. As I gawked,

Alyce explained, "She's a prostitute."

"What's a prostitute?" I asked, twisting my head to take a last look at this mysterious new being as Alyce hustled me into the Broadway Department Store. I had never seen anything like her in East Syracuse.

"Never mind. It's nothing you should know about."

"You sound just like Mom," I said. I thought Alyce was beginning to look more like her, too.

There was always something I shouldn't know about. I walked around with my mouth open for the next year observing these shouldn't-know-abouts.

On one of her days off Alyce took us to the star-studded sidewalks of Hollywood Boulevard instead of the beach. I tried every actresses' cement-embedded hand and footprints on for size. Unfortunately, my aristocratic feet were just too big for those petite prints. Spirits unhampered, I felt as though every honoree was there in person sharing the excitement with me. I could actually hear the crowds cheering their appreciation and did a deep curtsy in recognition of that honor. My flamboyance went unnoticed, because there were far too many other oddities in Hollywood to make my behavior stand out.

In late August, Chuck visited us while on a short leave from his Army post in St. Paul, Minnesota. He bunked on the floor of the boys' bedroom and drove Alyce to work so we could have the car to explore the area. In the evenings we sat on our front stoop listening to the music coming from our neighbors' apartments and planned our futures. We didn't mention Mom or East Syracuse.

Sometimes Chuck and I danced the samba, rumba or cha-cha to the music just as we had in our living room on Cutler Street. That summer in L.A., we danced once again in flawless choreographed movements, surprising the Garcias, who often joined us. Unlike our planned steps, the Garcias danced with a fluidity and confidence which seemed natural for a couple raised south of the border.

When Alyce didn't have to work in the evenings, she'd join Chuck and me on the stoop. We'd reminisce about the good parts of our childhood. Most were hilarious accounts of their days of playing hooky from school and church. Alyce recalled the years they lived in Newark before I was born. "Mom and Dad's friends were mainly the Negro League baseball players and their families. They played for the Newark Eagles when Dad played for the Newark Bears," she said. "Dad always told us that 'those guys are the best damn players in any league.' Remember, Chuck?"

158

"Sure do," he said in almost a whisper.

"I wonder what would've happened if Dad stuck with baseball?" I asked as I made circles in the dirt with a stick.

No one said anything. We all stared into the courtyard listening to the salsa music and the traffic on nearby Harbor Freeway.

The following day Chuck left L.A. I not only fretted over his departure but I also complained to him about going back to school. "I don't know anyone and L.A. is so large, especially compared to East Syracuse, " I whined.

With his arm around my shoulders, Chuck consoled me, "Don't mope about going back to school. After all, you could be in the Army."

"Ah, yes," I chuckled, "there's always a positive side to everything."

In a letter Chuck sent a few weeks later he told us that other than the pilot, he was the only man on the Air Force transport that took him from L.A. to St. Paul. The other passengers made up the Women's Air Force (WAF) softball team. On that flight, Chuck got a strong dose of what it was like to be in a minority. He was the brunt of many jokes, because he was the only male and in the Army rather than the Air Force. He wrote, "I kept expecting them (WAF's) to heave me off the plane at any moment. Fortunately, the pilot let me come up to the cockpit for the greater part of the flight."

To get him through that trip, Chuck drank too much and woke up the next morning at the barracks with a hangover and facing AWOL charges for returning to the base twenty-four hours late. He told us about his dilemma in the same letter he wrote us about the flight. "After some fast talking, I convinced the Charge of Quarters into signing me in the day before. This we accomplished by erasing half a dozen names from the sign-in book to make room for mine. And contrary to all rumors, I did not threaten him with the possibility of losing all his finance records and thus making it rather difficult to pay him."

Reading that letter, I believed he learned a lot from my clever and bold sister. Since I was related to them, I figured I was destined to be the same.

That morning after he returned, Chuck's bunkmate persuaded him to go on a blind date for tennis. As can be imagined, he was less than charming. Not only suffering a raging headache, he also borrowed tennis shoes that were a couple of sizes too large and he forgot his racket. Though he should have been humble given his negligence, Chuck treated Joy, his date, like one of the WAF softball team members he preferred to forget.

A few weeks later Chuck wrote that he somehow persuaded Joy to marry him. "I fell in love with her the moment I saw her," he said.

I treasured every letter Chuck sent to us that summer. His stories about humorous Army experiences were often the only light-hearted moments we had.

Within a week of Chuck's departure, Alyce got a letter from Josie that said she was heading to L.A. with her three sons to live with us. Josie was also fleeing from her abusive husband, Pete. With the little money Josie sent and Alyce had saved, they bought a small, well-maintained house in the Pacific Palisades, three houses from a cliff. Alyce and Josie got the house cheap because it was built near a park that had collapsed onto the Pacific Coast Highway the year before during the heavy rain storms. When that slide brought the house closer to an ocean view, the sellers were convinced they should live somewhere else.

Josie swore to Alyce she didn't slip up and tell Angelo where we were as she had done when we lived in Las Vegas. Still we weren't sure how much information she or her sons let Pete know, consciously or unconsciously. After all, Josie's sons probably didn't understand why leaving their only home had to be a secret. Alyce was satisfied that Josie hadn't given away our location even though Josie admitted Angelo had been pressuring her.

We piled the orange crates into the station wagon along with our other possessions, waved good-bye to the Garcias and moved to the Pacific Palisades. In that one wave, the Garcia family and my doll, Ginger, became history.

Our new home was a mint green, stucco, three-bedroom-ranch on a street lined with palm trees in an upwardly mobile middle-class neighborhood. It also had an attached two-car garage, the first I had ever seen. Not only did the house have a dining room, but it also had a breakfast nook. I couldn't conceive of why anyone would need two places to eat. The lush postage-stamp-sized yard brimmed with lemon and avocado trees and rhododendron bushes. As was common in California, ivy covered the front yard instead of grass. After the enforced couple of days in Nebraska, I felt blessed to live in a tropical paradise that I had only dreamed about.

To celebrate our move, Alyce took us to the first McDonald's in the U.S., which served up a new cuisine concept—fast food. As we rejoiced in our good fortune, gobbling up our cheese burgers and fries, Alyce joked, "My restaurant, Meals Away, could have been the first McDonald's."

On the day we moved into our mint green dream house, I roamed from one large sunny room to another, basking in the splendor. I could see only one drawback. I had to take a school bus to University High School in West

Los Angeles.

While unpacking, Josie carted in several boxes, announcing, "These are all I could salvage from your house."

Alyce stopped humming. She laid down the rag she was cleaning a kitchen cupboard with and walked to Josie. She took a box from her and quietly asked, "What do you mean?"

Josie's eyes twitched. She looked nervous when she said, "Angelo broke into the house. He destroyed or threw out almost everything," she said. "I'm so sorry."

Alyce pointed to the four boxes. "This is all that's left?" Her eyes moistened.

Josie nodded.

"Let's see what's in them," I said to Alyce.

She hesitated but retrieved scissors and ripped the tape. We sat in the middle of the living room floor among all the other packed boxes and went through the four that held what was left of our family history. We pulled out pictures that had been long forgotten. When we found the one of me at two years, Alyce and I recited together the poem Mom did every time she saw that picture. "There was a little girl who had a curl right in the middle of her forehead. When she was good she was very good. But when she was bad she was horrid." We laughed until we had to go to the bathroom.

We grew quiet looking at pictures of Mom and Dad when they were young. One showed Dad in his baseball uniform and another showed him in his railroad denims. The last one we found of him was of an emaciated figure just before he died. He had his arm around Mom, who stood unsmiling between him and me.

Alyce and I could only find a handful of pictures of Mom. All of them were either black and white or shades of brown and beige. I had three favorites. One was her confirmation picture. Mom stood serious-faced and saintly in a white lace drop-waist dress, white veil, shoes and socks. She held a white candle in one hand and a white Bible in the other. I fingered her face. Her image in that picture made me believe she must have always been devout and had taken a temporary detour when she eloped with Dad.

Another picture showed Mom as a young beauty in the 1930's, looking like Greta Garbo. The third picture was taken with me just before Mom died. In that one, Mom was smiling and appeared euphoric. No one would have dreamed her fate looking at her in that picture. I was resting my chin on her shoulder and was wearing an Easter dress. Mom wore a soft gray dress with a small rounded collar and a double row of white buttons down the front of the fitted bodice. The dress showed off Mom's beautiful figure. I held it up to show Alyce and said, "You got Mom's breasts. I got Dad's."

We both laughed again until my laughter turned to soft sobbing when Mom's words resounded in my ears: "You can be anything you want to be." Though I could hear the words Mom spoke, I realized that no matter how I struggled, I couldn't remember the sound of her voice. I couldn't even remember how it sounded when she sang. The only reminder I had of her was the scent from a wig or Ivory soap. Nothing except her smile remained truly vivid with me.

I studied that picture of Mom and me. I remembered every detail of the dress I wore. It had a pink organdy top and navy-taffeta skirt with pink flowers. Mom and I were laughing, and she looked radiant. I wanted to know what happened to those people. Was Mom a fraud smiling at us as though the world held only good times and treasures? What hidden madness changed her from the person in the photo to the one who killed herself? What clues had I missed about her that would have helped me understand who she was and why she didn't want to live?

I traced her handwriting on the pictures describing who, what, where and when. Though I had seen her writing many times when she was alive, looking at it years after she had died was both strange and familiar. It was sobering to realize that Mom's handwriting could last far longer than she did.

"We never talk about suicide, do we, Alyce?" I asked as I shuffled through the pictures again. "Or about why Mom killed herself."

Alyce bent over the box she was opening pressing her hands heavy against it. "I think," she said to the wall, "I think it scares us."

"What do you mean?"

Alyce turned to me with sympathetic eyes and said, "We may do the same thing. If we don't talk about how Mom died, maybe that fear will go away."

"I didn't know you felt the same way I do," I said. I was shaking. "But I also miss her and wanted the world to know her. I wanted to know her. I can't even hear her voice anymore."

Alyce circled her arms around me. "I know," she consoled and rocked me. "I know."

I pushed away from her and summoned the courage to ask her a question that had been tucked away deep inside me. "Did you believe me when I told you I thought something was going to happen—just before she died?"

Alyce's face wrinkled into one that looked like an old woman's. "I've wondered that, too. Many times," she answered in a soft voice. "I was so worried about Angelo, I don't know what I thought anymore."

"Do you think we could have saved her?" I asked as I repacked the pictures.

"No. I don't," Alyce said with certainty.

I wasn't so sure. And I didn't want to hear Alyce say, "It's a vicissitude of life."

After a few quiet moments, Alyce and I tore open the rest of the boxes and found Chuck's yearbooks and Dartmouth sweater. Sadly, the World War II scrapbooks were not among the cache.

Tears streamed down my face as I sang an unpredictable song, one Mom used to sing trying to cheer me up because it was so silly: "Flat Foot Floozy with the Floy Floy."

Alyce filed for divorce that fall, which meant Angelo was notified. So he knew we were in Los Angeles, but not exactly where. Waiting the prescribed six long months for the divorce to be final seemed like an agonizing eternity filled with the fear Angelo would find us and stop the separation again.

CHAPTER TWENTY

Surf's Up

Once again our furnishings were makeshift, but Kyle and Todd finally had beds of their own. It was my turn to sleep on the floor in the muskrat coat. Since it had come in handy, I decided Alyce was right about taking the coat despite its origins.

Shortly after we moved, I walked two blocks to the bus stop, boarded the yellow school bus and headed to my first day at University High School in West Los Angeles. Alyce drove Kyle to school and dropped Todd off at a daycare center. Kyle, who was in second grade, stayed after school in daycare until either Alyce or I picked him up. Usually it was me because Alyce still worked a second job as a cocktail waitress most nights.

On the bus that first day, I met Barbara Montero. She lived about a half mile from me. Though she was like most of the other wealthy girls I would meet who had large, well-furnished homes, closets filled with expensive clothes and large allowances, she was down to earth, had a healthy sense of humor and a deep laugh that could have been heard back in New York. Barbara was my height, perpetually tanned, had naturally platinum blond hair and wore braces with confidence.

A month after I met Barbara, her parents gave her a red Mustang convertible for her birthday. After that, we traded riding the school bus for driving the Pacific Coast highway in her car, top down, humming to "The Theme from *A Summer Place*" playing on the radio.

Most days after I cleaned up the dinner dishes, I walked the half block to the cliff and sat on the edge of jagged asphalt that once had been a road. I'd watch the sun set over the ocean. Rainbow colors filled the endless miles of sky and danced over the horizon. When the sun settled into the dark night water, I'd wish on the stars just peeking out that my life would always be like this. Never again like the one I'd left behind in New York.

Gradually the orange crate furnishings we brought from East L.A. were replaced with items purchased at thrift shops and Salvation Army stores. One find was an eight-foot table made of dark mahogany and held up by large, bulbous-looking things the seller called "fat lady" legs. Over the years, prior owners had carved initials into the table top. I used to tell everyone we had the first hand-carved table in the neighborhood.

Though the large size of the pieces in the set which included the table, eight chairs and a five-foot side-board made it seem more appropriate for the Hearst Castle than our house, we managed to squeeze it all into our dining room. It turned out to be the perfect gathering place for friends and family throughout the year, so we spent a great deal of time around it, preferring to eat there rather than in the nook off the kitchen. Many Saturday mornings I served pancakes to my nephews and up to ten other kids living in the area. Our neighbors and my friends who shared time and meals with us at that table often remarked, "There is a lot of love in this house."

My heart swelled with the thought that love was far more important than furniture.

University High School (Uni) was a far cry from East Syracuse High. Uni had over four thousand students attending tenth through twelfth grade and they came from every imaginable social-economic level, Mexican immigrants to Bel Air elite. Unlike the single building that had been my school in New York, Uni's campus consisted of several multi-level buildings and temporary trailers sprawled across an entire city block.

Since the weather varied little, every day I bought my lunch, a peanut butter and honey sandwich on whole wheat bread and a carton of milk, at the kiosk in the commons and ate at a picnic table. If it hadn't been for Barbara, I would have been eating alone.

All the other girls wore sundresses the colors of sherbert with cute little jackets and matching socks rolled down their ankles, a similar fashion to that worn by the Las Vegas girls. So once again I stood out in my sweater sets, plaid pleated skirts, knee-high socks and bucks. Yet no one could recognize a new person in the midst of four thousand students. Lunch in the commons was an unidentifiable mass of color like a filmy, multi-patterned quilt spread over the pavement. In that atmosphere I went from being the Pied Piper of East Syracuse to an obscure curiosity.

Though I was lonely, I had no idea how to break into that intimidating society. I watched from the sidelines, jealous of the perky girls half-heartedly thwarting advances from jocks like my brother in their letterman jackets. In East Syracuse I would have been in that crowd. At Uni, I was an outsider, an oddity who would never fit in. Each day when not with Barbara I sat alone munching peanut butter and honey sandwiches and wondered what had happened to all that self-esteem I once gained under Mom's tutelage. But I knew the answer. It started to wane with Gigi. It was almost erased by Angelo.

Barbara was an only child whose parents yielded to her every whim. Since I would not give in to her, they thought I was a godsend and used me to manipulate her into less self-centered behavior. For instance, one Saturday she wanted me to go shopping with her. When I told her no because I had to do housework, she got huffy and said, "Can't you get out of it?"

I frowned at her insensitivity and yelled, "NO, I can't. We don't have Jeanie, the maid, and cooks like you do. Even with two jobs, Alyce can hardly put food on the table."

I leaned to within inches of her and said, "If you want me to go with you, help me clean."

Barbara did help me clean. Her mother was so awed by this she rewarded me. She and her husband took me on their family trip to San Francisco. I ate bouillabaisse for the first time, which became a favorite, at a restaurant on the wharf facing Alcatraz Prison as it emerged menacingly from the fog.

When we weren't in San Francisco, Barbara and I spent many lazy afternoons sitting at her kidney-shaped pool sipping Cokes. The pool was centered between her house and her grandparents'. Both houses were surrounded by a high concrete wall masked by bougainvillea vines, yucca and palm trees. We entered the compound through an electrified gate controlled by a man in a booth. None of this security bothered me until someone threatened to kidnap Barbara. After bombarding her with questions, Barbara told me some gangster wanted to buy her father's supermarket chain and he wasn't going to sell. When bodyguards followed Barbara everywhere, I put two and two together and decided the gangster was from organized crime.

Barbara survived and I was thrilled Mr. Montero didn't sell his market chain. To the disappointment of the family's cook, Barbara and I gave up her meals in favor of two items new to markets—frozen TV dinners and frozen fruit-filled turnovers. The cook disapproved of our lack of taste, but delivered the meals to us at pool-side. I was getting a lesson on how the other half lived. I was hell-bent on living as close to that lifestyle as I could. I began making plans for college and a career that would get me there.

Every day while roll call was taken and announcements were made over the PA in home room, the girls strolled in carrying huge purses that looked like overnight cases. With great effort, they hoisted the purses onto their desks and hauled from their depths enough products to supply a beauty salon: stand-up mirrors, brushes, hair spray and makeup that would take care of the entire population of L.A. County. Those girls performed hair and makeup rituals foreign to me so I could do nothing but gape with my mouth open. They, in turn, glared at me, thinking I was either from another country or a nerd. Once they got to know me, they decided on nerd.

One day, few students showed up for home room and I thought maybe the rest of us had missed an assembly. When our teacher, Miss Smythe, arrived, she straightened out the mystery. "Surf's up," she announced. The absent students were surfing. I soon learned that was a normal activity for the students who could afford surfboards and the cars to tote them. I couldn't compete with the Beach Blanket Bingo bunch, so I never learned to surf and any crush I had on a local beach hero went unnoticed.

When I wasn't studying, most of my after-school hours were spent as usual caring for Todd and Kyle, preparing meals, and cleaning. Unlike my chore-ridden days in New York, though, I had the freedom to take part in extracurricular activities when Alyce was home with the boys. On many occasions I sailed with the Mariners, a girls' sailing group similar to Girl Scouts except they stayed on land and we didn't. My first ocean sailing experience ended in my being thrown overboard while I was hauling in the head sail. My mates were not thrilled that my rescue delayed our anchoring in Avalon Harbor at Catalina Island.

Two of my favorite Mariner-related events were the Christmas progressive dinner parties and the year-end bashes. I went to some of the most beautiful homes in the area and, unlike the pizza parties I left behind in New York, those Mariner parties were catered.

Laurie held one of the year-end celebrations. I thought she was only slightly better off financially than I because she usually wore the same brown tweed skirt and white blouse to school every day and had little concern about her appearance. Her dishwater-blond hair was cropped in an unfashionably short style, reminding me of Peter Pan. Her nails, less appealing than mine, were as short and as ill-kept as a carpenter's. When her party invitation said Bel Air, I assumed her parents were caretakers at that address.

The night of the Mariner party, Barbara and I drove up a half-mile driveway which ended in a circle around a goldfish pond fed by a fountain. In front of double mahogany entry doors, I stumbled out of Barbara's car, mumbling, "So this is how the other half lives."

The maid answered the front door just as a woman flowed into the foyer in layers of blue chiffon like Loretta Young making her weekly entrances on her TV show. Like a ballerina, the woman swooped her right arm across her body and into the air above her head and announced "I'm Laurie's mother."

Barbara poked me in the ribs with her elbow and whispered, "Close your mouth."

The contrast between Laurie and her mother baffled me. Later I recognized it as Laurie's rebellion against a stick thin, well-coiffed, perfect-featured mother because she felt her plain face and fireplug body could never compete. I liked Laurie better for that spunk, but believed she quietly suffered as I did from her inability to meet the advertisers' and Hollywood's standards for beauty.

As I met more and more girls through our Mariner gatherings, I became painfully aware that everyone I knew had two parents. I felt odder and more isolated than when I was seen as a nerd. This oddity seemed to endear me to my girlfriends. I became someone they needed to take under their wings. Often I felt like a charity case when they showed up at my house with clothes they thought were more appropriate than mine for a dinner or sailing. One time Barbara offered me a pink-checked, spaghetti-strapped, full-skirted sundress. She held the dress over outstretched arms and offered it to me like a gift from one of the three kings visiting Christ's manger. She told me, "It doesn't fit me anymore." Her braces sparkled in the sunlight. "And pink is such a good color on you, especially if you ever tan."

Her good intentions made me feel small. "Thanks, I think," I mumbled and took the offering. As I hung the dress in my closet, I recalled the three men toting the Christmas basket so many years earlier. I had thought we came further than that. Obviously I was wrong, at least in Barbara's eyes.

With that dress and other such "gifts," I soon had an acceptable Californian wardrobe free of charge, but not free from hurt. Though I'm sure they meant well, my friends' gestures lowered my self-esteem and emphasized my sense of not fitting in. But I declared to the girl in the mirror wearing the pink-checked sundress, "I will one day enjoy a lifestyle similar to theirs."

It was bad enough that I had missed the brilliant fall colors that engulf upstate New York. But when flowers filled the neighborhood's yards rather than snow at Christmas, I was homesick. Whoever heard of Christmas without snow? Chuck couldn't come for the holidays because he had no money and couldn't risk being AWOL again if an Air Force hop wasn't available. I was happy he could spend the holidays with Joy's family in St. Paul. Financially and emotionally, that Christmas was difficult for all of us.

A couple of days before Christmas, I stood in the living room window watching the rain, a welcome sight since I couldn't have snow. I could hear Barbara's voice in my head reminding me that I lived in California and to stop talking about "my New York home" and how much better it is. "California's your home now," she once scolded.

As I watched the rain soak the ivy in our front yard and weigh down the palm fronds, a man parked his car at the end of our driveway. I couldn't make out the driver well enough to describe him, but he stayed there for over an hour surveying our house. That night I told Alyce. Thinking it was someone Angelo had sent, we both panicked. In our fearful state we didn't notice that our gas stove was leaking. When I lit it to make dinner, it exploded and set me on fire.

Remarkably calm, Alyce ripped the drapes from the dining room windows and wrapped them around my flaming head, arms and shoulders. Once she was sure the fire was out, she extinguished the flames on the stove. Within minutes she had me in her car racing to the ER. I was fortunate that Alyce's employer provided health insurance, under which I was covered.

While in the ER waiting area, a boy about four years old stood in front of me, mouth agape, examining my charred face and hair. His startled eyes told me not to look into a mirror because what I saw would probably worsen the pain. It was bad enough when the nurse asked me to sign the registration papers and I couldn't pick up the pen. My hands were raw, exposing parts of bone where there was no skin left.

Furious with the nurse, Alyce grabbed the pen and shouted, "What's the matter with you? She can hardly see, let alone write."

Alyce signed the forms and thrust the clipboard at the silent nurse. "Besides, she's a minor and I have to sign for her," she said and led me back to the chair.

Once in a room, the nurse swabbed my face and soaked my hands in a watery solution. Though I immediately felt a soothing sensation, it was also the first time the true pain had registered. I clearly recall saying, "That feels so good."

I suffered with second and third degree burns on my face and hands and lost most of my hair. But I was alive and would recover. On the third day of treatment, doctors rushed in and out of my room, displaying my hands to each other as they grunted disbelieving "umms." They huddled in the corner like football players going over their next play. None shared their diagnosis with me. I only heard the "umm" and watched them nod to one another. While asleep, I dreamed those ghoulish doctors came out of their huddle and approached me with a huge hacksaw, ready to amputate my hands.

Finally, during a consultation, my doctor let me in on the secret. The skin on my hands, which had suffered third degree burns, was regenerating and there was no medical explanation. So I wouldn't need skin grafts after all and could go home. While the doctors may have been puzzled by this remarkable turn of events, I was thrilled not to have to endure more pain from the surgery.

When I was released from the hospital, Alyce took me to a movie to help distract me from my injuries. I can imagine what everyone thought when they saw me hobble by them with my swollen face, my hair covered in a bandana and hands wrapped in huge bandages which looked like white boxing gloves. I had to take medication every four hours, so I asked the usher, "When does the movie get over?"

"Why?" He eyed me as though looking at a distorted creature from a B-rated horror film.

"I turn into a rare beauty at midnight."

His mouth dropped open as Alyce took a hold of my elbow and escorted me to our seats. "When will you ever learn to keep your mouth shut?" she asked.

"I dunno if I have to." My mouth, healing from the burned skin, tightened as I talked.

When Kyle and Todd saw me for the first time, they said, "You don't look like Aunt Tekkie."

They made a game out of feeding me while my hands were still wrapped. I, however, felt like a newborn. Alyce bathed me and wiped my bottom. It was a loving and humiliating experience for both of us. It was a task only a mother could endure.

Within a month I was back at school. Because my doctor wanted the air to help heal my burns, my unprotected hands looked like a mutant's. Tiny black scabs grew like spots on a red dog. If classmates weren't gawking at their ugliness, they asked, "Will your eyelashes grow back?"

No one asked if I'd ever be able to write again, as I used a small recorder instead of taking notes. So much for what really counts in life.

When the doctor gave his ok, Alyce took me to her hairdresser, Michael, for my first professional styling. He chuckled when he saw the mess that was my hair and said, "Next time you don't have to burn your hair; I'll do it for free."

Shortly after New Years, Josie's estranged husband and his girlfriend were killed in a car accident. That spring, Josie announced that she and her three sons were moving back to East Syracuse, which left Alyce solely responsible for the house mortgage. Alyce held on as long as she could, but by fall she filed for bankruptcy. She rented an apartment for us across the street from University High School. Once again, things were happening too fast for me to grasp. Once again when life seemed as though it was stable and going well, something stepped in our way.

CHAPTER TWENTY-ONE

Visits

Our new apartment was in a three-story, white, glittery stucco, u-shaped complex. A courtyard and pool filled the center. From the street we entered through a wrought iron gate, while the covered parking was at the rear facing the alley. Our apartment itself was a two-story, three-bedroom affair that had a curved wrought iron staircase to the second floor. Though we lived in a lower-middle-class neighborhood, I thought the building was very Hollywood.

I missed watching the sunsets from the cliff near our Palisades home and riding down Chataqua Boulevard to Pacific Coast Highway in Barbara's convertible. I missed having our own home in a swank neighborhood.

As it turned out, our move was an economic plus for me. There were so many children living in that complex, I took up babysitting and had as many as twelve at any given time in my little daycare center. It was an ideal moneymaker. The parents in the complex were confident in my abilities and thankful not to have to rush home from work or take their children to babysitters and other centers.

One spring day before the end of the school year, Alyce came home early from work as I was preparing dinner. "Why are you home so early?" I asked as I studied her face. She smiled and raised her eyebrows up and down as though hiding a secret. As she passed by me, the faint smell of White Shoulders cologne filled the air.

"I have a surprise for you." She was out of breath and had apparently taken the stairs two at a time. When she did that, I always knew something big was going to happen.

I rolled my eyes. "Now what? We're moving again?" I hung up the dish rag and closed the apartment door she'd left ajar.

"Nooo," she said with an impish smile. "But you are leaving."

"What do you mean?" My stomach felt queasy. "Where am I going?" I bellowed.

Alyce giggled, took hold of my hands and twirled me around the living room. Her giggle became a deafening laugh that reminded me of Mom's when we had danced the jitterbug.

"You've gone crazy, right?" I asked. As soon as I called her crazy, I regretted it. Those words still held a lot of pain for me.

"No. But I have saved enough money to send you back to East Syracuse High for the prom."

"What?" I yelled a little too loud, which halted our spinning.

Alyce dropped my hands. "You did say Gary wrote to you and asked if you could come as his date. And you have been homesick, right?"

"Gary did write, but what qualifies as homesick?" Since her divorce would be final within a few weeks and Angelo appeared to have resigned himself to its inevitable conclusion, Alyce allowed me to write a few friends, including Gary. Besides, Angelo knew we were in L.A. He just didn't know exactly where.

"You miss your friends from home."

I looked away to hide my quivering mouth. "Who will take care of all the kids?"

"You'll only be gone for a long weekend. We can all manage without you for that period of time." Alyce pressed my cheek between her forefinger and thumb. "What do you say, booby?"

Booby had become her new endearment.

"I hate spending the money." Yet the possibility of going back thrilled me.

"This sounds like the conversation you had with Mom about going to camp." Alyce suddenly turned serious.

"That was different. She would have been all alone if I went."

"Did you ever consider she wanted to be by herself for a while? Besides, everything was paid for by the church."

"Well, I didn't go because..." I plopped down on the couch.

Alyce sat next to me. "You were afraid for Mom." Alyce put her arm around my shoulders. "You knew she was depressed and didn't know what she would do, right?"

My eyes stung as I fought back tears and nodded my head.

"It would make me happy if you'd go." She turned to me and lifted my face with her hand so I had to look at her. "You've been through so much since Mom died. I want you to have at least one chance at being a normal high school teenager. And I am quite capable of taking care of me and the boys, if you haven't noticed."

"You'd send me to some stupid finishing school if you could," I told her as I realized Alyce was leaving her role as my sister and entering with great care the job of mother. While I am sure she never wanted to take Mom's parental memories from me, Alyce was savvy enough to realize I needed a mother figure to look to for help even more than a sister. Alyce slipped further and further into that function each day.

"You're absolutely right," Alyce agreed. "Anything to get you out of those cut-off jeans." She tugged at the pair I was wearing and bounced up the stairs like a young girl, shouting, "We've got a lot to do in the next two weeks." She stopped halfway up and turned around. "Oh, you better telephone Gary before he gets another date."

I smiled as I watched a woman that sounded and looked more like Mom than my sister. Alyce grinned back as though acknowledging my thoughts.

With Alyce's help I made my prom dress from royal blue taffeta I bought at McCrory's Five and Dime on a special sale for fifty cents a yard. Several months earlier Alyce had purchased a second-hand sewing machine that was much easier to operate than Mom's old treadmill.

Despite the low cost, the gown was acceptable. It was floor-length and sleeveless and had a scoop-neck. With the leftover yardage, I made a floor-length shawl that I wrapped gracefully over my shoulders. To complete the outfit, I borrowed Alyce's elbow-length white gloves and fake pearl necklace and earrings. When I tried on the ensemble and appraised the results in a mirror, I had to admire my sewing talent and was pleased that finally some of Mom's seamstress skills rubbed off on me as they had on Alyce.

Standing before the mirror for longer than planned, I inventoried the image of the young woman. "Not bad," I said and turned to see all sides of my reflection, "for a girl with fat ankles."

In keeping with her usual character, Alyce saved a big surprise for the last. When I got to the L.A. airport, I discovered I was leaving on one of the first passenger jets to fly. I approached the ride on this space-age invention with both trepidation and enthusiasm at the prospect of being a pioneer in the new world of travel. As soon as I boarded the jet, my fear was replaced with a haughty feeling of superiority because so few people had done what I was about to do. I flew to East Syracuse for the only prom I thought I would attend.

Gary, looking exactly as he had when I left—gangly, blond hair falling in his eyes which are blue like glacier crevasses—picked me up at the airport. He drove me on the portion of the New York State Thruway where someone had painted my name across two eastbound lanes. He pulled the car onto the shoulder so I could get a good look and said, "It's a tribute to East Syracuse's only celebrity. After all, you're now one of those mysterious California girls."

"When did you do that?"

Gary looked puzzled and shook his head. "I didn't."

"Who on earth did if not you?" I pressed my nose to the window to get a better look.

"A secret admirer, I guess."

Willy was my admirer. He was a year older. I believed he was enthralled with me because I had escaped to the land of sunshine "where the streets are paved in gold."

Painting the thruway wasn't enough for Willy. When I showed up at the prom with Gary, Willy challenged him to a duel. Actually it was a fist fight in the high school parking lot as we were all piling into cars and heading out for breakfast after the prom. Neither one came out the victor because I managed to separate them before either one got too carried away.

I was both flattered and annoyed, but it was a heady experience leaving East Syracuse as a Pied Piper and returning as a celebrity. Though disappointed that life had not change in my hometown, I was complimented by the attention. I didn't get such notice competing with the beach beauties of Southern California.

My friend Tasha didn't go to the prom. When I telephoned her, she said she was dating an older man. "A prom is out of the question," she chuckled. "After graduation, he's setting me up in a Manhattan apartment. I'll work for his escort service."

"What about college or art school?" I asked. "You can get a scholarship."

"This is better for me right now." She sounded distant. She hung up without saying good-bye.

Tasha and I took very different roads out of East Syracuse.

The night I returned from my jet adventure, Alyce and I sat at the breakfast bar drinking coffee as I gave her a minute-by-minute account of the fairytale weekend. We had completely forgotten the man parked in front of the Palisades house at Christmas until we were startled by a knock at the door. I stopped in mid-sentence to see if Alyce's face registered the fear I felt. It did.

My heart raced at the thought of any unannounced late-night caller. Not knowing what to do, Alyce and I remained in place while the knocking became louder and more persistent. "It's probably one of the neighbors locked out or something," she said.

Her offhanded comment didn't convince me, and I smiled weakly. Alyce's hand held the doorknob for several seconds before she finally opened the door, just a crack. Her hair glowed like a copper halo as a slice of outside light snuck through the opening. A figure came dimly into view. I remembered the man in the car. My heart sank into my stomach when I saw Tommy, Angelo's motorcycle buddy, standing there.

"Hi! Can I come in?" he asked as he looked around Alyce and at me with a "you thought you could get away" look on his face.

Illuminated by the light above the door, his beady eyes seemed more pronounced against the dark stubble of his unshaven face. Paralyzed by those eyes, I froze, the coffee cup halfway to my mouth.

Alyce took charge. She held the door with both hands and braced her right foot against the part near the floor to allow only a narrow opening. I was in awe of Alyce's impressive composure. Unlike her, I was unable to move. Tommy's contemptuous expression—the same look he had that night in my bedroom—made every muscle in my body tense. I was horrified by the possibility that he would overpower Alyce and get to me just as he had in East Syracuse. The soured contents of my stomach rose and stung my throat. I held my hand to my mouth and swallowed.

"What are you doing here?" Alyce asked in a deliberate and strong tone. I could see the slight tremor in her hands.

"I thought you'd be happy to see someone from home," Tommy taunted as he put both hands on the jamb so Alyce couldn't shut the door. The familiar naked lady tattooed to his lower arm rose into the darkness like a boat's flare signaling danger.

Alyce's grip tightened as she pressed against the door. "We're not," she said, keeping her mouth firm.

Tommy's hair had grown to his shoulders. It was grimy and unkempt as though bathing was not in his daily routine. Though always thin, he looked like he had lost weight. His eyes had sunken deep into his narrow face.

"Don't you want to know how I found you?" he asked in a childlike sing-song teasing.

"Not particularly," Alyce answered and pushed harder against the door. Tommy's muscles flexed from the pressure. He showed no sign of giving in.

I wanted to know who told him, because if Tommy knew where we were, we couldn't be safe. I was positive Chuck would have never told Angelo, even if Angelo knew how to get a hold of him. So the only other person had to be Josie again. Seeing Tommy standing on the threshold of our home, I knew we couldn't break free of our past.

"I don't care how you got here," Alyce said. "But I do want you to leave now and never come back." She bore down on the door, mashing Tommy's hands. He winced as she continued without letting up on the pressure.

"If you do come back, I'll call the police and tell them you tried to break in," Alyce said more as a fact than a threat. "I'm sure you don't want them looking around in your past."

Tommy hesitated for a minute. "Have it your way." He removed one hand and flicked his forefinger against his head in a good-bye motion. As he removed his other hand from the jamb, he added, "For now."

Alyce slammed the door shut, double locked it and leaned against it for several minutes breathing deeply, gasping for air like a fish thrown onto the beach. We both had the same thought. Without any conversation, we dashed around the apartment making sure all the windows were closed and locked, even upstairs.

Once everything was secured, Alyce and I held onto each other, our bodies trembling in rhythmic motion as though in a religious trance. Clearly we were not as safe as we had thought we were and tried to be, but we couldn't afford to move again.

I broke the silence and said, "I should never have gone to that damn prom."

Alyce took my face in her hands and reminded me, "It's only a short time before the divorce is final. Angelo will find out where we live anyway."

"He already knows," I whispered and snuggled against her shoulder.

Trying to console me, Alyce stroked my back and said, "We'll just have to stay prepared."

Though I shuddered at the thought of facing Angelo under any circumstances, we couldn't despair. If we gave up now, panic would immobilize us and we would make foolish mistakes. Yet after Tommy's clandestine visit, I sensed that a confrontation with Angelo was likely.

CHAPTER TWENTY-TWO

What Price Freedom

A month after the final divorce decree, Kyle and Todd left for New York on their first visit to see Angelo. As part of the settlement, Angelo had custody of the boys for the summers. Angelo had moved in with his sister Maria and her husband, Paul, which lessened our trepidation about the reunion between the boys and their father.

My throat tightened as Alyce and I saw the boys onto the plane. In contrast to my sadness, the boys' faces beamed at the thought of being allowed to travel unaccompanied by adults. As the stewardess took each boy by the hand and attempted to lead them quietly onto the plane, Todd and Kyle skipped to the plane's door, nearly pulling her down to their level.

I had misgivings about their summer visit. Earlier that week Kyle appeared apprehensive when he was told he was going to stay with his father. "Why do we have to go there?" he asked Alyce. "We'll be good if you let us stay."

Alyce tousled his hair. "You're always good. Just think of the fun you'll have playing with your cousins. And you're going to fly on a jet all by yourself like a big man."

Kyle's eyes widened. The idea of flying alone so appealed to him, he forgot his other concerns. I believed it was only a temporary cover-up for the fear he still had of his father and for good reason.

As the boys disappeared into the plane's cavity, Alyce and I pressed our faces against the glass that separated the waiting area from the plane. If we got close enough, we could see into the plane and perhaps the future.

When the plane taxied away from the gate, we remained at the window and cupped our hands around our eyes to shut out the glare. We watched the plane until it merged into the group of other planes waiting for someone in the control tower to tell the pilot it was his turn to take off.

At last, Alyce and I pulled away from our vigil. We were the only people left in the waiting area, but we couldn't leave. The thought of going back to the apartment without the boys seemed unbearable. Finally Alyce took a deep breath, choked back her tears and circled her arm around my shoulder. "We might as well go home," she said and led me from the terminal.

That summer I continued to babysit, and Alyce worked two jobs. Somehow, she also found the time to start night school, at the urging of Gene Stanton, who told her, "As much as I depend on you and your secretarial skills, you are too bright not to get a degree." Besides, for California state residents, college tuition was affordable for just about anyone.

Even with all that activity, we desperately missed the boys and counted the days until we would meet them at the airport, which would happen a week before I started my senior year. The night before Kyle and Todd were due to fly home, Alyce spoke with Angelo to finalize the schedule. Hardly able to sleep anticipating our reunion, we stayed up most of the night talking about the boys. I took a photo album from the living room shelf and thumbed through it as Alyce and I chatted.

"How much do you think they've changed?" I asked as I looked at a picture of them sitting by our very Californian aluminum Christmas tree. I chuckled at their crew cuts and wide, hopeful eyes, waiting for the signal to open their gifts.

Alyce raised her right hand parallel to the floor and giggled, "A foot, I imagine. We probably won't recognize them."

"I doubt that we could miss those bouncing bodies." I jumped up and down trying to imitate them.

The following day, we were at TWA's gate an hour before the scheduled flight arrival. Every few minutes I checked the time and gate to be sure neither had changed. We both kept checking our watches as if to hurry the minutes. As I watched Alyce walk back and forth across the waiting area, I laughed at what a contrast in fashion we were. My sister, of course, maintained eastern protocol, while I had settled into California casual. She wore an ivory shirt dress, brown leather pumps and matching purse and a brown fedora. I wore my favorite cut-offs and man's shirt. Mom, I thought, would not approve of my dress code.

Our heads cocked toward the PA when we heard their flight announced. My heart hammered against my chest as I watched the plane taxi to the gate. Once again we pressed our faces against the window to see better. When the engines were turned off, we hovered around the exit door and waited. One by one, the passengers left the plane.

Alyce barely registered each person who went by, her eyes ready to find two little boys behind the next arrival and the next one after that. Her breathing grew more rapid as each traveler passed and there was no Kyle or Todd. The faster she breathed, the slower I tried to inhale and exhale, thinking that would control our panic. We needed to stay calm, think clearly.

Alyce turned to me and then back to the plane and said, "The stewardess will probably take the boys off last."

I nodded without looking away from the corridor that led to the airplane's door. When the jetway emptied, Alyce searched the happy crowd of people greeting the arrivals. "Perhaps we missed them," she said in a high-pitched, anxious voice.

She twisted her gloved hands over and over and chewed the lipstick off her lower lip. When we saw the stewardess shutting the jetway door, Alyce ran to her. Her wing-shaped name tag said she was Miss Leonard. Alyce held her hand against the door to keep it open and screamed, "Everyone can't be off that plane, Miss Leonard."

The others in the waiting area turned to see who was yelling. Miss Leonard nodded to the plane as she spoke. "You can't go there."

Alyce forged past her down the corridor to the plane as Miss Leonard yelled, "It's not allowed."

Alyce didn't stop. So Miss Leonard and I followed her. By the time we reached the plane, Alyce was chasing up and down the aisle looking for Kyle and Todd in every seat. No boys anywhere. Alyce collapsed into a seat and cried. When the reality hit, I went numb. The boys weren't coming home that day. I puzzled over reasons why.

"You have to get off the plane, " Miss Leonard said. She tugged at Alyce's arm and tried to pull her up.

Alyce scowled and tossed Miss Leonard's hand aside. The stewardess went pale and backed away. We stayed like that for several moments, a tableau: Alyce crying, I fidgeting with a seatbelt and Miss Leonard eying us as if we were mass killers.

Alyce raised her head and blew her nose. "I'm sorry for causing you any trouble," she said to Miss Leonard. She followed her apology with a chaotic and hurried explanation about her missing sons.

Miss Leonard's face softened. She took Alyce's hand in hers. "Let me see what I can do to help." She looked at me as though asking for forgiveness.

She escorted us to her supervisor and detailed the situation. After the supervisor reviewed the flight records, she sighed, "I'm sorry." She laid the roster down and said, "No one by either boy's name was scheduled for that flight."

She stood up and put her hand on Alyce's shoulder. "The records show that the tickets were turned in for a refund."

Tiny black mascara rivulets streamed down Alyce's cheeks. She turned to me and shrilled, "He'll never send them back." She had the eyes of a crazy woman.

I felt like someone had punched me in the stomach. "How can that be?" I asked. My voice was strained and loud. "What about the court order?"

Alyce glanced at the airline supervisor and didn't answer. "Let's go," she said to me. "We've got work to do."

As we left the office, Alyce yelled out over her shoulder, "Thanks."

Alyce's finger tapping against the steering wheel was the only sound as we drove back to our apartment in silence. I was confused and didn't grasp the seriousness of the situation. Alyce screeched the car to a stop across two spots, left the driver's door open and bounded up the stairs two at a time before I could get out of my seat. When I reached our apartment she was mumbling and pacing across the living room floor, with one hand on her forehead and the other on her hip.

I stood in the doorway. When she came to my side of the room, she said, "Close the door. I've got to talk to you." She motioned me to sit.

From the edge of the couch, I watched her move back and forth for several minutes, waiting for her to tell me what was happening. I had never seen her this frantic. After what seemed like hours, she stopped in front of me. "I'm going to New York to get the boys."

I jumped up. "Can I come, too?"

"No. You don't understand. Angelo doesn't want me to have the boys." She turned vaguely toward the window and brushed a piece of hair away from her face, a motion I had seen her do many times before. She faced me again. "He doesn't really want the boys, either, but it's a way to punish me."

"If he doesn't want you to have Kyle and Todd, how will you get them?"

"I'll kidnap them."

"What?" Kidnap? What are you saying?" I shook her shoulders as though that would bring her to her senses.

"It'll work, you'll see." As Alyce dialed a telephone number, she said, "The first order of business is to talk to my attorney so that everything will be legal once I return to L.A."

I flopped back onto the couch. For the second time that over-long day I felt as though someone had punched all the air out of me. "Do you think it will be safe?" I asked.

"Who cares? He has my sons." She twisted the phone cord as she spoke into the mouthpiece in a calm voice unlike what I had been hearing most of the day.

Two days later we were back at the Los Angeles airport, this time to send Alyce off. When her flight was called for boarding, I hugged her so hard she gasped. The sound of her breath reminded me of Chuck the last time Mom hugged him just before she committed suicide. Fearing I would never see her again, I didn't want to let her go. "I feel so helpless," I said as I released her. It seemed as though I was always holding on to her, not wanting to let go.

"Your job will begin when the boys and I get back." She gave me another quick hug. "Rest up for that and do what Mr. Greenwald tells you."

I wasn't sure what that meant because Alyce didn't tell me when she'd be back or what I would have to do. Taking orders from Clark Greenwald, her attorney, however, brought home the gravity of what was happening. I was scared. Alyce, on the other hand, remained composed and determined. And of course dressed to the nines.

I cried uncontrollably as the plane taxied from the gate and took off. I felt like I had never left the airport since the day we said good-bye to Kyle and Todd. As the plane joined the queue, I wondered if I would ever see any of them again. My head bounced in rhythm with the pounding of my heart as I rested it against the familiar windowpane. All I could think about was if she didn't come back, there was no one left but Chuck and me, and he was in Germany with Joy, his new wife. They were waiting the arrival of their first child and couldn't be expected to cope with me, too.

And what if Alyce didn't come back? What would happen to her and the boys? Contemplating the horror of what Angelo could do to them overwhelmed me. Though I had just turned seventeen, I felt I had aged a thousand years in three days.

Dusk arrived before I realized I had been driving up and down the Pacific Coast Highway for several hours. I couldn't face going to our apartment. While driving, I tried to think about happier times and laughed out loud about the many days Alyce spent teaching me how to drive—a task which brought out my stubbornness and identified me as a burdensome student. One particular day, I had difficulty accelerating and stopping smoothly. So in frustration I simply gave up and got out of the car. Perhaps that wouldn't have been unwise, except the car was still moving and Alyce had to jump into the driver's seat to take control before it headed for a stout palm tree at the curb. Thinking about that lesson, it became clear to me that Alyce was always jumping into the driver's seat to steer us out of harm's way.

Another time I froze at a busy intersection and couldn't muster the courage to drive through. While I had stopped for several minutes, ignoring opportune breaks in traffic, an impatient driver behind me honked his car horn. That time I did shift into park before I got out, strolled to his car and knocked on the window. Though the driver looked stunned, he rolled down the window. I asked, "Do I know you?" He was thrown off guard by my insolence and in frustration pulled out around me and our car, went through the stop sign and sped away.

Though I had embarrassed Alyce on those and other occasions, she never gave up on me, and I did eventually get my driver's license. Perhaps she also recognized that my obstinance would eventually be an asset in the rest of my life.

When I reached the Santa Monica Pier where Alyce, the boys and I had spent so many days riding the carousel and eating hot dogs on a stick, dread struck again. What would I do without Alyce? Who would be there for me like she always had been?

It was late night when I reached our apartment. I turned on the lights and stood in the doorway surveying the living room. The silence gave rise to fearful thoughts that Alyce was in danger and I had no way of helping her. I charged around the apartment like some crazed person locking windows and doors and closing all the drapes to shutter me from the outside. Afraid to move further, I sank to the floor in a corner of the living room. I drew my knees to my chest and rested my head on them. Willing for Alyce to call, I stayed there until daylight. I wanted so badly to hear her bright voice assuring me that everything was ok.

In the morning, I got up from the floor and made coffee and toast. I had given into the idea that Alyce's escapade could take a lot longer than I had hoped. Around ten o'clock the telephone did ring. Suddenly petrified to answer, I let it ring several times. It could be bad news: Alyce had been arrested, the plane crashed, Angelo hurt her. My spine felt as though it was being kneaded by icicles. After about the fifth ring, I picked up the receiver. It was Mr. Greenwald. He told me to meet him at the airport at two that afternoon. Alyce was on her way home with Kyle and Todd.

"What happened? Is she ok? Where's Angelo?" I rapid-fired questions at him.

"Alyce and I will fill you in later with all the details," he answered in a professional tone which contrasted to my squeaky-voiced barrage.

"Later?" I bellowed.

"You'll have to be patient." His brusque tone alarmed me. "I have to go. I have several things to tend to before we meet Alyce's plane. Don't be late."

I held the receiver in my hand, listening to the hum of the dead line.

At 1:30 that afternoon it was my turn to pace across the TWA terminal as I watched every person entering through the doors. Finally Mr. Greenwald, wearing his usual three-piece suit, burst through them waving his hand above his head. He hurried to me and grasped my arm, hustling me to a corner as he scanned the area. When we reached a vacant spot, he stopped and turned to me, his face close to mine. "Tekkie," he said as he pushed his sunglasses to the top of his head, "you must listen to everything I tell you. You must follow every detail of my directions. Do you understand?"

I nodded more frightened than I had ever been.

He opened his briefcase and withdrew an official-looking paper. As he handed it to me, he said, "All of your lives may depend on what we do from this point on."

I took the papers into my shaking hands and read them. Mr. Greenwald interrupted, "That is a restraining order. If Angelo should get here when Alyce does, you have to serve them on him so I can get Alyce and the boys to safety. Can you handle that?"

I nodded again, trying to process the information that was overloading my brain. "What do you think he'll do?" My skin crawled with the possibility we would face another Las Vegas scene. Or worse. Angelo, crazed by the kidnapping, would harm my sister and nephews.

"First of all, I doubt there was enough time for him to get here. But if by chance—well, who knows what could happen."

"Isn't there anything else I can do?" I thrust the restraining order at him, indicating it wasn't enough to protect us.

"No. The hardest part comes next."

"What do you mean?" The loud, desperate pitch of my voice caught the attention of travelers milling in the area.

Mr. Greenwald raised his finger to his lips, cautioning me. He leaned closer and spoke in a soft, gentle tone. "You and the boys are going to hide out in the mountains. You'll be there with my friend, Jeff. You'll be safe."

The kindness reflected in his manly face didn't reassure me. My shoulders slumped in defeat. "What about Alyce? Who will keep her safe?"

He ignored my questions. "They've announced Alyce's flight," he said. "Get ready."

I looked at the clock and followed him to the gate.

I stood back, anxious to see Alyce and the boys and confirm they had arrived safely. Like a sentry, I also kept a vigilant eye over the waiting area, but saw no sign of Angelo. What if I missed him and he got to Alyce first? I was sure everyone near me could hear my heart pushing blood through my veins as my sweating hands tightened around the restraining order.

What about Tommy?

Every nerve ending woke in warning when I remembered Tommy. He could still be in L.A. Angelo could send him to do his dirty work. What would stop him? I walked through the crowd waiting for disembarking passengers and checked the area for any sign of Tommy lurking in a dark corner. I didn't see him, but that didn't mean he couldn't jump out from some hidden place like Angelo did in Las Vegas. I couldn't face failing again.

There was no time to tell Mr. Greenwald about Tommy because Alyce and the boys were coming down the corridor from the plane. Their smiles and excitement distracted me from everything but the joy of our reunion. As Alyce and the boys dashed toward me, I chuckled at the sight. Though dressed in the same clothes she had left in yesterday, Alyce was still neat as the proverbial pin, outfitted in her perfect traveling ensemble, while the boys looked as though they had a hard day in a sandbox right down to their scuffed shoes, dirty t-shirts and holey jeans. Mr. Greenwald allowed only the quickest hugs before he whisked us away.

As we headed for the terminal's exit, Mr. Greenwald didn't break his stride when he introduced us to Jeff, who appeared from behind a pillar. Jeff apparently had also been guarding the area. When we reached the parking lot, Kyle, Todd and I were ushered into Jeff's Jeep. Alyce was guided into Mr. Greenwald's car.

"Jeff," Mr. Greenwald said as he climbed into the driver's seat, "will fill you in on where you're going and what you'll be doing next."

Alyce tried to smile when she said, "Tekkie, everything will be ok. This is for our good. I love all of you. See you soon."

"But..." I yelled as I was helped into the Jeep. Jeff rubbed his hand over his scruffy beard, gave one last visual sweep of the area and sat down behind the steering wheel.

As the two cars sped away in opposite directions, I consoled the boys who were both shaking and crying, "Mommy, Mommy!" The tempo and confusion of the day's events dizzied me. When would there be time to sort everything out? I hyperventilated and then vomited.

Jeff said, "We'll have to live with that. We can't stop now."

The odor from the vomit grew more pungent with each mile until it congealed into a firm gel. But there was an upside—the sight of me throwing up had stopped Kyle and Todd's tears. Was that the beauty Chuck told me about in his letter? The beauty I could find in everything if I looked? Defiantly, I crossed my arms over my chest and wondered if Jeff's unkempt ponytail should be counted among the beautiful, too.

CHAPTER TWENTY-THREE

Into the Mountains

Hour after hour, we traveled winding roads into the countryside until finally Jeff parked in front of an old log cabin in the San Gabriel Mountains. "We're here," he announced as though he was a tour guide and we were in some exotic vacation spot. "Come on, you three. Help me unload and I'll show you around."

I got out and stretched my cramped muscles. Kyle and Todd jumped eagerly from the back seat and sprinted to the creek behind the cabin. As I kept an eye on Kyle, I wondered what Jeff could show us—a cabin smaller than the garage we lived in? There wasn't much else there to see.

I turned back to lift out a bag filled with groceries. Jeff was holding a shotgun.

"What's that for?" I asked. The sharp scent of pine stung my nose.

"Protection," he answered and straightened his bushman's hat so it rested low on his forehead.

"From what?" Startled, I held the bag only part way out of the Jeep.

"No telling. Wild animals, Angelo or his buddy Tommy." He jammed an unlit cigar into his mouth. "No need to be scared, though. It's doubtful Angelo or Tommy will find us here."

I surveyed the thick woods that edged the property, looking for signs of bears and mountain lions.

"Besides," Jeff moved closer to me as though to assure me, "I made sure no one followed us."

So he and Mr. Greenwald already knew about Tommy. I studied Jeff. Though he seemed to be about the same age as Mr. Greenwald, mid-thirties, his mountain man look was a stark contrast to Mr. Greenwald's three-piece pinstriped suits. Were they really friends? It didn't matter. I trusted Jeff, which was saying something for me. I had a tough time being comfortable around or relying on any man.

There was no indoor plumbing in our two-room house. The boys and I slept in the bedroom and Jeff used the couch in the other room that also served as our kitchen and dining areas. Jeff carried his shotgun everywhere or laid it on the floor beside him when he slept.

While I hauled water from the creek and cooked over a wood stove, Jeff chopped wood and circled the area several times a day to check the woods, bushes and hills nearby. Kyle and Todd skipped rocks, built forts and generally had a good time. Since running away and hiding had happened so often in their short lives, they made an adventure out of it.

Kyle did ask me, "Will Mommy be coming?"

"No," I said. His face scrunched up and I added, "We have to be brave for a while without her."

"How long?" he asked.

"Not too long. Now go tend to Todd." I nudged him. "You don't want to make him scared, do you?"

Kyle bounded back to the creek and threw stones with Todd.

The day after we arrived, Jeff, still wearing the same jeans and jack shirt, handed me the shotgun.

I shook my head and refused to take it.

"You have to learn how to use it," he said.

"What for?" I asked in the snotty way teenagers challenge authority.

"In case you need to protect yourself." His speech seemed deliberately slow as though he was talking to someone who didn't understand English.

"I thought that's your job," I said as I formed my right arm into a muscle to mock him. I started to walk away from him.

"It is," he yelled after me, "but what if something happens to me?"

I returned and took the gun. "I better not have to use this thing." A hundred pins were stabbing my chest.

Jeff stuck the unlit cigar in his mouth and started the lesson. The rest of that day and the next I spent missing the target he had set up against a tree by the creek. Jeff's patience with my lack of skills as a mountain woman was comforting. He did flinch a couple of times when I swung around waving the loaded gun. He grabbed the barrel, pointed it toward the woods and said in a low, soothing tone, "Be careful where you point a loaded weapon. Always be sure it is at a target you want to hit." I detected a slight Texas drawl.

By the end of the third day, my right shoulder was in agony from the gun's kick, but I could hit the target's edge.

In the evenings after dinner, we read by candlelight just like Abe Lincoln. Sometimes Jeff told us stories. Once after the boys had gone to bed I pressured Jeff to tell me about Alyce's kidnapping caper. It was a daring tale and better than all those he had made up on previous evenings. It was even better than most the cliff hangers I saw at the Pit.

Jeff refilled his coffee cup and settled into his chair. "Alyce arrived in Syracuse late in the afternoon," he said, "rented a car and drove to Maria and Paul's farm. When she got there it was dusk. Kyle and Todd were playing in the yard." For the first time Jeff lit the cigar he had clenched between his teeth since our arrival. He took a long drag and continued, "There was no one else in sight. Alyce parked on the street and turned off the headlights, but left the engine on." He braced his feet clad in well-worn hiking boots against the porch railing as he balanced his chair on its rear legs.

"There's got to be more than that," I said as I crinkled my nose and fanned the noxious smoke away from my face.

"Sure." Jeff checked the end of his cigar while I grew impatient. Finally he began again. "Alyce sat for several minutes watching the boys play in the yard. She was looking for any signs of other people, especially Angelo." He took another long drag from the cigar and blew the smoke out the side of his mouth away from me.

"When she was confident no one else was outside, she ran from the car toward her sons. Before the boys knew what was happening she snatched them both, tore across the lawn to the car and escaped."

The breeze blew the smoke back toward me, so I got up and leaned against the railing away from the fumes. "Where was everyone else?"

"I'm not sure, but it was a miracle no one heard her," Jeff said.

"Hmmm," I said and took a sip of my coffee. "Angelo only heard the kids when they interrupted his TV watching. If they were outside, he couldn't hear them and couldn't care less about what they did."

"That was probably lucky for Alyce." Jeff stubbed out his cigar against his boot's sole, stood up and stretched and grunted from the extension.

"Yeah. It's the first time his TV watching was a virtue." I took his empty cup from the railing.

We laughed about that and laughed even harder when we talked about how Alyce and the boys must have looked to the other plane passengers—a narcissistic mother more concerned about her appearance than her sons. I laughed again as I pictured her dashing across the lawn in high heels, hat and gloves. I imagined a rising moon causing Alyce's aqua suit to shimmer in its reflection.

Most nights, Jeff, the boys and I sat on the porch facing the creek. The evening coolness was such a contrast to the scorching heat of the day we had to wear sweaters. I marveled at the sight of the stars never visible in the L.A. skies and happily listened to the crickets, frogs and the fast-moving water of the creek. Jeff would finger his shotgun when he heard bushes rustle or an animal howl in the distance.

The sounds were a wondrous serenade, but not when I had to work my way down a dark path in the middle of the night to use the outhouse. The beam from a flashlight only emphasized the critters and monsters I was certain lurked in every shadow. It reminded me of the night the cockroaches marched across our kitchen in Las Vegas. I shuddered at the thought.

My first night at the cabin, I tried to ignore the pressure building in my bladder. I had no intention of venturing to the toilet alone. When I finally gave in to the call, I tiptoed off the porch hoping no four or two-legged creature would be waiting for me. Stumbling down the dark path, I made it to the outhouse and was greatly relieved to be alive.

I emptied my bladder. Accepting the possibility of a splintered butt, I had almost decided to stay seated on the wooden toilet until daylight rather than risk my life again. I concluded it was my wild imagination preventing me from being rational. I breathed deeply and slowly unclasped the lock and shoved the warped door. Terrorized by the figure standing in the moonlight, I let out a fierce, bloodcurdling scream which aroused sleeping animals and birds into a frenzied commotion. "I'm going to die, I'm going to die," I repeated to myself between each hyperventilating breath.

"Jesus!" the shadowy figure said. "If they didn't know we're hiding here, they do now."

My eyes adjusted to the dark and focused on the shotgun. "You idiot," I yelled. "I could have had a heart attack." Jeff's face came into view.

"Not with those lungs," he chuckled.

"What are you doing here?" I asked.

"My job." He used the shotgun to motion me toward the cabin.

Though shaken, I was glad he was doing his job. Going to the outhouse was less frightening for me after that, but the venture never was a pleasure.

Every third day, we piled into the Jeep and made a forty-mile round trip to a gas station/mini-store for supplies. Jeff also called Mr. Greenwald for updating and instructions. Those trips were the only diversions we had.

The start of school came and went. Todd had missed the thrill of his first day in kindergarten. After the third week of 100-plus degree weather, no showers and wearing again and again the few pieces of clothing Jeff managed to get from our apartment, we wanted to go home. Besides, the most threatening thing we'd seen that whole time in the mountains was a skunk.

At the end of the fourth week, Jeff announced, "Pack up. We're leaving."

The boys and I shouted and threw everything into the Jeep without a care. We couldn't wait to get home and see Alyce. Within an hour we were ready to go.

As Jeff's dusty white vehicle wound down the mountain roads and into the San Fernando Valley, the sound of the traffic noise became excruciating. Unlike the cabin where we barely had to raise our voices to be heard, we shouted at each other. I was surprised how quickly we had acclimated to the mountain's serenity. For a brief moment, I wanted to return to that solitude. Though I was desperate to get back to a normal life, such as ours seemed to be, and school, I also dreaded what might be ahead of us. I had no idea what had happened to Alyce since I said good-bye to her in the airport parking lot. If Jeff knew any details, he never shared them. I also had no idea where Angelo was.

Riding through the Valley, I became self-conscious as people gaped at what appeared to be a man and his young wife and sons in a condition that rivaled any characters from *The Grapes of Wrath*. How we appeared to others became most evident to me when we stopped at a traffic light and the man in the next car shouted, "Go back to the hills where you belong."

Jeff touched his forefinger to his hat, smiled and said in that now-familiar accent, "Love to."

Alyce was waiting for us in front of the apartment complex. The four of us embraced for several minutes, once again afraid to let go. It was a scene we seemed to play too often. Alyce laughed as she released us. "You look like Ma and Pa Kettle and their kids. You need baths and clean clothes."

Kyle and Todd, who usually had to be bribed to the tub, didn't even argue with that. We unloaded the Jeep in a hurry, said a brief farewell to Jeff and bolted for the apartment. I wanted Alyce to tell me everything that had happened from the moment she got to New York to our reunion. "But first," I said, "I need to take a shower and wash my hair."

I never saw Jeff after that. I suspected he was not a friend of Mr. Greenwald's, but some professional bodyguard he had hired. We did, however, see a lot of Mr. Greenwald. He and Alyce had originally met when she worked a part-time cocktail waitress job at Kelly's Steak House. When she needed an attorney, Alyce called him. While the boys and I hid out in the mountains, they began dating. From the time we returned from hiding out, he became a welcomed and stable fixture in our lives.

Despite Angelo's reluctance to send the boys home, Alyce never filed for sole custody. She harbored some romantic idea that the boys needed a father, good or bad. He never paid child support and the boys didn't visit New York without Alyce. Angelo never came to L.A.

CHAPTER TWENTY-FOUR

Cinderella

Though I welcomed the comforts of my home, especially an inside bathroom, I didn't look forward to my last year in a high school where few people cared if I showed up each day. Even the drill team coach, a petite blond ballerina from Latvia, barely raised an eyebrow when I attended my first practice of the year almost a month late. An odd longing grabbed a hold of me—this was no East Syracuse High. A raised Latvian eyebrow could never replace the care in a tongue-lashing from an Irish principal or Miss Gifford.

As I looked around at the thirty cheerleader-type girls gathered on the school's playing field that first morning, I wondered how they had spent their summer.

After being denied a position on the cheerleading squad at East Syracuse High School, I was thrilled to be selected as a pom-pom girl and drill team member for University High. Other than my ability to step in rhythm, I had no particular talent. I figured I was chosen because of my willingness to practice at six in the morning. I didn't mind the lack of competition because it left more room for me to be accepted.

At each Friday night football game, the drill team gathered with the marching band on the playing field at half time. We pom-pom girls wore orange pullover sweaters with Peter Pan collars and white pleated skirts that ended just above our knees. We carried orange and white pom-poms that we hoisted into the air in sync with our routine. That year we placed second in the city-wide competition for doing our synchronized drill to "You gotta be a football hero to get along with a beautiful girl."

My after-school hours were quite different. Each day I rounded up the kids from the apartment complex into our home and delved into some entertainment to keep them busy and content. For instance, on cooler days we baked cookies. An assembly line of busy hands mixed, rolled, cut and decorated cookie dough. While waiting for the cookies to bake, we snuck pinches of dough and licked the beaters. Often our kitchen floor was covered in green, blue and yellow sprinkles that had missed the cookies when the little bakers shook them from their containers.

On other days we held the Olympics at the pool in the apartment's courtyard or hiked to the nearby park. When school was on holiday or on an occasional Saturday, I gathered the group around a map of L.A. and surrounding counties. A different child was selected at each gathering to point to the map. The place his finger landed was the place we went on our adventure. I packed lunches, necessary supplies and loaded them and the kids into our red Mercury station wagon and explored the chosen destination.

The loud bang when I popped the clutch driving downhill was voted the best part of all our trips. I swore the kids to secrecy about that stunt, but I had to stop that amusement when the secret suddenly slipped from Kyle's mouth during his excited review of our day at Redondo Beach.

Alyce rolled her eyes at me and frowned. "You'll destroy our only transportation." She put her hands on her hips just like Mom would have. "Perhaps you'd rather not use the car."

I made a face "who me?" like a dog who had been caught sleeping on the couch. "Oh no, pleeeease, I won't do it again," I begged. The thought of being imprisoned in the apartment complex with twelve energized kids under the age of ten made me promise anything.

"One more time," Alyce shook her forefinger at me, "and I'll take the car away." I didn't pop the clutch after that and hesitated to share secrets with those rug rats again.

That station wagon not only saved our lives when we fled from New York and helped make babysitting easier, it served as an ambulance. One of the children's mothers went into an early labor, but had no way to get to the hospital. I loaded her, her son, my nephews and five other screaming kids into the car and sped off. I was thankful she didn't deliver until she hit the emergency room entrance.

Though Kyle and Todd called me Aunt Tekkie, during that time I became more a big sister to them. I was quite content with that role as I am sure Alyce was being the mother to three rambunctious kids.

Thanksgiving was a different celebration for us that year. Alyce took us to the Los Angeles International Airport. She was always finding unusual things for us to do as a family. The space-age restaurant built in the middle of the parking area had just opened. Alyce decided Thanksgiving dinner in such special surroundings was the perfect way to appreciate how far we had come in the past two years. Being alive was enough for me.

The restaurant towered high above the terminals. Its parabolic arches reached upward to hold the restaurant, which looked like a cylindrical flying saucer. An elevator at the center of the cylinder raised us to the top. When we stepped out through the door, I was ready for an intergalactic encounter.

Our table was in the outer portion of the low-profile circular eatery and as we ate, our section of the building moved clockwise. Fortunately, late November in 1960 had little smog and few high rises, so we saw miles of the surrounding area from the ocean to the valley. A harpist played classical music, adding elegance to the ambiance. But the best part of the day was taking home the leftovers and we didn't have to cook one thing.

Shortly after Christmas, while I filed a college application, the other pom-pom girls made plans for the senior prom. Feeling homesick for my unsophisticated town in New York and the kids I grew up with, I only applied to one college, Cazenovia, a two-year women's college outside Syracuse.

Since I had no hope of attending the prom, I was content planning my exodus from Uni and back to upstate New York. I hadn't dated, and no boy over ten years old noticed me since I landed in L.A.

"What are you doing about the prom?" Alyce asked one day, to my surprise.

"I guess you didn't notice, but I haven't exactly had a rush of calls since I've been here," I answered. "Who would I go with?"

"We'll see about that. You can't miss your prom," she said as she read my application over my shoulder. "You'll never forgive yourself."

"You already sent me to the one in East Syracuse, remember?" I felt safe with Gary who was more a brother to me than a date.

"That's different. That wasn't your prom. You go to a different school now."

Though I didn't miss dating, I felt more an outcast not being asked to the prom than I had when I didn't make the cheerleading squad in New York. Or worse, on my first day at Uni High, when I showed up wearing a fading blue sack dress. Having arrived looking like one of the Beverly Hillbillies, I wasn't on top of any boy's list to ask out. As a teenage girl, getting good grades didn't get as many points as looking good in a bikini. With my straight A's and limited wardrobe I was out of luck. I hid behind a proud smile and told

Alyce, "The prom is nothing special in the scope of my entire life." I made a swooping gesture with my arm and covered my head in a pretend faint.

"I'd rather study." I held up the stack of school books I was carrying. "You know how important getting a college scholarship is to me. And I need to babysit as much as possible. How else will I cover expenses?" Besides, I thought not being among the popular girls at school, studying and babysitting posed no threats. In both those pastimes I didn't have any fear of losing someone I had become attached to like Mom, Dad and Grandpa, and I didn't have to fight off an oversexed teenage boy or man like Tommy and Gigi.

Alyce pursed her lips and she passed a hand through her shoulder-length hair which had straightened into a flip. "I wanted this to be a graduation surprise, but I think this is a better time to tell you."

"What? I'm not going to college?"

"No, silly. I've sold Mom's house. To the renters. The money will help you with tuition."

Even though it only brought us sadness, the thought of not having Mom's house any longer shook me. It had been the last tangible thing we had of Mom's. Everything else—Grandpa's rocker, the hope chest filled with European linens, most family pictures and Mom's World War II scrapbooks— had already disappeared when Angelo ransacked the house shortly after we departed. There was nothing left.

Alyce put her arm around my shoulder. "What's the matter? Aren't you happy about this?" If I could have remembered Mom's voice then, I was sure Alyce's maternal pleading would have sounded like her.

"Of course." I choked back tears. "I'm especially thankful that you care enough about my future to sell Mom's house."

Alyce encircled her arms around me. "I know what you're thinking." She patted my back. "It's all we have left of her. But do we want that kind of memory?" She leaned away from me and pointed to her heart.

I didn't answer.

While the rest of that semester I studied extra hard to be sure I got a scholarship to Cazenovia, Alyce apparently was beating the bushes for my prom date. One day she came home from work and announced, "I've found him."

I was draped down the stairs talking on the phone to Barbara. "Who?" I put my hand over the receiver.

"Your prom date." Alyce's face was lighted by a smile that sprawled from ear to ear. Again I was startled by how much she looked like Mom.

"Gotta go, Barb," I said and hung up the phone.

"What?" I asked Alyce and raced down the stairs to face her. "You can't be serious. I have no intention of going to some dumb prom, and absolutely not with some guy you bribed."

"I didn't bribe anyone." She looked like a teenager herself as she explained, "He's the son of a colleague. I think you'll like him."

"I can't believe you're doing this." I stomped my foot. "I'm not going."

She produced a gold satin tea-length dress that I could only imagine Princess Grace wearing. The dress had cap sleeves, a scoop neck and a bodice that would snug my torso. The full skirt gracefully flared from the waist, which was accented with a matching gold satin sash and a satin rose.

"What's that?" I pointed at the gown.

"Your prom dress. That is if you like it. When I saw it at the May Co. I knew it was perfect for you."

It was beautiful, and after a lifetime of wearing hand-me-downs, the thought of appearing in this—my first truly elegant dress—melted the horror of being escorted by a store-bought guy.

"Try it on." Alyce dangled the folds of gorgeous fabric in front of me.

I didn't take it. I tried not to look at the tempting frock

"Go ahead," she said. "Just see how it looks."

I knew what she was up to. She believed once I had the dress on, I would change my mind. She was right. I was caught off guard and should have considered her stubbornness. Yet standing there with that gorgeous gown held in front of my face, I had temporarily forgotten her past. My sister was and is an expert in obstinate persistence.

I glared at the gold satin dress suspended in front of me and held my arms tight against my sides. But I knew better than to buck Alyce's determination. The picture of her running across the farm kidnapping her sons flashed into my head. I yanked the dress from her and retreated to my bedroom to try it on.

As I slipped the fabric over my head and down my body, I shuddered with delight at the luxurious softness of the satin. I closed my eyes and caressed the gown's silky bodice and skirt. I twirled around so I could listen to the rustle of the new material.

I suddenly remembered Angelo's insult about my fat ankles. I couldn't imagine why those words still haunted me. Though I often saw myself as an intelligent girl with large ankles, I announced to the person in the mirror, "Who cares?" and twirled around again.

When I came back to the living room to model the dress, Alyce pulled out the matching high-heeled satin pumps and bag. I shook my head in disbelief. Alyce as always knew her younger sister well. When she held up the new white wool coat, I surrendered.

"You've thought of everything," I said.

"Almost." She raised her eyebrows up and down several times. "I've got to make an appointment with Michael to get your hair and nails done. You're going to stun them at this ball."

"Hmmm," I said ungraciously. "At least it's not one of your hand-me-downs."

I vanished into my room with my bounty. I sat on my bed fingering each item laid out before me and dreamed about the prom. "What if I hate my date?" I asked myself. "What if he's a greaser or worse yet, a four-eyed nerd with buck teeth and pimples?"

I yelled out to Alyce, "By the way, what's my date's name?"

"Troy. Troy Marvel."

"Ah, the marvelous Troy," I chuckled, wondering if she had invented the name, just as perfect as the dress. Later that evening I discovered Troy was a student at UCLA and he drove an MG. Not only did I have a date, but he was an older man, a college man.

On the day of the prom Alyce kept her pledge and took me to Michael's to get my hair and nails done. As soon as I entered the salon door, Michael walked over to me, rubbed his hand in my hair and smiled. "I'm glad I don't have to work a major miracle like the last time with the fire." He flirted with Alyce, as always. He didn't charge her full price for his services and never accepted a tip from her.

Michael scrubbed my hair with a fragrant shampoo that made my head tingle. I began to feel the transformation from a char-woman to Cinderella. While I sat under the hair dryer, a manicurist turned my hands—raw cuticles, shaggy nails and all—into ones that I'd only seen the likes of in *Seventeen* magazine.

As I admired my new pearl polish, a woman in a pink lab coat carrying a suitcase approached. She took hold of my newly perfect right hand. "My name is Bobbie," she said and pulled me toward a bar stool in front of a mirror.

"Sit," she said as she pointed to the stool.

I did as I was told. She placed the suitcase on a shelf beneath the mirror that faced me. She opened the case and revealed tiers of colorful makeup containers.

"Oh no," I screeched and glared at Alyce. "It's bad enough I'm going through this date thing, but this?" I pointed to the tubes and bottles.

"This won't be painful," Bobbie laughed. "Besides, you need a little color."

"Who needs color? I don't want to be a clown."

"Trust me," Bobbie said with a wink. I groaned but gave in when Alyce hovered nearby.

When Bobbie finished her task, I didn't recognize the girl in the mirror. Michael had created a soft yet sophisticated up-sweep hair style, and Bobbie's magic gave my skin a glow which looked completely natural. And my eyes seemed huge. I had never imagined looking like this.

"It's not bad," I said, tilting my head from side to side. Secretly I felt like a swan rather than the ugly duckling nerd I thought I was. For once, I didn't stick my tongue out at the image staring back from the mirror.

Promptly at seven that night, Alyce and I heard a knock at the apartment door. I wanted to fade into the wall, but Alyce was too quick. She flung the door wide and produced Troy, a drop-dead gorgeous twenty-one-year-old with black curly hair and teeth too perfect to be real.

"This is going to be quite an evening," I mumbled to myself.

"I couldn't wait for this evening," he said and handed me a corsage of white baby roses held together by gold satin ribbons that matched my dress. I wondered if Alyce had bought them too and if she scripted his lines.

In one fluid motion Troy helped me on with my coat, took my arm and led me out the door. He had class and a lot of practice at the smooth use of it. I was charmed.

Troy's MG sped into the school parking lot. He jaunted around the car to open my door as I sat waiting like a queen. Several students stopped to see who he was. He reached his hand toward me and helped me out. I tried to remember Alyce's lesson about swinging both legs out at the same time so as not to expose my privates.

I heard the gasps from the group when I rose from the car and several recognized me. Low murmurs came from the onlookers as we passed them and entered the school. With every step I took, I carried myself more haughtily.

Troy and I strolled into the gym, which had been changed into a Hawaiian resort complete with miniature clam shell-shaped waterfalls, fountains sculpted like fish, potted palm trees, flaming torches and non-alcoholic punch served in coconuts. However, the obligatory crystal ball twirling from the center of the ceiling seemed out of place in Hawaii as it scattered glowwormlike images about the room. A hush filled the room, and with everyone staring at us, Troy circled his right arm around my back to dance.

As though I was the teen movie star, Sandy Dee, the same girls who had ignored me in the past two years surrounded us and greeted me, their new best friend. I laughed and shook my head at them in ridicule. When I turned to introduce Troy, he interrupted me, "I'm Troy Marvel, Tekla's boyfriend."

Prince Charming had rescued me and completed my metamorphosis. For one night I was a princess, Cinderella touched by her fairy godmother—and it was wonderful.

Like all fantasies, that one came to an abrupt end. All too soon I was home again, pulling off the beautiful dress and stepping out of the matching shoes.

Prince Charming did take me out again, but when he discovered I wasn't the glamorous woman manufactured by Alyce, Michael and Bobbie, he moved on to others. Unlike the fairytale Cinderella, the glass slipper didn't fit my aristocratic foot.

I went back to babysitting, making plans for my high school graduation and college, a serious student once more. Still that evening will forever be special to me because I learned to what lengths Alyce, who had quietly become my mother, would go to make my life magical.

A month later we had a small gathering at our apartment to celebrate my graduation. With a thousand students the ceremony was neither intimate nor memorable. However, a week before I learned that I won the scholarship to Cazenovia, news which sweetened the celebration. Mostly it was Alyce's friends, including Clark Greenwald, who came to my party to give their congratulations and share champagne.

Though Chuck and his wife Joy were new parents preparing for their return to the States, they sent a gift. It was a musical German beer mug that played "Lilly Marlene," one of Mom's favorite WWII songs. We sang the words as Mom had taught them. I'm sure my eyes were as red-rimmed as Alyce's when we listened to the tune.

When the melody finished, I sighed, "I wish Mom was here."

"So do I," Alyce said in a shaky whisper.

Before I left for an open house at Barbara's, Alyce handed me a huge box wrapped in silver. It reminded me of the box Angelo had given her on her graduation day. I suspected she was up to something out of the ordinary again and hesitated to open it. Finally, after being urged by our guests, I ripped the paper away, lifted the top off the box and laughed. As I pulled the contents out, everyone but Alyce, who was laughing too, asked, "What's so funny?"

I put on the muskrat coat that Angelo had given Alyce. She had it altered and updated. "It's a little warm to wear for this time of year," I said, mimicking the way Mom said that to Alyce on her graduation day.

Alyce chuckled and pointed her finger at me in acknowledgment but turned serious when she said, "You'll need a warm coat for those New York winters. Besides, I told you it would come in handy one day."

"Yeah. You sure did. Thanks, Mom," I said as her eyebrows raised, acknowledging her new title. I played "Lilly Marlene" again on my beer mug. Then we hugged and laughed until the tears started, while the guests gave each other puzzled looks.

We couldn't explain the journey that brought us to that joyful and poignant moment. Instead we shared our happy anticipation of both being college students. We already knew then our educational paths would lead us into different careers. Alyce was studying accounting and business, and I was leaning toward social work. Our chosen fields of interest mattered little. It was fulfilling Mom's and our dreams that counted; all three of Mom's children would go to college as she had intended.

That night I slept with the muskrat coat wrapped around me, thinking about all the years it had been with us and all it had been through. I could smell the pain and joy it held. I wondered what our lives would have been like if Dad played ball for the Yankees, if Mom graduated from college, if Alyce had become an attorney and if I had not been parentless.

Even with all the mothering Alyce had given me, I had lost the concept of parents. I had a difficult time seeing people as having parents or being parents. Despite that ambivalence which would live with me, I was more than grateful for my sister's love and care.

Rubbing my face into the fur, I sang, "The best things in life to you were loaned, so how could you lose what you never owned? Life is just a bowl of cherries. Don't take it serious. It's too mysterious. You live, you work, you worry so, but you can't take your dough when you go, go, go. So keep repeating it's the berries and live, love, and laugh at it all."

* * *

Printed in the United States
57863LVS00003B/329